ACTING

BEHIND
THE SILVER
SCREEN

BEHIND THE SILVER SCREEN

When we take a larger view of a film's "life" from development through exhi-
bition, we find a variety of artists, technicians, and craftspeople in front of and
behind the camera. Writers write. Actors, who are costumed and made-up, speak
the words and perform the actions described in the script. Art directors and set
designers develop the look of the film. The cinematographer decides upon a
lighting scheme. Dialogue, sound effects, and music are recorded, mixed, and
edited by sound engineers. The images, final sound mix, and special visual effects
are assembled by editors to form a final cut. Moviemaking is the product of the
efforts of these men and women, yet few film histories focus much on their labor.

Behind the Silver Screen calls attention to the work of filmmaking. When
complete, the series will comprise ten volumes, one each on ten significant tasks
in front of or behind the camera, on the set or in the postproduction studio. The
goal is to examine closely the various collaborative aspects of film production,
one at a time and one per volume, and then to offer a chronology that allows
the editors and contributors to explore the changes in each of these endeavors
during six eras in film history: the silent screen (1895–1927), classical Hollywood (1928–1946), postwar Hollywood (1947–1967), the Auteur Renaissance
(1968–1980), the New Hollywood (1981–1999), and the Modern Entertainment

Marketplace (2000–present). *Behind the Silver Screen* promises a look at who does what in the making of a movie; it promises a history of filmmaking, not just a history of films.

Jon Lewis, Series Editor

1. ACTING (Claudia Springer and Julie Levinson, eds.)

2. ANIMATION (Scott Curtis, ed.)

3. CINEMATOGRAPHY (Patrick Keating, ed.)

4. COSTUME, MAKEUP, AND HAIR (Adrienne McLean, ed.)

5. DIRECTING (Virginia Wright Wexman, ed.)

6. EDITING AND SPECIAL VISUAL EFFECTS (Charlie Keil and Kristen Whissel, eds.)

7. PRODUCING (Jon Lewis, ed.)

8. SCREENWRITING (Andrew Horton and Julian Hoxter, eds.)

9. ART DIRECTION AND PRODUCTION DESIGN (Lucy Fischer, ed.)

10. SOUND: DIALOGUE, MUSIC, AND EFFECTS (Kathryn Kalinak, ed.)

ACTING

Edited by Claudia Springer and Julie Levinson

RUTGERS
UNIVERSITY PRESS
New Brunswick, New Jersey

For Geoff and Jack Adams and to the memory of Annemarie Springer
For Al, Elena, and Molly Weinstein

Library of Congress Cataloging-in-Publication Data
    Acting / edited by Claudia Springer and Julie Levinson.
        pages cm. . — (Behind the silver screen ; 1)
    Includes bibliographical references and index.
    ISBN 978–0–8135–6433–3 (hardcover : alk. paper) — ISBN 978–0–8135–6432–6
(pbk. : alk. paper) — ISBN 978–0–8135–6434–0 (e-book (web pdf)) —
ISBN 978–0–8135–7267–3 (e-book (epub))
    1. Motion picture acting. I. Springer, Claudia, 1956–, editor.
    II. Levinson, Julie R., editor.
    PN1995.9.A26A26 2015
    791.4302'8—dc23

2014041362

CONTENTS

ACTING

INTRODUCTION   Claudia Springer

Film actors leave us with indelible impressions by bringing characters to life. Audiences often cherish a film for its memorable performances, and reviewers typically pay particular attention to acting when they evaluate a film. Effective acting may appear effortless, but it is actually a product of a performer's careful labor and the changing conventions in performance styles, which are continually being transformed by technological, industrial, aesthetic, and social developments. During the early film era, filmmaking technology excluded the actor's voice; actors relied on a gestural style that made dramatic use of their bodies and facial expressions, drawing on the rich tradition of the theater and adapting it to the screen. When synchronized sound technology was introduced during the mid-1920s, actors modified the gestural style's heightened physicality for a new realist approach. Over the next decades, acting techniques developed alongside broader changes. During the classical Hollywood period, actors adapted to standardized production and film censorship, and when the postwar years brought progressive social movements, a loosening of censorship, and an increase in independent filmmaking, acting styles underwent a major change. Recently, new technologies such as CGI and the Internet have profoundly altered the way films are made, distributed, and watched, and approaches to acting are again undergoing a shift. The chapters in this book offer new scholarship on the craft of film acting in the United States from 1895 to the present; by analyzing each historical period in depth, the authors illuminate the dynamic role of acting in the creation and evolving practice of American filmmaking.

Performance Styles

When Philip Seymour Hoffman won the Academy Award for Best Actor in 2006 for his role in *Capote* (Bennett Miller, 2005), another nominee for the award—Heath Ledger—is purported to have said, "I thought it was for best acting, not the most acting."[1] Whether true or apocryphal, the comment identifies one of the enigmas at the heart of the acting enterprise: What is a great performance? The standards for evaluating performances have changed and will continue to be modified. Late nineteenth- and early twentieth-century grand gestures appear excessive to our twenty-first-century eyes; similarly, Method acting as it was practiced in the 1950s appeared fresh and authentic at the time but now can look stilted. Good acting is a relative concept described differently over time. What is considered a great performance is a product of changing tastes. It is also dependent on individual preferences, and while it is sometimes characterized by subtlety, in other cases it involves a heightened display of gestural and vocal virtuosity—the kind of acting that Ledger supposedly attributed to Hoffman.

Film scholars find it productive to go beyond evaluating the quality of actors' performances to analyze the way acting functions within a film's entire formal system. A performance does not take place in a vacuum; it is part of a complex arrangement of cinematic techniques involving the setting, lighting, costuming, cinematography, editing, and sound, and it is inflected by the requirements of particular genre or narrative conventions in addition to a director's working methods. Yet no matter how much these factors guide a performance and how carefully the acting is integrated into a film's mise-en-scène, an actor's individual technique—the presentation of body and voice—is often a central factor in the film's creation of meaning.[2] Actors' performances are a crucial thread in the woof and warp of a film's fabric; sometimes the thread blends imperceptibly into the overall pattern and sometimes it is conspicuous and loud. Film scholar James Naremore reminds us that effective screen performances are not always subdued: "Though it is true that movies have helped to foster a restrained, intimate style, it is wrong to assume that 'good' film acting always conforms to the low-level ostensiveness of ordinary conversation."[3] There is no universally ideal approach to film acting; every performance represents a confluence of distinctive influences and choices.

Pinning down the ambiguous shades of meaning in an actor's performance can be difficult. There have been attempts to create taxonomies of gestures, most notably in the work of François Delsarte, a nineteenth-century French instructor of acting and singing whose system of associating gestures with corresponding emotions was taken up by stage actors in Europe and the United States. Mechanical application of the Delsarte Method led some actors to engage in melodramatic posturing, and by way of rejecting their techniques, the Russian theater director Constantin Stanislavsky developed an approach during the early twentieth century based on internalization; he encouraged actors to inhabit a character by drawing on their imaginations and emotions to empathize with and emody their characters' actions. Stanislavsky's teachings inspired the school of Method acting popularized in New York by the Group Theater in the 1930s and by Stella Adler and Lee Strasberg, among others, in the 1940s and 1950s. Adler and Strasberg differed in their interpretations of Stanislavsky's techniques, but between their two schools they trained many highly successful film actors, including Marlon Brando, Robert De Niro, Al Pacino, Jane Fonda, Steve McQueen, and Dustin Hoffman.

In contrast to Stanislavsky's early emphasis on realism at the Moscow Art Theater—on actors seamlessly "becoming" their characters—the German playwright, poet, and theorist Bertolt Brecht advocated a modernist approach that sought to expose the artificiality of drama and its characters. Initially working in the German Weimar Republic in the 1920s, he promoted an acting style in keeping with *Verfremdungseffekts* (alienation effects): techniques to distance the audience in order to encourage contemplation of a play's social implications. Brecht's goal was to prevent audiences from becoming mindlessly absorbed in plays; he wanted to transform them by making them aware of social injustices and their own complicity. Stage actors working in a Brechtian style remind audiences of the gap between the actor and the character by acknowledging the audience's presence, sometimes speaking directly to them or breaking character or carrying placards that comment ironically on the plot. In films, Brechtian distanciation techniques exist most obviously in comedies with their playful upending of conventions and winks to the audience, but they are also found in films with loose characterizations (such as those of the French New Wave), overtly political goals (those of Jean-Luc Godard, for example), or highly stylized aesthetics, such as *Dogville* (Lars von Trier, 2003). Brechtian film acting reminds spectators that they are watching a performance, and actors are not required to draw from a deep well to discover backstories or motivation for a character.

In some ways, as James Naremore argues, distanciation techniques bring us back to Delsarte's codified gestures, and Naremore makes the point that Delsarte could be considered a proto-modernist if we think about his approach in relationship to the twentieth century's avant-garde movements.[4] Contemporary film acting tends to combine elements of internal and external styles, with individual actors leaning toward one or the other end of the spectrum, depending on their own personal approach and training. In practice, the line between internal and external technique is ambiguous, and it is difficult for viewers to distinguish a Method from a non-Method performance. Moreover, recent research indicates that Stanislavsky's and Brecht's approaches were not entirely divergent; there is more nuance and less fixation on naturalism in Stanislavsky's concepts than is apparent in the version popularized by Lee Strasberg's Actor's Studio.[5]

Contemporary work in computer-generated imagery (CGI) has facilitated a revival of codified gestural acting by recording and then digitally reproducing an actor's every movement and facial expression. Actors, in effect, provide the physical raw material that technicians transform into a performance; the actor's contribution is one step in the special effects team's process of creating a character. A fascinating example is Brad Pitt's appearance in the film *The Curious Case of Benjamin Button* (David Fincher, 2008), about a man who is born old and grows younger. Pitt's head was computer generated for the scenes in which he is elderly, a process that involved 325 shots. He acted the part in a studio with each facial expression recorded and transferred to a three-dimensional digital head that was based on what he might look like as an old man, given his bone structure and musculature. Brad Pitt does not actually appear in the first third of the film; instead, the spectator sees his expressions on the digital head modeled from his head. Not only do we not see his actual face, but the bodies onscreen are those of children and little people with the digital head added.[6] Pitt's acting was a key element in the creation of the aged Benjamin Button, but digital artistry is capable of rendering actors obsolete, as journalist Laura Sydell indicates: "Given the long history of demanding, egotistical movie stars, there's no reason to think that Hollywood won't take advantage of the new technology to cut the big names out of the picture."[7] Time will tell the extent to which actors will continue to appear in films. At some point in the future, this book on film acting might be considered quaint.

Anybody appearing in a film, even in a *cinéma vérité* documentary, can be said to be participating in an "act," however unplanned the performance, simply because viewers inevitably interpret onscreen gestures, mannerisms, facial expressions, and vocal inflections, finding significance in minute details. The earliest films made in 1894 by Thomas Edison and William Kennedy Dickson in New Jersey lasted only about one minute and typically showed vaudeville and other types of performers (including dancers, boxers, acrobats, strongmen, and the sharpshooter Annie Oakley) presenting their skills. The craft of screen acting was nascent in their performances because they presented themselves purposefully, unlike the French crowds filmed in 1895 who were often just going about their business, perhaps unaware that they were being filmed. In these *actualités* filmed in the streets by the brothers Louis and Auguste Lumière, the people preserved on film were not acting in the sense of having prepared in advance to perform a role, but once they had been captured on film, they were turned into signifiers that represented types or evoked responses from viewers. Other Lumière films, however, did involve participants' conscious self-presentation, as in *L'Arroseur arrosé* ("The Waterer Watered," Louis and Auguste Lumière, 1895), in which a gardener hosing a flowerbed is surprised by a boy's prank when the flow of water stops and then squirts into his face as he examines the end of the hose. The gardener grabs the boy and spanks him before returning to his task.

The craft of screen acting appeared when people who were filmed took control over their performances to achieve specific effects, a tendency visible in the short film *The Kiss* (Thomas Edison, 1896), which comprises a medium-close-up shot of May Irwin and John Rice reenacting the kiss that closes the play *The Widow Jones*. Sustained film acting emerged with the introduction of storytelling in films. By the first years of the twentieth century, short narrative films with people playing roles circulated around the world. Actors, however, did not become widely recognized by audiences until after 1908, when movie production companies learned that their films could make the most of an actor's talents to appeal to audiences, as film historian Charlie Keil documents in his study of Vitagraph films from 1907 to 1913 featuring Florence Turner, who "became one of a handful of performers apparently selected by the public as an early motion picture favorite."[8]

It was another Florence—Florence Lawrence—whose immense popularity made her the first full-fledged film star in 1912 and demonstrated to film studios that publicizing actors' names and information about their lives (factual or invented, it hardly mattered) helped draw audiences. Lawrence worked with director D. W. Griffith at the Biograph studio starting in 1907 where, as was the custom, she was identified only as "The Biograph Girl." But when Independent Moving Pictures Company (IMP) producer Carl Laemmle hired her and led reporters to believe that she had been killed in a streetcar accident, and then published an irate retraction announcing that she was alive and would be starring in a soon-to-be-released IMP film, the public embraced her and she became a screen sensation pursued by reporters and fans, who sent her voluminous mail.[9] Thus the film star system and fandom were born in the second decade of the twentieth century and, ever since, assessing an actor's performance in a particular role has been one of the pleasures of going to the movies. This type of informal assessment can exist on the same spectrum as theoretically informed analysis, as film scholar Aaron Taylor points out when he writes that "what we might begin to recognize is that these casual deliberations can frequently serve as tacit substitutions for (or self-reflective entry points into) more explicit and coherent theories of filmic engagement and/or appreciation."[10] Investigating the specifics of a performance and its aesthetic, technological, cultural, social, or industrial context can expand our appreciation of the intricacies of film acting while deepening our understanding of individual films.

Scholarship on Film Acting

There is an impressive body of scholarship on film acting, but much of it was written relatively recently after decades during which film scholars prioritized other aspects of cinema, including film genres; auteurist directors; national cinemas; industrial, technological, and aesthetic developments; social, political, and cultural contexts; the historical exclusion of African Americans and other persecuted groups from Hollywood; the semiotics of film language; the psychoanalytic experience of the spectator; the ideological underpinnings of the apparatus; the gendered address of classical Hollywood conventions; and the potential for queer readings; among others. Acting took a backseat in film scholarship in part because it was the purview of film reviewers in the popular press and on television, and because it was associated with everyday discourse instead of perceived as a topic worthy of systematic analysis. Furthermore, as film scholars Cynthia Baron and Sharon Marie Carnicke make clear, there is a longstanding misunderstanding that the only true acting takes place on stage, with actors appearing live in front of audiences, while film actors just behave naturally and lend their bodies and faces to the multiple elements that constitute a finished film. This view assumes that filmmakers create performances through framing and editing, with minimal artistry from actors. Baron and Carnicke are among those who dispel this misrepresentation, stating that while "nonperformance elements" do influence how we interpret a character's presentation, "framing, editing, and production design do not *do all the acting* in screen performance. . . . Films create meaning not by the combination of inert physical and vocal elements but instead through the selection and combination of recognizable human gestures and expressions that carry dense and often highly charged connotations that can be variously interpreted."[11] Studies of film acting have indeed elucidated how actors contribute to films' meanings and opened up specific films to new interpretations.

A fascination with the phenomenon of stardom ushered in some important film scholarship starting around 1970, and although acting technique was not the central focus of these studies, it was included as a component of the image projected by a star to his or her fans. Alexander Walker's book *Stardom: The Hollywood Phenomenon,* from 1970, takes a historical view of the rise of early film stars. He emphasizes that before sound technology required silence on the set, directors coached actors while scenes were shot, creating beautifully collaborative performances in which the director's vision and the actors' skill produced art.[12] Ironically, he writes, the talkies put an end to verbal prompting; sound prescribed silence. Walker's book also debunks the notion that the talkies destroyed many actors' careers. Instead, "sound gave some fading stars a new if brief lease on life; it increased the artistry of some of the established stars once they had proved they could 'talk'; and it helped create new stars from among some, though by no means many, of the stage players whom Hollywood had recruited."[13] Walker examines the acting styles and trajectories of Lillian Gish, Richard Barthelmess, Charlie Chaplin, Greta Garbo, John Gilbert, Bette Davis, Joan Crawford, John Wayne, and Sidney Poitier, among others, linking their star personae to their performance styles. His analysis demonstrates how acting styles are linked to industrial and social changes, and how the phenomenon of stardom is a major factor in constructing viewers' relationships to films.

Richard Dyer's book *Stars,* published in 1979, combines sociological explanations for film stardom with analyses of specific films, and identifies how the discourses surrounding a star can support or challenge dominant ideologies, sometimes simultaneously. Dyer describes actors' physical and vocal traits when they are playing a role as "performance signs" that can be interpreted based on connotations specific to their time period and culture as well as their context within a film.[14] Included in *Stars* are analyses of star images, such as the meanings created by Jane Fonda's naturalistic Method acting style and the material circulating in the media at the time about her relationship with her father, her status as an "all-American" sex symbol, and her political radicalism.[15] Dyer considers how we understand screen performances within the larger discourses surrounding an actor, over which the actor has little control, a project that he continues in his subsequent book *Heavenly Bodies: Film Stars and Society,* from 1986, in which he scrutinizes the star images of Marilyn Monroe in terms of sexuality, Paul Robeson in the context of "crossing over," and Judy Garland in relationship to gay men.[16] Dyer reveals the power of stardom—its capacity to shore up or undermine a culture's ideological assumptions—and raises the possibility that stars, like directors, might be considered auteurs of their films, but cautions that while actors can have a substantial influence on the way a film is made, it is rare for an actor to exert the kind of overarching control that typically characterizes an auteurist director.[17]

An influential book on film acting, as opposed to stardom, is *Acting in the Cinema,* by James Naremore, published in 1988. Naremore elaborates on the continuity between an actor's calculated performance of a character and our everyday performance of ourselves from day to day; we are all actors to an extent. He examines screen actors' techniques in the context of larger notions of theatricality and performance, showing how different conventions govern the expressive techniques used for each type of performance—in the theater, on television, on film, and in our everyday lives. While we ordinarily expect characters—and ourselves—to maintain expressive coherence by not presenting wildly inconsistent personality traits, we get to see expressive incoherence when a character in a film is "wearing a mask," or giving a performance within a performance, such as Mary Astor's when she attempts to deceive Humphrey Bogart's Sam Spade during their first meeting in *The Maltese Falcon* (John Huston, 1941).[18] Naremore divides screen performance into five concerns: performance frames that separate actors from the audience, rhetorical conventions, expressive techniques of voice and physicality, a "logic of coherence," and the actors' interplay with the mise-en-scène (with chapters devoted to the expressiveness of objects, costumes, and makeup). His readings of specific performances (James Cagney in *Angels with Dirty Faces,* Katharine Hepburn in *Holiday,* Cary Grant in *North by Northwest,* among others) and ensemble acting in *Rear Window* and *The King of Comedy* provided a valuable model for future studies. Scholarly interest in film acting has grown, and the literature on film acting is now quite extensive.

The focus of this book is on acting techniques and methods in American film history rather than on the phenomenon of stardom or the lives of celebrities. Some actors become stars, and Hollywood stokes our fascination with their celestial existence with massive publicity as well as with films about stardom, such as the first two versions of *A Star Is Born* (William Wellman, 1937; George Cukor, 1954). (A third version directed by Frank Pierson in 1976 transposes the story to the world of rock music.) Hollywood stars do rise to amazing heights and sometimes plummet spectacularly. But most film actors are not stars; they are hardworking craftspeople who devote time and energy to honing their skills and building on the achievements of their predecessors.

Actors in the Hollywood Studio System

American film actors have had a notoriously fraught relationship with the industry that made their profession possible. Much as the Hollywood studios and actors have depended on each other, they also have been embroiled in conflict over the decades. From about 1929 to 1948, when a few powerful studios (MGM, Paramount, Twentieth Century–Fox, Warner Bros., RKO, Columbia, United Artists, and Universal) ruled the film industry, actors struggled for any semblance of control over their lives and careers within a system that required most of them to sign long-term contracts to work exclusively for a particular studio for five to seven years. Contracts included a six-month option clause, meaning that every six months the studio had the right to drop actors who were not considered sufficiently profitable. Actors, however, did not have the option to break their contracts and were bound to a studio's dictates over when to work, how many and which films to appear in, and when to be loaned to another studio. Studios paid their actors for forty weeks a year and determined when an actor would not be paid, adding up to twelve unpaid weeks per year.

Actors forfeited control over much of their personal as well as professional lives under studio domination, as film historian Ronald L. Davis explains: "Studios sometimes encouraged contract personnel to go into debt, assuming that financial obligations would insure subservience. Even when actors weren't busy on a picture, they were not free to leave town without their studio's permission. Since they rarely knew for certain when they'd be working and had little or no control over what roles they played, character actors like stars complained they felt like property."[19]

Frustrated actors occasionally refused to cooperate or sought redress in the courts. James Cagney, for instance, took Warner Bros. to court in 1936 over the roles they had been assigning him, and succeeded in getting released from his contract. Bette Davis also objected to the parts Warner Bros. gave her and was angered by their refusal to loan her to RKO for a starring role she wanted. She took an unpaid leave in 1936 and fled Hollywood for New York, announcing that she would return only on certain conditions. The studio responded by suspending her. Months of negotiations followed during which Davis decamped to London to appear in British films, but Warner Bros. sued her in the British courts for breach of contract. Davis lost the case and returned to Warners.[20] Her rebelliousness may not have been in vain, though, since Jack Warner welcomed her back by giving her the lead in the film *Jezebel* (William Wyler, 1938), for which she won the Academy Award for Best Actress, and during the 1940s she was given her own company, B. D. Incorporated, within Warners, along with 35 percent of her films' net profits (see figure 1).[21] Her resistance may have inspired Olivia de Havilland, also under contract to Warner Bros., to sue the studio in 1943. This time the tide turned and de Havilland won the case as well as the 1944 appeal to the Superior Court of California. Her case revolved around the studios' practice of subtracting days during which actors were not at work on a film from their

FIGURE 1: Bette Davis's Oscar-winning performance in *Jezebel*.

contracted years and tacking the accumulated time to the end of the contract. The courts deemed this sleight of hand illegal in a ruling that is known unofficially as the de Havilland Law.

Actors who challenged the system received support from the Screen Actors Guild (SAG), founded in 1933, the year the studios slashed salaries for their personnel, including actors, ostensibly to comply with President Franklin D. Roosevelt's efforts to lift the country out of the Depression. When SAG was created, studio bosses dismissed any actor found to be a member; the union had to hold secret meetings at first to avoid studio retaliation.[22] Rapprochement was reached in 1937, when 99 percent of film actors surveyed said they would be willing to go on strike unless the studios accepted SAG's existence.[23] The studios were forced to recognize SAG but nonetheless continued to exert control over their stable of actors and resist efforts to reform, while SAG pushed for such improvements as better working hours and a pension plan for its members.

There were advantages to being under contract—actors derived some job security and could benefit from studio publicity on their behalf. It was undoubtedly reassuring for many actors to cede control over their careers to a well-oiled studio machine. Other actors, however, sought autonomy by staying unattached to a studio and selecting roles for themselves. Well-established stars had an easier time going freelance than lesser-known actors, but some up-and-comers boosted their careers by making wise decisions. As film scholar Richard Jewell points out, Cary Grant's stardom rose after his contract with Paramount ended in 1936: he chose to sign non-exclusive contracts with RKO and Columbia, giving him the flexibility to also appear in films produced by MGM, Warner Bros., and Twentieth Century–Fox during the 1930s and 1940s.[24] Resistance to industry domination also took the form of actors starting their own companies, most famously United Artists established by Charlie Chaplin, Mary Pickford, Douglas Fairbanks, and the director D. W. Griffith in 1919 to distribute independently produced films. In 1942, James Cagney and his brother William created William Cagney Productions after years of clashing with Warner Bros. In 1947, Burt Lancaster and producer Harold Hecht created the successful Hecht-Lancaster company. In 1948, Humphrey Bogart formed his own production company, Santana Productions. Striking out on their own did not endear these actors to the studio executives, but they paved the way for many stars today who own their own production companies.

Far removed from the wealthy stars who had the means to become producers were aspiring actors whose entry into the kingdom of light and shadow was controlled by the studios' talent departments. Some aspirants were discovered by talent scouts sent by studios on a regular basis to Broadway and other big-city theaters to look for performers with a special flair. Scouts combed entertainment venues of all kinds to find a photogenic face or a charismatic personality, and also took note of people in such mundane places as the lingerie department of a clothing store, where a Warner Bros. scout found Lana Turner.[25] Scouts invited their discoveries to come to Los Angeles for a screen test, with the studio paying the way for those considered most promising. Studio drama coaches sometimes evaluated new arrivals before their screen tests, and a negative judgment could send them packing. Screen tests typically had two parts: a silent session to assess whether a person photographed well, followed by a scene with sound to assess acting skill. Producers and directors watched the tests within several days and decided whether to offer a contract and, if so, whether to change a new hire's name and how to style and clothe him or her, if not make actual physical alterations, such as a new hairline (for Rita Hayworth) or nose.[26] Talent departments prided themselves on their ability to detect talent, but it was not uncommon for an actor rejected by one studio to test successfully at another and become a star, as happened to Clark Gable and Burt Lancaster after Warner Bros. gave them a pass.[27] Even signing a contract did not assure all young actors a career; sometimes the studio did not know how to cast them and let them languish before dropping them at the first available opportunity. Insecurity was a factor for Hollywood actors at all stages of their careers, a situation that created disequilibrium and helped the studio executives maintain power.

Even so, the once-almighty studios started to falter in the late 1940s. The 1948 Supreme Court ruling known as the Paramount Decision required the studios to sell the first-run movie theaters they owned across the country to break their monopolistic control over the film industry. At the same time, movie attendance slid downward as more and more people bought televisions and stayed home to watch them. Home increasingly meant a house in the suburbs, far from the urban centers where movie theaters were located. Losing their theaters and a significant portion of their audience caused a crisis for the studio heads, but they continued to assert control over their employees. When the House Un-American Activities Committee (HUAC) targeted Hollywood in 1947 and in the name of anticommunism attacked left-leaning personnel, studio bosses chose to participate in the purge instead of defending their workforce, destroying the careers of several hundred actors, writers, directors, and technicians. Those who were subpoenaed by HUAC faced a choice between cooperating as so-called friendly witnesses by naming names of other Hollywood personnel for the committee to pursue or refusing and getting expelled from the industry. Blacklisted actors found that SAG, under the leadership of its then-president, Ronald Reagan, turned its back on them and supported the witch-hunt.[28] Government persecution and the Blacklist pitted actors against each other and created an atmosphere of hostility and fear that lasted through the 1950s. Beleaguered actors in some cases committed suicide—Philip Loeb was one—while others, including Charlie Chaplin, fled the country.

Even as actors suffered through the Red Scare, the studio system fell apart around them during the 1950s and the studios redefined themselves primarily as distributors of independently made films. Long-term contracts were phased out and actors gained the freedom to work with whichever production company they chose, including an increasing number of independent companies, and the power to manage their own careers. Ronald L. Davis explains that "by 1958, 65 percent of Hollywood's movies were made by independent producers, as stars moved from one to another, taking advantage of deals negotiated by agents, lawyers, bankers, and promoters. Rather than a studio publicity office, each actor began hiring his or her own publicist. . . . Stars with aggressive agents had become powerhouses, dictating packages to studio heads with little compromise."[29]

Talent agencies were indeed a major factor in the studio system's demise. Agents had worked on behalf of actors from early in Hollywood history and gained prominence with the transition to sound; they scoured the country for new talent, guided their clients' careers, made deals with producers, promoted their clients' interests, and had considerable power to broker high actors' salaries, from which they typically took 10 percent.[30] Many actors came to rely on the bargaining power of MCA (Music Corporation of America), which had moved to California from Chicago in 1937 to enter the film business and grew to become the world's largest talent agency. The agent Lew Wasserman, who later became MCA's president, developed enormous clout over his clients' careers and boosted actors' earning power.[31] Talent agents' success in advocating for their clients contributed to the end of long-term contracts and advanced profit-sharing as an alternative to a fixed salary after a landmark deal for James Stewart in the 1950 film *Winchester '73* (directed by Anthony Mann) gave him a percentage of the film's gross. The result is that today's biggest stars sometimes earn fixed salaries of $30 million per film, but if they opt for profit sharing instead, they may earn as much as $100 million, if not more, for a single film—exact figures are difficult to calculate.

Along with Hollywood's reconfiguration in the 1950s and 1960s came the lifting of censorship over film content and consequently a greater expressive range for actors, who had been held in check by the Motion Picture Production Code's rules. As early as 1906, the Women's Christian Temperance Union (WCTU) and other civic and religious organizations denounced what they perceived as debauchery in American films. The studios attempted to ward off external censorship by policing themselves and in 1930 introduced the Production Code, a document that listed precisely what would henceforth be inadmissible. Strict enforcement of the Code by the Production Code Administration (PCA) began in 1934 in response to a call from the Catholic Legion of Decency for a nationwide movie boycott; subsequently a film would only be released after it had been thoroughly examined and granted the PCA's seal of approval. Actors whose personae depended on wisecracks and sexuality were constrained, such as the spunky Mae West, who had to relinquish overt bawdiness in her films to comply with PCA demands, and the Marx Brothers, whose anarchic, irreverent humor was reined in. The Production Code loosened its grip during the 1950s when several films were released without its seal of approval (*The Man with the Golden Arm,* Otto Preminger, 1955; *Baby Doll,* Elia Kazan, 1956) and after the Supreme Court granted First Amendment protection to motion pictures in 1942. A fresh crop of actors became associated with newly risqué content, among them Marilyn Monroe, whose sex kitten persona was on display in *Gentlemen Prefer Blondes* (Howard Hawks, 1953), *The Seven Year Itch* (Billy Wilder, 1955), and *Let's Make Love* (George Cukor, 1960); Carroll Baker, who starred in *Baby Doll;* and Warren Beatty, who emerged as a sensitive sex symbol in *Splendor in the Grass* (Elia Kazan, 1961) and *Lilith* (Robert Rossen, 1964). Actors gained considerable freedom to develop multidimensional characters without fear of censorship in 1968 when the film industry replaced the Production Code with film ratings administered by the Classification and Rating Administration.

Discarding the Production Code did not, however, immediately alter the film industry's narrow characterization of minority groups. Lifting the Code's strictures (such as "miscegenation [sex relations between the races] is forbidden")[32] did not generate many new opportunities for African American actors nor immediately eliminate the demeaning types of roles they had played for decades. Hollywood films in the 1960s only superficially acknowledged the civil rights movement, and they tended to continue to rely on stereotypes, merely updating the old roles that emphasized subservience, buffoonery, or brutality. For most of Hollywood history, African Americans had to conform to a limited range of character types that dated back to minstrel shows, vaudeville, and white supremacist propaganda that diminished or demonized them. The earliest American films used white actors in blackface to portray African Americans; later, African Americans themselves were cast and tried to bring dignity to their limited roles. In the film *Hallelujah* (King Vidor, 1929), writes film scholar Donald Bogle, "the characters . . . were indeed stereotypes, blacks depicted as either sentimental idealists or highly emotional animals. But it should be said that to the credit of the actors, although many suffered from the blackface fixation, they still invested their characters with energy and a raw urgency."[33] Some African American actors became wealthy, but only by playing degrading roles, such as Lincoln Perry, who was known as Stepin Fetchit and throughout the 1930s played servile, ignorant characters who were constantly the butt of jokes. By the end of the decade he had lost his fortune and shortly thereafter fell into obscurity.[34] Servility defined the roles given to eminently talented African Americans Bill "Bojangles" Robinson, Hattie McDaniel, Butterfly McQueen, Louise Beavers, Clarence Muse, Louis Armstrong, and Eddie "Rochester" Anderson, among others (see figure 2).

Change came very slowly, and stereotyping also tainted the parts given to Paul Robeson during the 1930s and 1940s, Lena Horne from the 1930s into the 1970s, Dorothy Dandridge from the 1930s through the 1950s, and Sidney Poitier from the 1950s through the 1970s. With the blaxploitation cycle of films in the 1970s,

FIGURE 2: Louise Beavers plays the role of Mae West's domestic servant in *She Done Him Wrong*.

Hollywood sought to increase African American movie attendance by featuring tough, urban, aggressive, cool black characters, often pimps or other criminals. The films offered a break from earlier humiliating stereotypes, but the new roles were limiting in their own way, confined to a narrow dramatic range. Credit goes to the African American directors Spike Lee and John Singleton for getting studio backing to make films with greater nuance and relevance to late twentieth-century American life. Lee's *Do the Right Thing* (1989) and Singleton's *Boyz n the Hood* (1991) paved the way for African American actors to play a far greater variety of characters, and the stars Denzel Washington, Angela Bassett, Laurence Fishburne, Samuel L. Jackson, and Giancarlo Esposito were among the actors whose careers received a boost from appearing in these directors' early films. Now these actors along with such box office draws as Viola Davis, Morgan Freeman, Will Smith, Jada Pinkett Smith, and Halle Berry play a wide array of roles.

Across film history, actors have been lauded for their electrifying accomplishments on screen. However, writing about actors' performances is notoriously difficult, given the myriad components of each second of screen time: each aspect of voice, posture, gesture, mannerism, and facial expression, and each interaction with settings, props, sounds, and other actors. To complicate matters, spectators interpret neutral expressions on an actor's face differently depending on the previous and subsequent shots in a sequence. During the artistic ferment of the years immediately following the Russian Revolution, Soviet director and educator Lev

Kuleshov famously explored the power of editing to shape audience response by presenting the identical close-up of an actor's expressionless face three times, the first time followed by a shot of a bowl of soup, the second time by a shot of a woman's corpse in a coffin, and the third time by a shot of a young girl playing with her teddy bear. He reported that audiences complimented the actor's ability to convey the appropriate emotion for each situation. Kuleshov's student, director V. I. Pudovkin, wrote: "The public raved about the acting of the artist. They pointed out the heavy pensiveness of his mood over the forgotten soup, were touched and moved by the deep sorrow with which he looked on the dead woman, and admired the light, happy smile with which he surveyed the girl at play. But we know that in all three cases the face was exactly the same."[35] Despite the Kuleshov Effect, as it came to be known, actors do create meanings with the choices they make for each of their roles. In the continuity editing style, meanings are created as much by the mise-en-scène and characters as by the editing, and even in a rapidly edited montage, actors can make choices about how their characters will be seen.

A Case Study: Dick Powell

A charge made against film actors is that they are simply playing themselves, presenting larger-than-life versions of who they already are. An actor's ability to dramatically change his or her style should lay this misperception to rest. One such actor was Dick Powell, whose midcareer transformation makes him worthy of close analysis. Powell initially gained fame in Warner Bros. musical films in the early 1930s playing exuberant, wide-eyed young men. He sang and danced energetically and specialized in conveying high-octane enthusiasm, both for putting on a show and for the girl he loved. His face was malleable and his body limber, as if he could not restrain his zeal. This expressive style underwent a remarkable shift a decade later after Powell deliberately refused to take any more singing and dancing roles (breaking off his contract with Paramount in the process) and began to star in film noir movies, determined to escape juvenile roles and prove his acting acumen. Looking back, he described how frustrated he had become by his "corny" screen persona: "It got so I'd get a part, do my songs, and then do my best to forget all about the darned picture. . . . I made four or five of those things a year—and always the same stupid story. I just wore different clothes. Never had anything sensible to say—I looked and acted like a dope."[36] He had set his sights on the role of Walter Neff in Paramount's film noir *Double Indemnity* (Billy Wilder, 1944) and was disappointed when he lost out to Fred MacMurray. But he got his chance when RKO signed him to play private eye Philip Marlowe in a film based on Raymond Chandler's novel *Farewell, My Lovely,* which the studio renamed *Murder, My Sweet* (Edward Dmytryk, 1944) to prevent audiences from expecting another Dick Powell–type musical. The film did well at the box office and was critically acclaimed; the *New York Herald Tribune* observed that "Dick Powell plays the detective as he has never played any role before—the erstwhile crooner is perfectly convincing as a Humphrey Bogart type with overtones of light sarcasm,"[37] and the Mystery Writers of America selected him for their Edgar Allan Poe award. As Tony Thomas writes in his biography of Powell, "It seemed that all of a sudden he had become somebody else."[38] Powell himself wrote an article for the *Hollywood Citizen-News* in 1945 describing his transition as an opportunity to act: "From now on, I'm going to act. . . . I don't care what kind of characters they hand me, just so they don't have anything to do with putting moon together with June and coming out with No. 1 on the Hit Parade" (see figure 3).[39]

Of course, Dick Powell was indeed acting in both the musicals of the 1930s and the film noir movies of the 1940s; in neither genre was he simply himself, and for each type of film he crafted performances that fit the roles and the films' moods. It would be a mistake to assume that Powell only started acting when he began to star in film noir movies, as Powell suggested when he expressed scorn for having to do no more than put "moon together with June" in musicals. Studies of film acting should avoid simply reproducing the myths disseminated by the entertainment industry and actors themselves, as film studies scholar Kevin Esch argues:

FIGURE 3: Dick Powell as a film noir tough guy in *Murder, My Sweet*.

Re-envisioning a history of film acting . . . necessitates the examination of these actorly myths: the stories that we relate to define actors and the tales they tell to understand themselves (even those who define themselves in opposition to such myths, such as the pragmatic performer Spencer Tracy, or many British actors), and how those myths change over time. A mythis-torical approach would recognize film acting's indissoluble ties to its past mythologies, even as contemporary ideas of acting strain against those ties. It could help illuminate how these myths operate within, and respond to, the economic circumstances of the contemporary late-capitalist entertainment industry.[40]

Rather than dismiss Powell's musical film performances as non-actorly and applaud his acting chops in film noir movies, we can recognize his skill at successfully embodying both types of protagonists. What we see is a contrast between the Powell who got his start in entertainment relying on broad gestures as a singer, musician, comedian, master of ceremonies, and radio personality and the Powell who altered his approach to deliver a restrained, naturalistic perfor-mance.[41] He adjusted his body and voice for each film, in the process conveying how each genre envisioned the place of the individual within society. In musicals, he performed men whose energy and teamwork meant that their dreams would come true, and in film noir movies he played men who knew that brutality per-meated society and prevented a simple equation between effort and success.

His transformation from happy-go-lucky hoofer to tough guy is most appar-ent in his second film noir, *Cornered* (Edward Dmytryk, 1945). Comparing a sequence from this film to one from the earlier musical *Gold Diggers of 1933* (Mervyn LeRoy and Busby Berkeley, 1933) reveals how Powell's performance style changed to adjust to the new genre. Both scenes involve a confrontation between Powell's character and someone who has angered him, and in each performance Powell captures the essence of the film's thematic emphasis. The difference between the performances can be described as that between lightness and weight, between the springy excitement of a young man filled with hope and the world-weary heaviness of a middle-aged man with little to live for.

Gold Diggers of 1933 is a quintessential Depression-era musical, one of a cycle of films made by Warner Bros. about fighting the odds to put on a Broadway show. The typical *Gold Diggers* plot involves a young chorus girl getting a break and, through pluck and hard work, proving herself in a leading role. In *Gold Dig-gers of 1933,* a group of impoverished chorus girls get their break when a young man they know as a struggling songwriter named Brad Roberts (Powell) puts up the money for a new show, providing them with jobs and launching his career and that of his sweetheart, Polly (Ruby Keeler). Brad turns out to be on the run from his wealthy and disapproving family, but when he is forced to fill in for the male ingénue on opening night, his family discovers his whereabouts and

FIGURE 4: Dick Powell defending his passions in *Gold Diggers of 1933*.

sends his older brother, Lawrence (Warren William), and the family banker, Peabody (Guy Kibbee), to threaten to disinherit him if he continues to associate with low-life theater people and, in particular, Polly, whom they reject as a frivolous showgirl. The scene where Brad meets his brother and Peabody in the exclusive University Club displays Dick Powell's perky style and captures Brad's eagerness to achieve success, which the film defines as belonging to the realm of popular culture—Broadway musicals—rather than pompous high culture. Brad counters his brother's objection to his writing music for the theater by saying that the songs he wants to write are the kind that are "sung in shows and over the radio and on records . . . not the kind played by the Boston Symphony Orchestra, you have to be half-dead to compose that" (see figure 4).

Throughout their confrontation in the elegant club room, where Peabody, Brad, and Lawrence sit side-by-side on a sofa, Powell imbues Brad with energy; he strides into the room purposefully, smiles broadly, shakes hands, and maintains a straight back while he sits. He is like a coiled wire, ready to spring. He defends the theater and Polly against his brother's criticism by speaking quickly and forcefully with dynamic intonation. He crosses his arms across his chest as if to protect himself from attack, furrows his brow when his brother's comments annoy him, and gestures with his hands when responding. When he becomes fed up with his brother's threat to cut off his income, he stands, leans down toward his seated brother, and announces, "If that's all you have to say to me, you're just wasting your time; I've got more important things to do"; then he straightens up, turns his back, and strides out of the club in a long shot. Powell's performance infuses Brad with optimistic resolve; he strides into a Warner Bros. musical world where hard work and a willingness to collaborate bring success. His irrepressible energy promises to catapult him to his goal (see figure 5).

In contrast, Powell's portrayal of Laurence Gerard in *Cornered* is filled with despair. Gerard is a Canadian pilot who served in the British Royal Air Force during World War II, when he was shot down over France and held in a German prisoner of war camp. The film takes place just after the war ends, with Gerard newly freed and determined to avenge the death of his young French wife, Celeste, a member of the Resistance who was killed after being handed to the Nazis by a collaborator. Early in the film he sneaks into France despite lacking the proper documents and makes his way to his wife's village to find out from her father—Monsieur Roujon—who it was who betrayed her. Roujon evades Gerard's questions and urges him to abandon his quest for revenge, provoking Gerard's anger. Their confrontation takes place in Roujon's dark and cramped office where he works as the village prefect; deep shadows crisscross its walls, bathing the sequence in gloom and expressing the village's end-of-war desolation.

Powell's Gerard is characterized by sorrow and fatigue, a far cry from Brad Roberts's cheerful optimism in *Gold Diggers of 1933*. Gerard enters Roujon's shadowy office wearing dark clothing—an Eisenhower jacket, shirt open at the collar,

FIGURE 5: Dick Powell as an eager go-getter in *Gold Diggers of 1933*.

and slacks—unlike Brad Roberts's tie and tailored gray suit with an elegant hand-kerchief peeking out of the pocket. Gerard has dark stubble, a long scar on the left side of his buzz-cut head, and his face is creased, with wrinkles around his eyes and grooves running from his nose to his chin. After he enters, he slumps back against the door as if he cannot bear the weight of life (see figure 6). His arms hang limply and he stares silently, remaining at the door until Roujon leads him to a chair and seats him. Brad Roberts's bouncy step has been replaced by heavy plodding and the need to be pushed. Gerard is silent while Roujon babbles nervously, until finally Gerard says that he knows about Celeste's death: "Your letter came to the hospital." He speaks with effort, as if painfully dredging up words in a voice several registers lower and less nasal than the one he used for Brad Roberts. When Roujon hands him a glass of wine, he downs it in one gulp, unable to savor it. However, he is not without resolve, as he proves when he demands to know how Celeste was killed, jumping up and grabbing Roujon's arm and shouting furiously, "Someone was responsible; who was it?" It is while he shouts that we can see a trace of Brad Roberts, for Powell's voice rises and sounds momentarily more like a querulous child than a cynical man. But seconds later Gerard resumes his stooped heaviness to accuse Roujon of being an opportunist who is satisfied to have gotten his old job back. Roujon objects, and adds: "Who are you to tell me that your wife is dead? Your wife of twenty days who is dead was my daughter of more than twenty years!" Gerard takes a deep breath, turns his back, and remains

FIGURE 6: A world-weary and battle-scarred Dick Powell in *Cornered*.

silent, as if unable to find the appropriate words. Facing away from the camera, he finally says despondently, "Where is the grave? I would like to see it." When Roujon stalls, Gerard spits out, "I would like to see it now!" while clenching his fists. This is followed by a cut to the two men in an extreme long shot outside the cave where Celeste was killed.

It is possible to watch *Gold Diggers of 1933* and *Cornered* and not realize that Brad Roberts and Laurence Gerard are played by the same actor, given Dick Powell's transformation, which is not entirely explained by his having aged. In each performance he embodies a different genre inflected by a different *zeitgeist*: eager confidence versus disillusioned anguish. In a variation on film scholar John O. Thompson's notion that it is instructive to commute one actor for another in our imaginations,[42] we can swap Powell's two performances and recognize how inconceivable it would be for Brad Roberts to stand with his back to the camera in helpless resignation, unable to find the words to express himself, and how inappropriate it would be for Laurence Gerard to bound into the room with a huge smile and an arm extended for a handshake. Powell's transformation in fact indicates how the commutation test may not take account of an actor's ability to defy our expectations, going beyond typecasting in unexpected ways. Who would have thought that chipper young Dick Powell of the *Gold Diggers* franchise would come to represent postwar bitterness a decade later? Ironically, Powell once again chafed at being typecast and in the early 1950s declined to play any more roles in the film noir genre, turning instead to producing and directing.

Chapter Overview

The six chapters in this book examine the dynamic developments in American film acting from 1895 to the present, spanning the birth of moving pictures to their current omnipresence on screens of all sizes. In chapter 1, Victoria Duckett introduces the silent screen years (1895–1927) by investigating the American poet Vachel Lindsay's claim in 1915 that European stage acting was unsuited to film. This critique held sway for decades, during which commentators celebrated American, as opposed to European, contributions to the new craft of motion picture acting. European acting became associated with mannered staginess in contrast to a more subtle American style. Building on recent scholarship that questions this dichotomy, Duckett skillfully analyzes the screen performances of two women actors: the French Sarah Bernhardt, arguably the most famous late nineteenth-century actor, who electrified theater audiences but made relatively few film appearances, and the American Lillian Gish, who began her career as a child in stage melodramas but whose fame derived from her appearances in films. Duckett's nuanced reading of Bernhardt's performance in the film *Camille* (Film D'Art, 1911) and Lillian Gish's in *Broken Blossoms* (D. W. Griffith, 1919) reveals that despite their differences, they both used their bodies expressively to convey meanings and emotions. Their styles, rather than totally divergent, intersect in fascinating ways, indicating the crucial importance of the language of gestures for silent films and their successors in the sound era. Contrary to Lindsay's hostility to *Camille* at the time of its release, American audiences generally reacted favorably, Duckett shows, recognizing it as an opportunity to watch the famous French tragedienne display her dramatic techniques, just as Lillian Gish would be applauded for her emotive range a few years later.

In chapter 2, Arthur Nolletti Jr. identifies the classical Hollywood period (1928–1946) as a time of significant change in American filmmaking, when sound technology was introduced along with a regimented new industrial production mode within which actors' careers were controlled by powerful producers. This is the period that gave rise to the Hollywood studio acting style. A combination of naturalistic and theatrical acting, the Hollywood studio style was tailor-made for genre films, with their reliance on conventions within which slight variations could be registered. Nolletti demonstrates that in the period's genre films we can see how film aesthetics influenced performances and how gestural acting techniques persisted, embedded within the dominant naturalistic style. He offers astute close analysis of the performances of Herbert Marshall, Kay Francis, and Miriam Hopkins in the comedy *Trouble in Paradise* (Ernst Lubitsch, 1932); Ginger Rogers in the musical *Swing Time* (George Stevens, 1936); Beulah Bondi in the family melodrama *Make Way for Tomorrow* (Leo McCarey, 1937); and Fred MacMurray in the film noir *Double Indemnity* (Billy Wilder, 1944). Nolletti's sensitivity to the meanings conveyed by subtle performance signs is revelatory, and his approach encourages us to appreciate the varied work of actors appearing in genre films.

In chapter 3, David Sterritt describes the postwar era (1947–1967) as bridging a transition between one cultural ethos and another in American society, the first originating in economic depression and world war and characterized by conformity and consensus, the second arising from prosperity and characterized by self-doubt and discontent. Film acting changed alongside these cultural shifts. At a time when young people sought authenticity as an antidote to what they perceived as the older generations' superficial values, performances built on technical polish and charisma gave way to character idiosyncrasy and interiority. Guided by Method acting techniques, actors plumbed their own experiences to prepare for their roles, aspiring to make their performances as immediate and deeply felt as possible; this produced the sometimes jarring novelty and eccentricity of actors such as Marlon Brando and James Dean. Film aesthetics underwent a similar shift away from obvious technical refinement under the influence of Italian Neorealist and French New Wave cinema, which strove for documentary-style authenticity and spontaneity. Sterritt conveys how the era's values and tensions infiltrated performance styles with his case studies of the female stars Marilyn

Monroe, Shelley Winters, and Elizabeth Taylor and the male stars Montgomery Clift, Marlon Brando, and James Dean. Sterritt also reveals that even though individuality was triumphing over social sameness for Americans, especially for young people, not everyone jumped on the Method bandwagon, and some of the most popular stars of the postwar period spurned Method acting in favor of traditional performance techniques.

In chapter 4, Julie Levinson characterizes the Auteur Renaissance (1968–1980) as a time of upheaval both culturally and artistically, and analyzes how these disturbances shook out for American film production and acting styles. Ironically, although the period is well known for its immensely talented directors—the auteurs of the era's title—who revitalized filmmaking in the United States, actors also gained significant power as the creative force behind film projects, with certain actors rivaling directors for being cinematic visionaries. Performance styles reflected the new status accorded actors; European-influenced, loosely structured American films gave actors an opportunity to improvise their lines and influence narratives, and even in more conventional projects actors were given unprecedented control over their self-presentation. This sometimes took the form of Method-induced self-probing and at other times included actors learning a skill required by a role, shadowing real people to study their mannerisms, or gaining or losing massive amounts of weight. One of the iconic actors of the era, Robert De Niro, famously engaged in all of these activities to prepare for his roles. Levinson explains that actors were caught up in the larger cultural fascination with self-actualization and its promise that with sustained effort one could discover one's true, authentic self. The search for authenticity, driven by youth culture's rejection of social conformity, was a guiding principle; it found expression in films' greater freedom to depict sex and violence as well as in an appreciation of plain looks over glamour and overt ethnic markers over homogeneity. In a time of heady artistic ferment, the era produced unconventional films that allowed actors to experiment alongside films that took their cue from the technically polished past. Levinson points out that disparate film styles were accompanied by equally divergent performance styles, sometimes within the same film. Her incisive analysis combines depth with breadth to illuminate how film acting kept pace with cultural trends during one of the most volatile periods in American history.

In chapter 5, Donna Peberdy concentrates on three significant modes of acting in the New Hollywood (1981–1999): transformation, excess, and the ensemble. Although present earlier, these modes came to the forefront in the last two decades of the twentieth century, a period often described as stable and prosperous in the United States, but also marked by worries about excesses in business and politics. In American films, actors went to increasing lengths to alter themselves for their roles, creating performances in which their bodies and faces were hidden or distorted, thereby making traditional signs of acting difficult to discern. Some actors also engaged in wildly exaggerated performances, perhaps to play with genre expectations (as in the case of Jack Nicholson) or push the acting lexicon's boundaries (as in the case of Nicolas Cage). In addition, actors in ensemble films had to adjust to the emphasis on character interactions as well as the goals of unity around a particular theme and balance between individual performers. The unconventional nature of these three acting modes posed challenges when it came time to evaluate performances for Academy Awards, and the antirealist tendencies on display created a rift between film critics who enjoyed the novelty and critics who bemoaned what they saw as bad acting. Peberdy provides a masterly analysis of how transformation, excess, and the ensemble manifested themselves in the work of particular actors, and establishes that a number of the films in which they appear deserve recognition for their creative and prescient social commentary.

In chapter 6, Cynthia Baron maps the exciting new directions taken by film acting in the modern entertainment marketplace (2000–the present). She shows that this is a good time to be an actor; challenging and energizing opportunities have opened up in our digital world as a result of new platforms such as video games and an array of technological innovations. CGI and performance-capture techniques have created work for actors instead of replacing them, facilitating intriguing collaborations between actors and animators and reviving interest in traditional acting techniques, especially those that emphasize the expressive power of facial expressions and physical gestures. Baron analyzes how animated gestures convey nuanced meanings in the film *Wall-E* (Andrew Stanton, 2008), and how actor Andy Serkis did meticulous work in coordination with the performance-capture team for the *Lord of the Rings* trilogy (Peter Jackson, *The Fellowship of the Ring*, 2001; *The Two Towers*, 2002; and *The Return of the King*, 2003) to create a layered performance for the character of Gollum. There is also newfound appreciation among audiences and acting professionals for performances in big-budget action films, despite the films' emphasis on explosions and rapid editing and their departure from realist acting. What the films call for is a restrained, minimalist style with sudden bursts of highly expressive acting. Emblematic of this fluctuation between calm and agitation, Baron argues, is the work of Denzel Washington, whose performance in *Man on Fire* (Tony Scott, 2004) she discusses in an enlightening close analysis. Baron points out that we now encounter the work of actors on many types of screens, not just in the theater, and actors' performances are increasingly influencing our daily behavior and mannerisms. Acting, she skillfully shows, is thriving both on- and offscreen.

As film spectators and as people who choose how to present ourselves in public, we benefit from learning about trends and transformations in film acting. These six chapters enrich our understanding of how the American movies we watch have gotten where they are, and prompt us to speculate about where they might be going.

1

THE SILENT SCREEN, 1895–1927 Victoria Duckett

Vachel Lindsay's *Art of the Moving Picture* was first published in 1915. One of the earliest attempts to assess acting in silent film critically, it today serves as an important guide to the nascent reception of screen acting in America. Lindsay not only asserts that acting on screen is an art form that must be taken seriously, but also argues that theatrical stars who exhibit the gestural style of the European theater have no place in the American cinema. Only those European films that can be recuperated through their impressive sets (Giovanni Pastroni's 1913 *Cabiria* and later Robert Weine's *The Cabinet of Dr. Caligari*, 1919, as cited in Lindsay's 1922 edition of *The Art of the Moving Picture*) are considered innovative and cause for celebration.[1] Otherwise, it is individuals such as Mary Pickford, Douglas Fairbanks, William S. Hart, Mae Marsh, Blanche Sweet, and Lillian Gish who are presented as examples of actors who successfully negotiate the demands of the new medium. In 1915 (and also in 1922) these actors are all young, they all developed and honed their acting skills before the camera, and they together point to the ongoing development and success of film as both an artistic and a commercial industry.

Lindsay's emphasis upon the "moving picture" reiterates the link he is drawing between the traditional fine arts (painting, drawing, sculpture, and architecture) and film. In his vision, the European theater and, with it, European actors have no place on screen. Lindsay cites Sarah Bernhardt's performance in *Camille* (*La Dame aux camélias*, André Calmettes and Henri Pouctal, 1911), a film that was released in America in March 1912, as an example of Europe's theatrical failure. He describes the film as a record of live stage acting and suggests that action was not modified for the camera, that it can be "compared to watching *Camille* from the top gallery through smoked glass, with one's ears stopped with cotton."[2] Lindsay was not just critical of the silence of Bernhardt's film. He also believed that the film "lasts as long as would the spoken performance."[3] With the most famous living European actor thus cast as anachronistic intruder in an art form that Lindsay otherwise associated with youth and experimentation, Lindsay creates a division between continents, generations, and even art forms. Acting that had its provenance on the European stage and that was developed in the live theater not only stood in contrast to acting in the American cinema, it was its nemesis.

It has taken roughly a century for Lindsay's criticism of Bernhardt in particular and of European acting more generally to be revised. Indeed, it is only recently, since the mid-1990s, that acting on silent film has been explored in terms of artistic exchange or collaboration with the live theater and that European acting on film has been explored as something more than a theatrical anachronism. Prior to the research of scholars such as Jon Burrows, Eric de Kuyper, Annette Förster, Christine Gledhill, and (in particular) David Mayer, acting on silent film was conceived in terms of a teleology that saw film take over the illusionism of the nineteenth-century stage, reaching maturity only when the American film industry dominated the world market during World War I. At this crucial juncture—which is precisely the moment in which Lindsay is writing—acting on film is associated with youthful actors trained in the cinema and screen acting becomes as "invisible" or "natural" as possible.[4]

In his pioneering article entitled "Acting in Silent Cinema: Which Legacy of the Theatre?" Mayer explains that acting on early film cannot be reduced to a single teleology and that film acting cannot be divorced from the live stage. Further, anachronistic "old style" theatrical acting expresses theatrical agency that we easily miss today. He states:

> Conditioned as we are to performance through our late-twentieth-century experience of what we view as more-or-less realistic acting within a more-or-less realistic mise-en-scène, we are unable or unwilling to accept early actors' work as an effective means of explicating narrative, clarifying character relationships, expressing appropriate or valid emotion, or providing aesthetic pleasure. We are conditioned to the camera as an instrument for recording truth and the actor's performance as a means of validating that truth.[5]

Although Mayer focuses on the impact that Nicholas Vardac's 1949 study *Stage to Screen: Theatrical Method from Garrick to Griffith* has had on sixty years of thinking about acting, his comments might also be addressed to the arguments that lace Lindsay's book.[6] Clearly, it is the separation between stage and screen acting, as well as the division between European and American actors and the Old and the New Worlds, that must today be redressed. Rather than repeat the model of an old European theater being usurped by a modern American cinema, or reiterate the idea that European actors and acting had no place on the nascent American screen, I contrast two of the actors that Lindsay himself isolates— the French actress Sarah Bernhardt in *Camille* and a young Lillian Gish—and explore the different acting styles they bring to American silent film. Both enormously famous for the idiosyncratic way they act on film, these actresses evidence very different gestures, acting tempo, and use of screen space. While Bernhardt's films were developed against the backdrop of her experience on the late nineteenth-century stage, Gish's films indicate the ways that acting began to capitalize upon small idiosyncratic actions and domestic props in the development of cinematic gestural language.

Rather than separate these actresses into a binary of old versus new, theatricality versus naturalism, good versus bad, and so on, I want to explore their differences in terms of their variety and change from the live theater. Indeed, we cannot discuss acting in the American silent cinema without acknowledging the very differences that were at play. Although today we consider "natural acting" appropriate to the screen, silent cinema is fascinating precisely because it illustrates both the directions taken *and* not taken in the development of screen acting. It is in this context that I have chosen to explore Sarah Bernhardt alongside Lillian Gish. I can think of no better way to illustrate that actors with different and even competing ideas were welcomed, celebrated, and even encouraged in the American silent cinema.

The European Enlightenment: Acting in Late Nineteenth-Century America

Acting in early American film must be understood not only within the context of diversity and difference; it must also be understood within the broader context of the Enlightenment. Indeed, as Joseph Roach demonstrates in his book *The Player's Passion: Studies in the Science of Acting*, theatrical gesture was rationalized in the seventeenth century when the human body was theorized as a machine. René Descartes, in his *Les passions de l'âme* (1649), decisively proposed that the human body is a machine moved by emotions. Identifying wonder, love, hatred, desire, joy, and sadness as passions that functioned as triggers to external physiological expression, Descartes broke from earlier models by articulating a Cartesian division between body and soul. Later, Julien de La Mettrie in *L'homme machine* (1747) argued that "man is a machine." As Roach explains, emotional expression was considered "the mechanical effects of internal physical causes, much like hours showing on the face of a clock."[7]

The impact of this thinking on the theater and its reception was tremendous. The actor could imagine the body as a formal and regular mechanism with laws that mirrored the physical laws of the universe. S/he could therefore direct the physiological expression of the passions and these could be universally deciphered and understood. The old oratorical style of acting that had associated physical gesture with the animation of spirits that accompanied a song-like chant of verse was replaced by a new emphasis upon the physical body as an expression of rational intellect. This provided a paradigmatic shift in thinking that ushered in expressive gesture as the new language of theatrical performance. The Royal Society, responding to these changes in scientific thinking that swept away ancient physiological theory, adopted *nullius in verba* as its motto. Roach states:

> In *L'homme machine* ["man is a machine"] of 1747, [Julien de] La Mettrie carried to its radical conclusion a scientific revolution begun over a hundred years before. This revolution emerged from the struggle of the new science to view the world afresh, to cast down the idols of received opinion and ancient authority. Its new policy was self-consciously dramatized by the uncompromising motto adopted by the Royal Society in 1662—*nullius in verba*, "on the word of no one." The so-called "mechanization of the world picture," which was the collective achievement of seventeenth-century science and philosophy, presented the universe as matter in motion. . . . Physics and psychology intersect in the study of the human body, identifying emotion with motion.[8]

This thought impacted visual literature. Printed publications that included sketches and diagrams circulated; these demonstrated the emotion that could be attached with a physical attitude or facial expression. For example, studies such as the painter Charles Le Brun's *Méthode pour apprendre à dessiner les passions* (1702) depicted the passions in detail. For the first time, Cartesian physiology motivated the artist's study of passions. A modern body of visual literature emerged upon which the actor could draw. The interplay between this literature and acting on the stage is extremely rich. Roach cites Franciscus Lange's *Dissertatio de actione scenica* (Munich, 1727), François Riccoboni's *L'art du théâtre* (Paris, 1750), Roger Pickering's *Reflections upon Theatrical Expression in Tragedy* (London, 1755), and Goethe's *Regeln für Schauspieler* (Weimar, 1803) as examples of the literature that can illustrate this interchange between Cartesian thought, drama, and the visual arts.[9] For my purposes, it is sufficient that Le Brun's images still circulate in acting handbooks in the late nineteenth century, even in books that argue that gestural language was not universal but "has its typical features in every nation."[10] As I discuss below, American silent film saw the coincidence of this idea that emotions can be visually relayed with the idea that emotions were universally legible. Although we cannot parallel the "homme machine" with the apparatus of the cinema, we can identify the ways that silent film became a particularly rich place for the physical expression of the passions.

Discussing Delsarte

Frenchman François Delsarte (1811–1871) had a strong impact on acting in America in the late nineteenth century. A bridging figure who illustrates the spread, application, and acceptance of Enlightenment thought and European aesthetic gesture in America, Delsarte taught a method of physical expression that gave attention to the expressive voice and the practiced used of gesture. Tired of the idiosyncratic and variable way that acting was taught to him in the Paris Conservatoire, he sought to establish a method of aesthetic acting that expressed naturalness, that was available to all artists (including sculptors, painters, and so on), and that could be shared as an acting method. His basic belief was that the body expressed inner thought and feeling and that every movement and gesture materializes inner thought.[11]

Although he never published a book summarizing his teaching, publications explaining and translating Delsarte's methods of physicalizing and therefore expressing emotion through an action or specific stance or look were published in America in the 1880s,[12] were reprinted into the early twentieth century, and made their way into simple middle-class acting manuals for home and school use.[13] Diagrams of full-bodied gesture with titles such as "Horror," "Listening," "Admiration," "Impudence" and so on detailed the pose and gesture that actors must achieve. In *The Home and School Speaker*, for example, "Bashfulness" is designated by a sketch that shows a woman with her right leg stretched out to the side, her foot peeking out from under a cascade of her draped dress. Her right hand reaches her mouth, wrist twisted inward, elbow bent. She does not look at us but faces slightly downward; her left arm, with its palm resting against her body, hangs languidly at her side. In gestures where emotions change, a negative inflection is always represented by the turning away of a head or hand from the direction initially adopted, so that the palm of a hand turns from upward to downward, or the body moving to one side turns back onto itself.

As the *The Home and School Speaker* indicates, these are "Delsarte exercises," not poses or attitudes. Performers must move between gestures and not freeze the body into an unnatural and illegible stiffness. To emphasize the importance of movement, *The Home and School Speaker* states that "music, to secure perfect unison in action, is a great help in Delsarte exercises. . . . The transitions [between poses] should each be made, of course, during one bar of music and the gesture sustained during a bar."[14] As I discuss below, music was fundamental to performance on stage and on screen. Our incapacity to identify and acknowledge the gestural impact and power of much silent screen acting can be linked to our ongoing tendency to see early film as truly "silent."

Nancy Lee Chalfa Ruyter explains in a discussion of Delsarte's impact on turn-of-the-century acting in America that it was particularly white, middle-class urban ladies, students, and amateur actors who developed Delsarte's system of aesthetic expression. Delsartean attitudes or *poses plastiques*, drills, pantomimes, and dances became expressive forms that saw bodies choreographed so that they naturally expressed an emotion or state.[15] While the voice was also given attention by the teachers and practitioners of Delsarte—*The Home and School Speaker* is subtitled, for example, "For the Cultivation and Preservation of the Voice and Use of Gesture" and explains that oratory is especially important in America because of the principle of free speech—it was in the physical expression of emotions that Delsarte's influence was most widely felt. As Ruyter explains, in America "bodily expression [was] not only included but emphasized—in the communication of narratives, character delineations, and thematic ideas."[16]

While amateur actors were important in bringing Delsartean attitudes and poses into the schools and parlors of America, professional actors also made use of him in their teaching and training. Actor Steele MacKaye, who helped establish the first school of acting in America (the Lyceum theater school that later became the American Academy of Dramatic Arts), was a famous advocate of Delsarte after he met and studied with him in Paris in 1869. As MacKaye's student Genevieve Stebbins explains, in the 1870s MacKaye returned to America "to prepare the New World for the coming of Delsarte."[17] Stebbins herself became a student of MacKaye, eventually founding (with Mary S. Thompson, an oratory coach) a Delsarte school in Boston and New York. She went on to establish the New York School of Expression at Carnegie Music Hall.[18] Stebbins believed that physical expression and transition between attitudes was important; physical change between poses must be natural and occur like a wave in the sea or like melody in music.[19]

While acting in the late nineteenth and early twentieth century was an international practice, emerging out of the reciprocal impact that European acting had in America, identifiable "theatrical" gesture was later caricatured and ridiculed. Delsarte's idea that emotions can be expressed naturally and that "excess is to be avoided" gave way to the presumption that gestural acting was preordained, stiff, regulated, and unnatural. Writing in the 1920s, Percy MacKaye (Steele MacKaye's son) explains how Delsarte was "commercialized and travestied by the distorted and ludicrous perversions of ignorance or half-knowledge. . . . A pure science and its disciplined embodiment in art had become a laughing stock of the vulgar and a source of vexatious sorrow to the few informed, who were aware of those gracious lineaments of Beauty which the mob had defaced beyond all recognition."[20]

Delsarte's demise in America, as well as Lindsay's incapacity to enjoy Bernhardt's performance on film, reminds us of the ease with which changing taste can retroactively dictate what is appropriate to theatrical acting. Rather than see studied and rehearsed gesture as an anomaly in America, as a foreign import that has no place in the nascent cinema, we might remember that American acting was in dialogue with developments in France and owed much to the idea that the actor could indeed express a great deal through gestures and movement. Like Gish, Bernhardt was certainly not alone in presuming that her gestures and actions were legible and even familiar to American audiences.

Beginning with Bernhardt: An Actress's Formation

Born in Paris in 1844, Bernhardt was the child of a Dutch Jewish courtesan, Julie Bernard. Bernhardt was accepted into the elite school of acting, the French Conservatoire, in 1860, at the age of fifteen. The Conservatoire was the leading school of dramatic declamation, established in France in 1786. Much has been written about Bernhardt's early life, her professional development within the Conservatoire, and the negligible impact that her debut at the Comédie Française had on Parisian audiences. For our purposes, it is her later years, after Bernhardt left the Comédie Française in 1879, spurred on by the praise and success she enjoyed on her first tour to London, that is significant. At this point Bernhardt launched a career of her own and began a series of tours that took her to Europe, America, and Australia. Bernhardt toured nine times to North America between 1880 and 1917. It was especially in America, on these long and demanding tours where she performed in a variety of venues before popular audiences, that Bernhardt developed a performance style that was visually pantomimic. Famous for her vocal skills and speaking always and only in her native French on stage, Bernhardt became equally famous for her capacity to engage popular and foreign audiences through her physical acting. As French theater critic Francisque Sarcey stated in his review of Bernhardt's *La Tosca* in 1887, the play was made not for Parisian audiences but for audiences (mainly "les Yankees") abroad; it was "above and before all, a good commodity for export." This was because Bernhardt no longer expressed psychological developments in her theatrical play through long conversation and vocal monologue but instead relayed facts that are "blindingly obvious" through physical gesture.[21]

Bernhardt did not engage foreign audiences through her gestures alone; it was also the expressive way she modulated her voice that helped express thought and sentiment. As Bernhardt explains in her book *The Art of the Theatre*, "The glance must precede the gesture, which must precede the word which is nothing more than the formula of thought."[22] Using the stabbing scene in *Tosca* to illustrate this point, Bernhardt explains how Tosca watches Scarpia sign his guarantee of her and her lover's safe passage. Reaching for a glass of wine on the table, she sees a knife. The thought comes to her: kill her torturer. She looks at Scarpia and then back at the knife. Her thought, freed by glance and gesture, is then realized as she stabs him, crying "Meurs! Meurs! Lâche!"[23] This vocal conclusion to action—where spoken lines reinforce acting—can be paralleled to the physical acting developed by the followers of Delsarte in America.[24] As Stebbins explains: "Expression of eyes precedes gesture, and gesture precedes speech."[25]

The importance of Bernhardt's engagement with film is not merely that film extended and ensured her fame in the twentieth century. Film demonstrates her physical gestures and in this sense provides a visible record of how a gesture might be expressed, modulated, changed, or achieved. Photographs of Bernhardt by Paul Nadar taken in the 1870s and 1880s show Bernhardt in theatrical poses, often also in the simple sleeveless and flowing white gowns that mirror the "costumes of the classical order" called for by Delsartean acting manuals. These images demonstrate an identifiable moment of a play that Bernhardt defines through physical gesture alone: the hypnotic and ritual closure that occurs as Tosca lays the final candelabras at the side of the murdered Scarpia, for example, a gesture that has become so important that it is still an identifiable part of performance today (see figure 7). Where photographs are like the sketches of Le Brun, or like the diagrams in acting manuals, film instead demonstrates physical flow.[26] We see the tempo and cadence of movement and appreciate that on film Bernhardt performed in a choreographed, timed, and not at all haphazard, posed, or stilted way. As *Motion Picture Story Magazine* explains, Bernhardt's film can therefore serve a pedagogic purpose:

> With the photographic lens these movements [of Bernhardt] could be caught, and, with them, the countless others which so glorify a Bernhardt impersonation, and they could be a factor in the training of generations of actresses. Bernhardt, supreme genius that she is, recognizes this and she has already posed for the "little pictures." . . . People do not go to the opera to see the dramatic exposition of the great roles, except in the case of a Mary Garden; they go to hear them sung, and it is for that, solely, that they will buy their phonograph records; with the artists of the drama they will buy their picture reels to see them act, and the dialog will be of as little consequence as it is in the Moving Picture theatre of today.[27]

In film studies we have long acknowledged that the "moving pictures" animate the still image. Erwin Panofsky famously removed theatrical acting from early film when he argued that "the earliest films added movement to works of art originally stationary, so that the dazzling technical invention might achieve a

FIGURE 7: Sarah Bernhardt in *Tosca*. Photograph by Paul Nadar, *Bibliothèque nationale de France*, 1897.

triumph of its own without intruding upon the sphere of higher culture."[28] Might the "moving" pictures also be considered, however, in terms of theatrical engagement? Might acting on film be seen as a way to make emotions legible to popular audiences? Can the acting that Bernhardt was so skilled at on the live stage be seen as part of her very appeal? Although Lindsay seems impervious to Bernhardt's acting in *Camille*, was it really illegible, silent, and foreign to an American public?

The Genius of Gesture: Cinematizing Camille

La Dame aux camélias was a film made by the French Film d'Art in late 1911 and released to French, American, and English audiences in early 1912. With a length of 2,275 feet, it ran for roughly forty minutes. In America, Canada, and Mexico, it was released as *Camille* and sold with Madame Réjane's *Mme. Sans-Gene* on a states' rights basis as part of a double bill. As a two-page advertisement in *Moving Picture World* announced, the program was a "Complete Evening's Entertainment of About Two and One Half Hours, Presenting the Divine Sarah, the World Renowned Emotional Actress, and Mme. Rejane, the Famous French Comedienne, at Their Best."[29] The impact of this program cannot be ignored. Not only was it rare for an actress of Sarah Bernhardt's caliber to appear on film, it was also rare for a film to be marketed to a middle-class audience as an evening's entertainment. *Camille* was therefore at the forefront of two related movements. It helped to expand the filmgoing public to include women and a more traditional theatergoing audience while it also offered a respected theatrical venue and program for an entertainment that had been largely associated with short films, the mass public, and the variety stage.

Camille debuted when Bernhardt was sixty-seven years old. It featured her in the role of Marguerite Gautier, the consumptive sixteen-year-old courtesan of Alexandre Dumas's 1848 book (and subsequent play) *La Dame aux camélias*. In the trade press, the film was advertised as "Making New Records for Selling State Rights"[30] and "The Fastest Seller Ever Offered State Rights Buyers."[31] In other publicity, Dumas's work was described as an "Emotional World Classic,"[32] a "soul shaking emotional drama,"[33] and an "Emotional Masterpiece."[34] It was Bernhardt's capacity to interpret Marguerite in an engaging and emotional

FIGURE 8: "Dumas' Heart-Gripping Drama." Two-page advertisement, *The Moving Picture World*, March 16, 1912.

way that was therefore publicized for audiences and which drove the film's success in America (see figure 8). Knowledge of Dumas, or even of the legitimate stage, was not necessary in this pitch to human emotions. As advertisements proclaimed, indicating that gesture would indeed be expressive and legible, Bernhardt was the "WORLD'S MOST FAMOUS EMOTIONAL ACTRESS."[35]

Reviews of Bernhardt's acting in *Camille* indicate her capacity to emotionally engage audiences. As the *New York Times* states in review of a performance she gave in 1910, "There were many tears when the final curtain fell, and there was no lack of evidence that the actress had again moved her people as she has done many score times before." This success was notwithstanding the fact that "after seeing the French actress at intervals for thirty years in this piece, her acting in it has become as familiar as the sun."[36] In contrast to the image we have in film studies of an out-of-touch, aged, and anachronistic Bernhardt recording her theater for film, I suggest that *Camille* was brought to film because it allowed foreign audiences to engage in Bernhardt's emotional performance.

In Vachel Lindsay's review of *Camille*, however, he focuses on the impossibility of hearing Bernhardt speak on film. Rather than interpret her gestures or concede the role that acting played in translating and expressing emotion, he speaks of his ears being "stopped with cotton." Bernhardt's *Camille* was largely famous, however, for the changes it brought to the physical acting of Marguerite. Indeed, at the play's debut in London in 1881, the *Times* notes that: "Mlle. Bernhardt introduces a curious novelty. She dies standing. Madame Doche, whose name is identified with the part of Marguerite, was accustomed to sink down upon a couch and die holding her lover's hand, but Mlle. Bernhardt remains standing till the last, and falls forward upon the bosom of her lover, who, with a cry of alarm, lays her down straight and stiff upon the floor. It may be presumed that Mlle. Bernhardt has fortified herself with some physiological authority for this unusual action."[37] The "curious novelty" is not just Bernhardt's fall to the floor, but the spiraling way in which this was achieved. Francisque Sarcey, reporting on Bernhardt's London performance to a French public, explains more fully:

"Mme Bernhardt stands—it is the movement imprinted, stamped in the [theatrical] program—but instead of sitting herself down again for her last words, and murmuring them seated, as was the tradition, she remains standing, breathing life in with all the strength of her being, defying death. Then, using herself as a pivot, she reels and makes a half-turn and, as if finally vanquished, she falls from her height in the most elegant and poetic pose imaginable."[38]

This turning fall to her death became a signature part of Bernhardt's *Camille* and is shown in the final scene of her film. Here we see her standing in Armand's embrace, her hands reaching around his neck as he holds her waist. She falls suddenly backward; he holds as she swings around him, coming to a rest in his arms on the floor. Her flowing white nightgown emphasizes this turn, spiraling around her feet as she lies dead on the floor. In a colorful poster for *Camille* this famous death is used to promote the work (see figure 9). Red type declares: "For the First Time in the Cinematographe."[39] Beneath this is Bernhardt's name—and not, tellingly, the name of Louis Mercanton as film director nor that of Alexandre Dumas as playwright—and the title of the film at the bottom of the frame. The image shows Bernhardt with her white dress wrapping itself around her thin frame as she lies dead with Armand grieving over her. Unlike Armand's father, who is shown covering his eyes behind them, as spectators we are offered the promise of witnessing this famous death flop. With "Le Film d'Art" written across the advertisement and camellia flowers stretching in S-shaped vines along each side of the frame, we are introduced to the work as a visual synthesis of the art nouveau movement. Bernhardt's body (on the poster but also on the film) creates a curving mobile line. She incarnates the tendrilic and spiraling momentum we are so familiar with in Hector Guimard's ornate cast-iron-balustrade entrances to the Paris Métro, for example, or in Alphonse Mucha's floral and spiraling poster designs. The tendril and its spiraling, curved movement were not just part of the decorative arts but integral to Delsarte and the gestural lines his method promoted.[40]

Bernhardt moves but she is also, notably, intensely moving: as mentioned above, Duval covers his eyes in response to Marguerite's death. What was once so unusual—to see the actress perform a spiral, to have Bernhardt physically describe Marguerite's

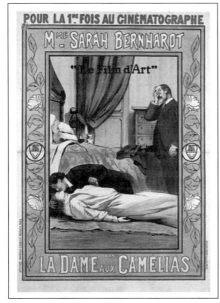

FIGURE 9: *La Dame aux Camélias.*

change from life to death and not rely upon words to relay this—was part of Bernhardt's physical vocabulary. Idiosyncratically, and before a new public, it made its way onto film.

Significance of Space

A fixed camera and indoor shots mark and define the space of *Camille*. We are inside the cottage that Armand and Camille share as their romantic retreat from Paris in the first scene, then at the elegant party hosted by Olympe where Armand sees Marguerite on the arm of the Count de Varville in the second, then briefly outdoors in the duel between Armand and the Count, then back indoors as Armand's father confides to him that he forced their separation, and we are finally in a modest bedroom when Marguerite dies in the arms of Armand. This focus on the indoors, with its suggestion of claustrophobia and bourgeois containment, confirms the moral of the story. After all, *Camille* is not just a tale of great love; it is about the incapacity of a courtesan to gain bourgeois respectability and the extent she will go to in order to respect the wishes of a bourgeois father. On the other hand, the use of theatrical indoor sets and the stillness of the camera frame Bernhardt in a continual long shot. It is as though we are seated in a theater with an unencumbered view of the stage action. We watch the choreography of Bernhardt's entire body; it is as though nuance has been lost in the effort to reach and record gestural emotion.

Reviews of *Camille* indicate that the fixed camera and indoor space were not central to the interpretation of Bernhardt's acting. Nuance and emotional detail were seen in full-bodied action. For example, the *New York Dramatic Mirror* relays how Bernhardt "is standing in Armand's embrace with her face hidden from view by her hand drooping and falling like the flower from which Marguerite's sobriquet was derived." The importance of this rising and falling hand, described as "tremendously impressive and convincing," lay in the fact that it condensed narrative meaning into one gesture.[41] A comment by W. Stephen Bush about a small gesture used by Bernhardt to indicate Marguerite's illness in the opening scene of the film similarly illustrates that viewers were watching and interpreting gestural nuance and detail. He states: "How subtle is the touch by which she gives us the first hint of the fatal nature of her malady, when the first reel has scarcely begun. This marvellous power in developing the tragic element is finely sustained throughout until it culminates in a veritable triumph of acting in the last scene."[42]

While this subtle touch might be the way Bernhardt pauses writing her letter to Armand to painfully wipe her brow, I am not certain that I see the gesture or moment recognized by Bernhardt's own contemporaries. Is it indeed this brow gesture? I do not know. Part of my problem today lies in the fact that I struggle to interpret theatrical nuance in the context of a fixed camera and through the distant, full-figure view of a gesturing actress. In this context, Mayer is indeed correct in arguing that we are "conditioned to the camera as an instrument for recording truth and the actor's performance as a means of validating that truth." When the camera does not individuate gestural details for us, we watch acting in a static space that makes the full frame our point of reference. In this context, I do not know where or how to look or to truly see. Instead of catching nuanced detail, I notice outstretched arms and the more obvious horizontal and upward-moving moments of gestural extension: Bernhardt stretching her arms out in despair when she writes her letter of farewell to Armand, Bernhardt falling suddenly backward just before she twists to the floor, Bernhardt filling the full stretch of the screen as she lies dead with Armand kneeling at her side. Indeed, Bernhardt's falling handkerchief asks for attention to what Delsartean actors called "the feather movements" that—unless forewarned—we can easily miss.

Performing Passions

The idea that Bernhardt theatrically overacted, that she brought to film gestures we today can identify for being artificial or too obviously "performed" on screen, misses the nuance of her movements in *Camille*. It also overlooks the very speed of her acting in the film. Indeed, we know that Bernhardt's live performances (like many performances by celebrities on the live stage) were often interrupted with applause from audiences. Her *entr'actes* were also lengthy: reviewers speak of these being "unusually long" and how "the performance was not finished until a late hour."[43] These interruptions were not part of film. Moreover, physical action on screen was quick. When *Moving Picture World* states that "someone has said that the pictures fairly crackle with life and send wireless messages to the specta-tor,"[44] it indicates that action in *Camille* was fast and (at the same time) legible. In another discussion, *Moving Picture World* explains how "*Camille* was rehearsed a few times with the watch in order to get it timed right. . . . The result is a long series of photographs that are staccato in their expressiveness."[45] Another review notes a "hurried flight" when Bernhardt painfully leaves the house she shares with Armand.[46]

This acceleration represents a departure from Bernhardt's live performance. In order to understand why this is so, we must briefly return to her voice and appreciate its use on the live stage. Bernhardt's voice was considered an import-ant part of her performance. Audiences at the opening of the twentieth century were galvanized by her expressive use of voice. W. B. Yeats, describing Bern-hardt's importance to the Irish stage in 1902, therefore explains how:

The other day I saw Sara [sic] Bernhardt and De Max in *Phèdre*, and understood where Mr Fay, who stage manages the National Theatri-cal Company, had gone for his model. For long periods the performers would merely stand and pose and I once counted twenty-seven quite slowly before anybody on a fairly well-filled stage moved, as it seemed, so much of an eyelash. The periods of stillness were generally shorter, but I frequently counted seventeen, eighteen, or twenty before there was a movement.[47]

Yeats was trying to eliminate action on stage in order to return a lost, common voice to the theater.[48] His comments are useful since he tells us that Bernhardt held a pose in a performance in 1902 for up to twenty-seven seconds as she spoke. What must be remembered, therefore, is that a silently mouthing Bernhardt who moves quickly and is in constant action on film is not equivalent to Bernhardt performing on the live stage. For Yeats, Bernhardt's voice is a tonic to the mechanical restlessness of industrialization. As statements indicate above, however, film is instead "crackling with life," sending "wireless messages," an industrial product that might even be experienced negatively in terms of the violence of modern life.[49] Other advertisements explain that Bernhardt's film is "AS VIVID AS LIGHTNING."[50] Perhaps more tellingly, her film places the photoplay "in competition on equal terms with the living Stage of Stars."[51] In this context, Bernhardt's *Camille* promotes the actress as a figure that is equivalent to yet quite different from the actress on the theatrical stage. Her gestures, moving quickly and quite differently in terms of their tempo on film, indicate the extent to which film modified and in a sense modernized the gestures of the nineteenth-century stage. As one reviewer notes: "My God, what will this hectic cinema do to this gentle figure of charm and pleasure? What is it that Electricity will do to Gesture? to the beauty of gesture? Admirable mime! Behind her vanishes the hanging sets, the carton furniture, the piano in black wood. Lips speak and if the public hears nothing, it nevertheless listens."[52]

Moving Picture World reiterates this view when it explains that "the story is revealed as plain as print. 'Camille' was never more pitifully eloquent than in this dumb record."[53] Indeed, David Mayer argues that passions were never performed in silence on film; just as music played a fundamental role on the nineteenth- and early twentieth-century stage, so too was it fundamental to the performance and reception of the passions in early film. He states, "Music is to the actor what water is to the swimmer." It provides the tempo, coloring, tonality, force, rhythm, direction, and impulse for gesture. As Mayer goes on to explain, there is evidence that some rehearsals for early narrative film were conducted with musicians. Presumably, this music continued to be played when the actor performed for the camera. Later, when the films were screened, musical accompaniment was provided by the house orchestra or by the piano.[54] In this sense, we must recognize that although Bernhardt is silent *and* emotionally legible on the silent screen, she likely performed for the camera to music just as she was seen on film to the accompaniment of music. We might therefore think of Bernhardt's films as works that underscore the gestural legibility of Bernhardt's actions even as they affirm the ongoing association of music and theater.

We know that in rehearsals for her stage performances Bernhardt relied on music and herself directed what was to be heard. The London *Sporting Times* recounts, for example, the efforts made to time Marguerite's death "to slow music, and with the curtain descending in the very nick of time."[55] The importance given music in Bernhardt's rehearsal indicates its importance in her live performance. This use of music carried into film. Although I do not know what music accompanied the screening of *Camille* in America, it was never screened in silence. Martin Marks, in his book *Music and the Silent Film*, suggests that the composer Walter Cleveland Simon—who crafted piano scores for Kalem—could have composed music for the Réjane/Bernhardt double bill, but there is no evidence of this musical score.[56] In an article in *Moving Picture World*, Clarence E. Sinn prints a letter from "our old friend Will H. Bryant" who had been "managing the house and leading the orchestra" in Terre Haute, Indiana. He lists the excerpts he used of familiar pieces of music to accompany *Camille* and indicates the point at which the music was to change. In all, twelve excerpts are chosen.[57]

It is at this point that we can depart from a discussion of Bernhardt and her first narrative film. Emotional, legible, and fast, it is an engaging work that indicates that Bernhardt both modified theatrical gesture and maintained theatrical agency on screen. Reaching a global audience, she was legible to a public she never saw and could not physically visit. In contrast to Lindsay, I believe that *Camille* frames Bernhardt anew, in a new medium and before new audiences, bringing Enlightenment thought to the cusp of a new century.

Cinematizing the Cinema: Lillian Gish's Formation

Lillian Gish was a child actor who was engaged—with her sister Dorothy and mother Mary—on the professional melodrama stage in late nineteenth-century America.[58] Born in Ohio in 1893, she did not train in acting school and had none of the formal education that Bernhardt enjoyed. Indeed, the tradition of a national acting school headed by some of the most famous actors of earlier generations passing on their knowledge and expertise to young students was, at this point, specific to Europe. By all accounts, Gish literally learned on the job. In her first professional appearance she was nine years old. Charles Affron explains that it was on this occasion that she claimed she received her only acting lesson: "Speak loud and clear, or they'll get another little girl."[59] James Naremore, in his chapter on Gish in *Acting in the Cinema*, provides little more information about the impact that theatrical training in American theaters might have had on the actress. He merely states that "Gish was influenced by the pantomime, or mimetic, form of acting she had learned in turn-of-the-century theatre."[60] What this pantomime or mimetic acting might entail is not discussed; note is only made of the fact that English actor David Garrick made famous an acting style in which "players struck elaborate poses" and that sentimental Victorian comedies indirectly influenced Hollywood narrative.[61]

Gish was introduced (with her sister Dorothy) to D. W. Griffith by Mary Pickford at the Biograph studio in New York in 1912. Accounts of why they were employed by Griffith are vague. They were put in pictures because of their acting experience; they were immediately cast as extras in a scene that required an audience.[62] Whatever the circumstances, Gish appeared in thirty-one films between 1912 and 1913. In June 1913 *Motion Picture Story Magazine* for the first time announced—in a simple phrase in a twenty-three-page "Answers to Inquiries" section—that the names of the sisters in *An Unseen Enemy* (Griffith, 1912) were Lillian and Dorothy Gish.[63] The following month Lillian Gish featured in a full-page photograph in the *Motion Picture Story Magazine*'s "Gallery of Picture Players," her image appearing beside an untitled photograph of fellow Biograph actress Claire MacDowell. One of the few actresses to look squarely back at the camera, Gish looks calm and confident. A simple dark shirt and modest hat frame a white face that is dramatically accentuated by side lighting.[64]

Gish came to national attention when she played Elsie Stoneman in Griffith's *The Birth of a Nation* in 1915. She was mentioned in this role in Lindsay's *Art of the Moving Picture*; in contradistinction to Bernhardt, Lindsay sees Gish as an actress who illustrates the "intimate photoplay," who traverses the distance between spectator and screen and whose magic "could be given wings and a wand."[65] As Kristen Hatch explains in her article "Lillian Gish: Clean, and White, and Pure as the Lily," however, it was not until a few years later, when Gish played in Griffith's *Hearts of the World* (1918), that she "emerged as a fully established star." The following year Gish played Susie in *True Heart Susie* (Griffith, 1919) and Lucy in *Broken Blossoms* (Griffith, 1919). Hatch states that it was at this point that Gish became "one of the screen's leading tragediennes."[66] Affron puts this argument more forcefully. He argues that *Hearts of the World* "showcased her star performance," while *Broken Blossoms* "used Lillian to raise the movie melodrama to the category of art film." In his view, after *Broken Blossoms* "Lillian Gish would be identified not merely as a charming, beautiful, and talented actress, but as a great screen tragedienne, perhaps the first movie star to merit the label."[67] As I explain below, *Broken Blossoms* indeed gives evidence of Gish's agency as an actress and can provide a productive counterpoint to the style of Bernhardt's acting in *Camille*.

Unlike Bernhardt's, Gish's fame came only after she had appeared in many films and had explored and developed her skills before a camera. By most accounts, her acting was greatly influenced by Griffith, a director who exerted a great deal of control over his actors. Scott Simmon explains that Griffith minutely coached his actresses in order to elicit emotions from them; Simmon goes so far as to argue that Griffith chose adolescent non-stage actresses as they were "presumably more pliant."[68] A photograph in Eileen Bowser's *The Transformation of Cinema* gives evidence that Gish received instruction from Griffith. Taken on set for *The Battle of the Sexes*, the first Mutual film Griffith directed in 1913, the photograph shows Griffith with a pointed hand, holding papers in the other, with action frozen around him.[69] Film itself gives us further evidence of Griffith's active direction of Gish, at least in these early years. In *A Cry for Help*, a work finished in November 1912, we see in MoMA's fragmented print a young Gish playing the supporting role of a fainting maid. Receiving off-camera instruction, Gish successively repeats the emotions she must perform: dismay, confusion, and fear (culminating in a faint). The fact that Gish has to repeat these actions indicates the extent to which the watchful eye of Griffith monitored rehearsal. Indeed, this rare sight of repetitive acting onscreen gives evidence of the way in which Griffith dictated Gish's acting. Rather than review herself on film, however, Gish explains that rehearsal was usually planned and timed to the second so that when she entered the film set there was just the single take to record her performance for film. In these circumstances, particularly as she emerges as a star in her own right, Gish is both creator and created, an actress who acts and is acted upon. Richard Koszarski sums up this duality in *An Evening's Entertainment*, where he states that Gish is both "a committed artist" and "a disciple, some say a creation, of D. W. Griffith."[70]

The Genius of Gish's Gesture

Bernhardt's *Camille* was a role that gave actresses across the world "the opportunity of showing off the variety of their histrionic gifts."[71] In contrast to this, with *Broken Blossoms* Gish performed a role that was little (if at all) known to international audiences. Based on a story called *The Chink and the Child* in Thomas Burke's collection of stories *Limehouse Nights*, it was first published as a short story in the English journal *Colour* in October 1915. *Limehouse Nights* was subsequently published in London in 1916 and then in America in 1917.[72] While therefore available to readers—and while certainly suggesting and using familiar literary and theatrical tropes within the story itself (the Chinese shopkeeper, the innocent child, the battling working-class father, and so on)—Burke's narrative nevertheless was new to a general American public. Gish's task, then, was to introduce and adapt Lucy, Burke's twelve-year-old girl, to film. In contrast to Bernhardt, who had to reanimate the familiar figure of an adolescent Marguerite Gautier, Gish had to make a character that is just one of three characters described in a short seventeen-page story believable in a feature film format. Moreover, she had to make a girl who is secondary to "The Chink" in Burke's original tale become a leading heroine that American audiences could understand, relate to, and empathize with.

The description of Lucy in Burke's tale gives an indication of how Lucy could be imagined and performed. Although Gish never mentions reading the tale in her writings, it clearly informs much of her gestural action. We are introduced to her as she walks, cowed, with a hunched back and bent knees, taking small tottering steps, her birdlike steps defining movement as a vulnerable, childish gait. Soon after this first sight of her, Gish sits on a coil of rope alongside a dock, her toes pointed inward, her chest leaning over her bent knees, one hand tucked under her shawl, the other curling upward, thumb and index finger pinched together in what will become a characteristic play of her hands in the fold of her shawl. This corresponds with Burke's story, where it is explained that she "crept," her movements were "birdlike," "impetuous," she had a "starved face" and "transfixed air," also a "shy grace . . . as she flitted around the squalid alleys."[73] This emphasis upon Lucy's birdlike manner is reinforced not just through Gish's gait, but through the quick and nervous movements that pepper her performance. About to go out shopping for her father's meal, she retrieves her piece of ribbon, foil, and letter from a hideout in the floor. Dusting it off, she does not brush the letter with an opened hand but with a single index finger. Repeating this tight gesture, she then holds the letter affectionately to her cheek; we can see in this small movement the enactment of what Burke describes as "the soft curve of her cheek that cried for kisses."[74] In the quick gesture of a finger, the fidgeting clasp of a hand around her shawl, the brush of a mother's letter against a face, and so on, we see Lucy's character emerge. Tellingly, her gestures begin at the elbow and extend to the hands (see figure 10). Her costume reinforces this tightness. Indeed, the shawl that covers her shoulders seems to pull Gish inward, into herself; it prevents expansive arm gestures while indicating her need for self-protection (both from her boxer father's brutal blows and out of a more general distrust of the world).

FIGURE 10: Lucy (Lillian Gish) holds the letter to her cheek in *Broken Blossoms*.

This use of costume and this reduction of movement to small, nervous, and often unexpected gestures is what James Naremore might describe as "actorly invention," "artistic labour," or the physical creation of *meaning*.[75] Developing this idea in the context of *True Heart Susie*, Naremore goes on to explain that Gish is an important actress because she allows us to see character depth on screen. Without the use of words, she expresses "cleverness beneath youth, strength beneath fragility, humor beneath spirituality, and sexual warmth beneath propriety."[76] Emblematic of this capacity to bring nuance and depth to simple and familiar characters is Gish's famous use of her index and middle finger to force her face into a physical semblance of a smile. The first time we see this, Lucy has returned home and her sadistic father demands a smile. He turns from her so it is only we, the audience, who see how she obliges: her right hand edges under her chin, her index and middle fingers open under her mouth to force both edges upward, so that a forced smile is on her face before Burrows turns back around. We see in close-up her opened, agonized eyes, bright with tears and the forced smile as she then turns to tend to the fire. Soon after, having finished the meal, Burrows asks her again for another smile. Once more her right hand creeps beneath her chin, bunched into a fist before it opens on the "V" that forces her mouth into place. After Burrows has left and just before she opens the door herself, Gish looks for a final time into the mirror and fixes her smile into place.

This smile becomes a leitmotif, index to the humiliation and pain that young Lucy must endure as well as the joy she can tentatively feel. When Lucy finally smiles of her own accord, without the need for her fingers to pull her face into place, she is lying on Cheng Huan's bed, newly attired in Chinese robes, her hair brushed with a decorative headpiece on. She looks at the mirror he proffers, holds it, and then offers a small smile. She points to her mouth with her index finger, indicating the smile that has appeared. She smiles once more, pats her hair in quick, short movements, pouts her mouth, looking calmly at "The Yellow Man" as she chatters to him. In her own idiosyncratic way, Gish has shown us what Burke directs in his story: to Cheng Huan Lucy is "a pale, lily-lovely child," his "White Blossom." Lucy was afraid of her father but not afraid of Cheng Huan: she "did not start away; she did not tremble," she was birdlike and full of "prattle" at his house.[77] At the end of the film, when we see her death, Lucy is in bed alone. Her hand now creeps up to her bloodied mouth, she gulps painfully. After stretching a final smile, her hand then covers her chest, her mouth opens, and her eyes roll unseeing upward.

As Gish recounts, this forced smile was her own invention, one that came about through experiment and chance in rehearsal.[78] What is interesting about her smile is that it is pantomime: in a small gesture and above all without words, layers of character and meaning are conveyed to an audience. In taking physical command of a role that might otherwise verge on the childish, Gish thereby ensures that the actress remains an intelligent figure who can demonstrate agency in the telling of a story. Gish's bent frame, scurrying walk, fidgeting fingers, tightly clasped shawl, and above all her often futile attempt to stretch her mouth into a smile are saturnine reminders that gesture remained at the forefront of developments in American cinema.

The Significance of Space

In *Broken Blossoms* the camera is static and remains largely indoors. The only moment we see Gish in an outdoor setting is when we see the outside of Lucy's house at the dockyard and when we see her nervously scurrying through the streets of London's Limehouse. It is in these open city spaces, where gesture has the spatial possibility of becoming more open and expansive, that we are made aware of how entrapped Lucy really is, of how ill at ease she feels in the relative openness of the outdoors. When she walks, she looks down, onto the road. If she stops to look at things, they are either on the ground (the foil she finds) or at chest height (the flowers she stops to touch, the dried fish she buys for dinner). She never looks up, or turns her head to look around, or releases her tightly clutched shawl. Even after Lucy is beaten by her father, when she stumbles out of her home and staggers against a supporting wooden beam on the dock, we do not get the sense that she is physically freeing herself from her terror at home. She instead falls into a doorway, almost trips as she crosses a road, sways on her feet, and eventually falls into The Yellow Man's shop. Collapsing on the floor, she finally rests. When she leaves The Yellow Man's shop and returns home, she is dragged through the streets by her father, forced to accompany him in his hurried fury. In this context, we might recognize how Gish's birdlike figure, even when released from the domestic space of her home, is never freed into flight; she never moves her arms or shops at leisure. She instead shadows walls, pauses at crossroads, and seems unable to enjoy her furtive freedom. Her ongoing entrapment is suggested, perhaps, by the architecture used to create the Limehouse district itself: streets open onto archways and dark corners, not open skies and trees.

Just as Lucy never stands upright in outdoor spaces, so too do her movements indoors remain bent, tight, and furtive. She scurries round and round the kitchen table, hurrying away from her father. She bends over the fire to cook dinner, she bends over as she serves her father dinner, she bends to the floor to clean Burrows's boots in an effort to abate his anger after she burns his hand. To no avail: Lucy is whipped as she crouches on the ground, her curled body becoming in this submissive gesture even smaller and more tightly crouched than before.

Performing Passions

Although Sandy Flitterman-Lewis has argued that in *Broken Blossoms* close-ups make the heroine's face "a mode of narration itself,"[79] I believe that it is both

Gish's full, expressive body and her face that together define the passions she is enacting in this film. Certainly, we are fortunate that the camera moves into her face and frames it in medium and close-up shots. Because of this proximity we cannot miss the whites that appear around her pupils as she widens her eyes in horror when her father demands his dinner or as she looks in fear at the clock on the wall. Because of the frequent use of medium shots, particularly in moments of unspoken tension, we also see Lucy's long unblinking stare up into the eyes of the Yellow Man when she first meets him crouching before her on the floor of his shop, her tentative smile hastily straightened as he approaches her, her eyes bobbing anxiously around his face as he moves even closer, and the eventual slide of her gaze onto the floor as he turns his head to break this advance.

Alongside these tightly framed and exquisitely performed expressions, however, we also see full-length shots that show physical gestures that are equally revealing and just as forceful. Often featuring props that represent and elaborate emotion, these shots cleverly displace the actions that once might have formed part of melodramatic acting onto everyday objects. Hence, in the scene in which Lucy burns Burrows with the dinner she has cooked, we see his hand knock against the pan she is holding. The next shot shows Lucy putting the pan on the table and twisting the cloth she had wrapped around its handle to protect her hands. A prop that was used to indicate the dangerous heat of the pan is therefore used to demonstrate and elaborate Lucy's distress (see figure 11).[80] She twists it in her hands, picks at it, wrings it, passes the cloth from hand to hand, scrunches it, places it on the table, picks it back up again and twists it, holding it with her hands meeting knuckle to knuckle against her chest. Finally, she folds her left hand across her chest while her right hand slips the cloth, now a limp roll, beneath her left elbow at her waist. This cloth is a clever way of indicating not just Lucy's fear but also her innocence and her surrender (the cloth is white, waved before an advancing enemy). Making the cloth an active part of her performance, Gish cows before Burrows in a choreography of gesture that echoes yet develops attitudes of distress, despair, and submission on the live theatrical stage. In the next shot, just before she pleads again not to be beaten, the cloth has gone.

In the closet scene, when Gish locks herself away from a furious Burrows, she enacts hysteria in a similar way. We cannot hear Gish's screams but we certainly feel and understand her madness as she twists, turns, and rocks in the cramped and claustrophobic closet. Tom Gunning, discussing an earlier Gish film (*The Mothering Heart*, 1913, and linking this also to Gish's angry denunciation of Lennox Sanderson in *Way Down East*, 1920), explains that Gish has the capacity to make an ordinary domestic item (a cultivated rose bush, in this case) become the trigger to unleash repressed emotion. While in *The Mothering Heart* it is fury and not fear she releases, Gish nevertheless transforms from a gentle and maternal figure to a woman who expresses her anger. As Gunning states: "Suddenly the action transforms and redefines this traditional image of motherhood and beauty,

FIGURE 11: Lucy twists the cloth in her hands in *Broken Blossoms*.

as Gish picks up a stick and begins to attack the rose bushes violently, flailing at them in fury and despair, the petals scattered by her blows."[81] In Gunning's opinion, Gish makes the screen "incandescent" in this moment of released emotion.

In the closet Gish similarly transforms. Cowering with fear she scampers inside. Once enclosed and locked behind the door, she begins to move and sound in a new way. Never having lifted her arm above elbow level, Gish now reaches her right arm high over her head as she pushes herself into the opposite wall from the door. With her right elbow remaining above her shoulder, she now reaches her hand back to her mouth and gnaws on it like an animal (see figure 12). Burrows takes the axe to the door. We now see Gish also in close-up. In this sequence, her right hand pounds her leg as she turns, in clockwise direction, around and around, shoulders hunched, her head down. This is followed by a medium shot of Gish screaming, her usually tight mouth open wide to reveal her teeth as she looks upward, turning from side to side, rocking and swaying deliriously. In close-up we then see Gish rotate her head; she turns left and right as she frantically rubs the side of her face. Her hair disheveled and unkempt, she continues to scream as she turns. We return to a medium shot and see Gish pound her leg again, her fist falling over and over with an oddly stiff and extended thumb. After another shot of Burrows pounding the door with an axe, we see Gish kneel, put her fist to her mouth, and rock on the floor.

Throughout all these actions, Gish clutches and protects the doll that The Yellow Man has given her. This prop again allows a quotidian object (a child's toy) to naturalize and justify theatrical gesture while metonymically developing the way in which Gish's character might be interpreted (she is a toy, a china doll, a mother, a child). Again, a range of gestures that would traditionally represent female hysteria have been choreographed into a believable sequence of naturally occurring actions and movements and linked to a domestic object. Taken out of the closet, put on a stage, and seen from a distance, Gish's actions would be identifiable and legible to audiences of the nineteenth-century stage.

Toward a Conclusion

The eight years that divide Bernhardt's *Camille* from Gish's *Broken Blossoms* do not necessarily see a change from European theatrical acting to naturalistic American acting on film. While Bernhardt and Gish saw changes and reveal differences, they also indicate overlap between films. Most obviously, the films that made both Bernhardt and Gish "tragediennes of the screen" describe the thwarted attempt of a young woman to leave home, show the impossibility for love if a relationship falls outside the boundaries of middle-class propriety, reveal the damaging impact that patriarchy has on the physical and mental health of the family, and use the flower to symbolize the purity and yearning of adolescence. In both films, the heroines die. The spaces that Bernhardt and Gish inhabit, though

FIGURE 12: Lucy gnaws on her hand, her elbow above her head, in *Broken Blossoms*.

different, are also interlaced: the home is a static chamber that highlights female entrapment, the bed or bedroom is not a solace but the place where women are whipped, are sick, and die. Even Bernhardt's and Gish's props might be compared: Bernhardt's white handkerchief is akin to Gish's white cloth, both held in the hands and used to choreograph and elaborate emotion. Finally, both actresses express extremes of passion. Bernhardt uses the horizontal frame, describing distress by opening her arms and chest or by swinging her body in a circular motion through space. Gish instead twists and turns in tight and frantic movements, she bobs up and down, and she uses the linear axis to indicate just how small she might become in moments of fear. With Gish, the circle is no longer a line of beauty but a desperate scamper around a kitchen table, a hysterical spin inside a closet. In both instances, narrative circumstances validate the gestures each actress performs. Bernhardt spirals to her death elegantly, finally supported by her lover. The two intertwine in this concluding turn. Her death is tragic but also beautiful in this physical description of their reunion. Gish instead enjoys no reunion with The Yellow Man. She is locked alone in a cupboard and hacked at by her father. Burke's tale makes no mention of this space or scene; in his short story Cheng Huan merely finds Lucy with her "pulse still." In *Broken Blossoms* we therefore have literal proof of Gish's acted "addition" or what Naremore calls "meaning." This closet scene provides evidence of what words do not (and perhaps cannot) recount.

We need to look for and acknowledge these moments of meaning, this physical proof of the work of acting, while we watch silent film. Although very different from each other, Bernhardt and Gish develop roles on film that allow (and even demand) a full range of emotional expression. Without this range, their characters and the stories they recount do not make sense. As David Mayer reminds us in his article "*Why Girls Leave Home*: Victorian and Edwardian 'Bad Girl' Melodrama Parodied in Early Film," acting that is outrageously clichéd and stagey was not performed by famous and skilled actresses on film. It was knowingly and cleverly included in film parody. Exaggerated performance was part of "a near-facsimile that is deliberately askew."[82] Our belief that semaphoric acting is derived from cheap melodrama and an outdated nineteenth-century stage blinds us to acting in the early cinema. Perhaps more importantly, it blinds us to the gestural maturity of an actress like Gish, who was developing new ways of incorporating physical expression and emotions on film. Rather than follow Lindsay and focus on the development of a specifically "cinematic" language in American silent film, we would do well to recall the ongoing importance of gestural drama. As Mayer reminds us, gestures were not relinquished: "The larger truth is that both stage and film acting was gestural, and remained so well into the 1930s and possibly beyond."[83]

2

CLASSICAL HOLLYWOOD, 1928-1946   Arthur Nolletti Jr.

The eighteen-year period from 1928 through 1946, which began a year before the Great Depression and ended with the aftermath of World War II, was a time of trauma and uncertainty for American society, as well as for American cinema. The stock market crash of October 1929 was followed by a decade of dire hardship that left millions out of work. In 1933 newly elected President Franklin Roosevelt initiated a series of federal acts and programs to get the economy back on its feet. At first, some Hollywood producers thought their business was "Depression-proof," but falling theater attendance and rising costs soon plunged the industry into crisis.[1]

On December 7, 1941, the Japanese bombed Pearl Harbor and America went to war. As the film historian Richard B. Jewell has noted, Hollywood's commitment to the war effort "stretched far beyond the creation of patriotic, morale-boosting movies."[2] This commitment included making public service shorts and training films and selling war bonds. Major stars including Clark Gable, Henry Fonda, and James Stewart joined the armed forces. Other stars also made important contributions, such as traveling overseas to entertain the troops.[3] Like other industries, Hollywood was forced to make sacrifices. Severe restrictions on film stock reduced the number of films being produced by 37 percent.[4] However, as the war continued and the economy surged, theater attendance increased and box office revenues rose. In 1946 grosses reached an all-time high of $1.7 billion, but this boom was short-lived. Popularly referred to as "The Golden Age of Hollywood," this period represented a unique coming together of talent, technical expertise, and financial and organizational conditions, without which the studio system could not have existed.

During these years, the studio system consolidated itself as an industry, genres rose to prominence, and sound film superseded silent film. Sound film brought a new dimension to film: "acoustic verisimilitude."[5] The result was the emergence of an acting mode that has been labeled "the Hollywood studio style."[6] This style is often erroneously regarded as one in which performers simply played themselves or behaved as they would in everyday life. More accurately, this role-centered (character) approach to acting was "a kind of prism through which character is refracted"[7] and in which an actor took conscious control of his or her instrument to necessarily color a performance.[8] It was naturalistic in that it put on the screen what seemed to be ordinary conversation and behavior, it sought to make technique invisible, and it endowed character types with individual traits and mannerisms. Yet it also embraced theatrical (or nonrealistic) acting in genres that called for heightened dramatic rhetoric, most notably comedy, musicals, and horror. There were various forms of theatricality, among them ostentatious performances and formal staging,[9] as well as voice-over narration and self-referential performance.

Fundamentally, performance is a creative act that depends on the actor's skill and powers of imagination, but it also is influenced by industry practices behind the silver screen. The first part of this chapter examines the relationship between film acting in the studio era and the following offscreen influences: the signature genres of individual studios, studio contracts, actor preparation and training, the star system, and the Production Code.

The remainder of the chapter offers a close analysis of the performances of Herbert Marshall, Kay Francis, and Miriam Hopkins in Ernst Lubitsch's sophisticated comedy *Trouble in Paradise* (1932); Ginger Rogers in George Stevens's musical *Swing Time* (1936); Beulah Bondi in Leo McCarey's family melodrama *Make Way for Tomorrow* (1937); and Fred MacMurray in Billy Wilder's film noir *Double Indemnity* (1944). Here the focus is on three interrelated elements: (1) what Richard Dyer calls "performance signs,"[10] that is, the choices an actor makes in terms of voice, intonation, gesture, body posture, body movements, and facial expressions; (2) formal cinematic elements that help structure performance, such as framing, editing, and shot size (close-up, medium, and long shots); and (3) essential forms that realism/naturalism and theatricality/nonrealism take in the above performances and genres. What emerges from the interplay of these elements is the film's meaning and signification.

Studios, Signature Genres, and Acting Styles

During the Golden Age of Hollywood, the leading studios—the Big Five, also known as "the Majors" (MGM, Paramount, Warner Bros., Twentieth Century–Fox, and RKO), and the Little Three, or "the Minors" (Universal, Columbia, and United Artists)—made genres the core of commercial production. Genres were standardized enough to satisfy moviegoers' expectations, yet, in keeping with changing fashions and attitudes, sufficiently different to give old formulas new vitality and relevance. Just as individual studios were identified with specific genres, so too were certain actors. In fact, genres played a central role in determining acting styles.

MGM, the biggest, most prosperous studio, boasted that it had "more stars than there are in heaven." This boast was only slightly hyperbolic, given its roster of players, which included perennial favorites Clark Gable, Joan Crawford, Marie Dressler, Spencer Tracy, Jean Harlow, Mickey Rooney, Greta Garbo, Greer Garson, Norma Shearer, Katharine Hepburn, and Judy Garland, all of whom excelled in at least one of the studio's signature genres. Hence Tracy and Hepburn in the comedy *Woman of the Year* (George Stevens, 1942), Garson in the melodrama *Random Harvest* (Mervyn LeRoy, 1942), Garland in the musical *Meet Me in St. Louis* (Vincente Minnelli, 1944), and Garbo in the adaptation of the play *Anna Christie* (Clarence Brown, 1930).

Unlike MGM, Warner Bros. made frugality its mantra. It had two signature genres: the backstage musical and the gangster film. The former included the prototypical *42nd Street* (Lloyd Bacon, 1933) with Ruby Keeler as an unknown who becomes an overnight success, and *Gold Diggers of 1933* (Mervyn LeRoy, 1933), which opens with Ginger Rogers and a line of coin-covered chorus girls singing "We're in the Money." The gangster film brought a new realism to the screen in such films as *Little Caesar* (Mervyn LeRoy, 1931) and *The Public Enemy* (William Wellman, 1931). Taken from newspaper headlines and modeled on real-life gangsters John Dillinger and Al Capone, these films were lean, taut, and fast-paced, and made stars of Edward G. Robinson and James Cagney. Determined "to be somebody," their small-time hoodlums struck a chord with Depression audiences, who felt the system was stacked against them.

Paramount cultivated a number of signature genres. In the 1930s, directors Josef von Sternberg and Ernst Lubitsch gave the studio a decidedly "European" flavor—sophisticated, naughty, faintly decadent. In his series of exotic melodramas with Marlene Dietrich, beginning with *The Blue Angel* (*Der blaue Engel*, 1930), Sternberg had the actress strike languorous poses, intone her dialogue enigmatically, and even look at a lamp as if she couldn't live without it. By contrast, Lubitsch's comedies of manners, such as *Trouble in Paradise* (1932), required actors to have polish, style, and a flair for dialogue. During the war, the studio set its sights on more identifiably American types. Bob Hope, Bing Crosby, and Dorothy Lamour delighted audiences in a series of highly profitable "Road" comedies, beginning with *The Road to Singapore* (Victor Schertzinger, 1940); Alan Ladd and Veronica Lake brought their special brand of somnambulism to film noir in *This Gun for Hire* (Frank Tuttle, 1942) and *The Glass Key* (Stuart Heisler, 1942); and Barbara Stanwyck, Henry Fonda, Claudette Colbert, and Joel McCrea, among others, invested director Preston Sturges's satires on American mores, such as *The Lady Eve* (1941), with crack timing, fun, and feeling. Another mainstay of the studio was Cecil B. DeMille. As he had done since the silent period, he made lavish historical epics such as *The Sign of the Cross* (1932) and *Cleopatra* (1934), which showcased larger-than-life performances from such stars as Charles Laughton, Claudette Colbert, and Fredric March.

RKO produced the landmark fantasy *King Kong* (Merian C. Cooper and Ernest B. Schoedsack, 1933) and *Citizen Kane* (Orson Welles, 1941), one of the most influential films of all time. However, its staple genres were literary and stage adaptations, among them *Little Women* (George Cukor, 1933) with Katharine Hepburn as Louisa May Alcott's headstrong, independent heroine, and Fred Astaire–Ginger Rogers musicals, the studio's consistently biggest moneymakers.

Twentieth Century–Fox had two superstars: curly-haired moppet Shirley Temple and sunny song-and-dance specialist Betty Grable. Virtually a genre in her own right, Temple was a beacon of hope during the Depression. The country's number-one star from 1935 through 1938, she was indefatigably plucky and eternally optimistic, and in films such as *Wee Willie Winkie* (John Ford, 1937) sang and danced her way into the hearts of even the most cantankerous characters. Audiences loved her. If Temple was largely responsible for keeping the studio solvent in the 1930s, in the 1940s that task fell to Betty Grable, who ranked among Hollywood's top stars throughout the decade.[11] Grable made over twenty highly popular Technicolor musicals, but her most memorable "role" took place offscreen. She was the favorite pin-up of servicemen overseas, her studio-insured million-dollar legs prominently on display.

Of the minor studios, Universal's signature genre was the horror film, which was primarily indebted to German Expressionism for its visual look, basic story line, and acting style. In the studio's most famous horror film, *Frankenstein* (James Whale, 1931), Boris Karloff remained human and pathetic, even when he was terrifying, as the monster created by overweening science. Denied the possibility of speech and despite the monster's grotesque appearance, with his deformed skull and deep-socketed eyes, Karloff managed to convey a wide range of expression. In accordance with Expressionist acting, he reduced a whole complex of thought and action to single, often abrupt gestures, and "exteriorized emotions and psychic reactions in the most extreme manner,"[12] stretching out his arms as the monster struggled to walk, a gesture that was less a threat than a protest at cruel fate.

Columbia's signature genre was the series of New Deal and screwball comedies that Frank Capra made throughout the 1930s. These included *It Happened One Night* (1934), *Mr. Deeds Goes to Town* (1936), and *Mr. Smith Goes to Washington*

(1939), which borrowed versatile stars, including James Stewart, Gary Cooper, and Barbara Stanwyck, from other studios. This series aside, the studio mainly relied on low-budget fare, B-westerns, and Three Stooges comedies until the appearance of its own major star in the 1940s, love goddess Rita Hayworth.

Unlike the other studios, United Artists was primarily a distribution company for the films of independent producers. One of its most important releases was the classic western *Stagecoach* (John Ford, 1939), which not only revitalized the genre but made a star of a struggling young actor named John Wayne.

Studio Contracts

During this period, the Big Five exercised firm control over actors; the Minors had much less control. Studio contracts, both short-term and long-term (usually seven years), required actors to accept whatever films they were assigned, rarely permitted them to choose roles for themselves, expected them to help publicize their films, stipulated that they could be loaned out to other studios, held them accountable to a strict morals clause, and monitored their weight and physical appearance.[13] In fact, an actor's offscreen life was carefully managed by the studio's publicity department to foster the illusion that it was no different from the actor's onscreen roles. Fan magazines such as *Photoplay, Modern Screen*, and *Screen Stories* gave moviegoers an inside look at the lives of their favorite stars, who were depicted as just plain folks—modest, unpretentious, and squeaky clean. To the movie-going public, actors seemed to live a charmed, glamorous existence. However, as film historian John Belton notes in *American Cinema/American Culture*, "During the early 1930s, in particular, the actors' lives were no picnic. They worked six days a week—often for 14 hours a day."[14] Bette Davis put the matter even more bluntly: "A day's work, and work it is—every minute of it."[15] Furthermore, it was not unusual for an actor under contract to make one film after another in a given year. For example, while in 1935 Fred MacMurray made seven films, a total scarcely imaginable today, Cary Grant made over three times that number.[16]

At best, the contract system was a double-edged sword. As arduous and grueling as contract players' schedules could be, they provided on-site training for performers to learn their craft and refine their technique. The studios also initiated training programs and hired dialogue coaches and dialogue directors to standardize Hollywood modes of vocal performance. This was part of the division of labor that went into the construction of performance,[17] and was designed to "mould vocal performance to narrative and generic codes."[18]

As mentioned, studios also had the power to loan out actors. According to James Stewart, "Sometimes they traded us, not for another actor, but for the use of a back lot. I remember someone told me that I was traded to Universal Studios to do a picture so that MGM could use a street Universal had built on its back lot."[19] Actors could also be loaned out as a form of discipline. In one of the most famous examples, when Clark Gable refused to accept a secondary role in a Joan Crawford film, MGM sent him to Columbia, then a decidedly minor company. Ironically, the film he appeared in was Frank Capra's Oscar-winning screwball comedy *It Happened One Night* (1934), which catapulted him to superstar status and established his onscreen persona as the iconic American male—honest, forthright, uncompromising, possessing a roguish charm and self-deprecating humor, and masculine to the core.

In the early 1930s, working conditions at the Big Five improved with the creation of the Screen Actors Guild, which unionized contract players, freelancers, and extras. Still, contract disputes did not come to an end. Actors who challenged the studios often found themselves on suspension without pay and were banned from working for any other studio. The battles of James Cagney and Bette Davis with Warner Bros. attracted widespread media attention, but it was the contract dispute initiated by Olivia de Havilland that had the most far-reaching significance. When her seven-year contract ended, Warner Bros. informed her that she owed them six more months for the time she had been on suspension. Deciding to contest this claim, she took Warner Bros. to court. For nearly two years, she pursued the case and was out of work. Finally, in 1944 the District Court of Appeals ruled that seven years, including any suspensions, was the maximum limit for any film contract.[20] This was a landmark decision that redefined actors' rights (see figure 13).

FIGURE 13: Olivia de Havilland, the actress who took Warner Bros. to court, in *The Private Lives of Elizabeth and Essex*.

Some actors, few to be sure, chose to freelance rather than depend on a studio to oversee their careers and provide steady employment. These included a number of Hollywood's high-paid talents who were prompted by "war-related income tax hikes."[21] Much-respected character actress Beulah Bondi freelanced for an altogether different reason. Distrusting contracts and determined to pick her own roles, she turned down an offer of a seven-year contract from MGM and Samuel Goldwyn. Only once during her thirty-year film career did she sign a contract: a one-year contract with Paramount,[22] where she made *Make Way for Tomorrow* (1937).

Actor Preparation and Training

The introduction of sound called for a new kind of movie actor, one who could handle dialogue skillfully and whose voice matched his or her physical looks. Silent film personalities who failed to make the grade, such as John Gilbert, Greta Garbo's favorite leading man, suddenly found themselves without work or relegated to second-rate talkies. During the 1930s, talking pictures brought an influx of actors to Hollywood from radio (Bob Hope, Bing Crosby), vaudeville (Mae West), and theater (George Arliss). Like all performers, these new arrivals had to familiarize themselves with the technical demands of the medium, such as framing, composition, and editing, in order to calibrate the size of their performance from the intimacy of the close-up and medium shot to the more public space of the long shot. They also had to learn that the camera had a logic all its own. While making his first film, *Shadow of a Doubt* (Alfred Hitchcock, 1943), Broadway actor Hume Cronyn took a step away from a character he was arguing with, whereupon Hitchcock told him he must step *forward*—or else his head would be cut out of the frame. Cronin felt the action was completely false, but when he saw the rushes, he realized Hitchcock had been right. The "false" move seemed completely natural.[23] As a newcomer to film, Henry Fonda also learned a valuable lesson about the difference between film acting and theater acting. When he proceeded to play a role exactly as he had done onstage, the director took him aside and told him he was mugging. Fonda then "pulled way back,"[24] realizing that film did not require projection. Rather, the camera needed to capture the actor *thinking*, which was conveyed primarily by the eyes. As the film scholar David Thomson writes in *America in the Dark*, "The most touching moments of films are when the camera shows us a human face 'lost' in thought and feeling."[25]

Preparation and training were as essential in the 1930s and 1940s as they are today. Often actors had little or no rehearsal time prior to appearing on camera and had to prepare on their own. Likewise, they had to adjust to the fact that films were typically shot out of sequence as a cost-cutting measure. Little, if any, consideration was given to how performance might be affected. This was yet another reason why actors needed to have a thorough understanding of their characters, and how those characters developed over the course of the film. Shooting a film also meant waiting on the set, often for hours, while technical matters (such as lighting and camera set-ups) were worked out. During this time, actors had to conserve their energy. When they finally stepped before the camera, they typically were called on to do take after take. Their job was to keep their performance fresh. Interestingly, what is frequently neglected in discussions of an actor's preparation is the importance of makeup, lighting, and costume tests—"externals" that are vital components in creating a fictional character. One has only to think of the hours that Boris Karloff spent being made up for *Frankenstein* (1931) or that Orson Welles required to be transformed into the aged, bloated Kane.

Influenced by twentieth-century acting theorists and practitioners, training and preparation may have varied from one actor to another, but the basics remained the same: a close study of the script in order to "explore their characters' given circumstances, objectives, and actions along with the dramatic structure of any given scene."[26] One of the most lauded actors of the 1930s was Paul Muni, whose credits include the gangster film *Scarface* (Howard Hawks, 1932), the social protest drama *I Am a Fugitive from a Chain Gang* (Mervyn LeRoy, 1932), and *The Story of Louis Pasteur* (William Dieterle, 1936), for which he won an Oscar. Known for his hard work and dedication, he "required months to research his character and prepare for his performance. If the character was a historical figure, he would read every available book on the subject. If the character required a certain dialect, he would rehearse into a recorder until he was satisfied with his accent. Once filming began he would remain in character between takes and even when he was off the studio lot. Muni would literally become the person in the script."[27] Oscar winner Joan Crawford, who was often considered to be more of a personality than an actor, approached her roles with no less seriousness. "If the script had been based on a book," she explained, "I'd go back and read the book. . . . Once in a role, I eliminated myself completely. I became the character I played. . . . I remember every one of my important roles the way I remember a part of my life, because at the time I did them I *was* the role and it *was* my life, for twenty-four hours a day."[28]

In contrast to Muni and Crawford, two-time Oscar winner Spencer Tracy downplayed the importance of the acting craft, at least in his public statements. Suspicious of such discussions, he urged fellow actors simply to learn their lines and not bump into the furniture. Yet he prepared meticulously, keeping to a rigorous schedule and isolating himself for days to study a script until he knew every word of it.[29] During his nearly forty-year career, he worked in an emotionally restrained mode, playing a wide range of roles that included a man who was falsely accused of kidnapping in *Fury* (Fritz Lang, 1936) and a Portuguese fisherman who befriends a spoiled rich boy in *Captains Courageous* (Victor Fleming, 1937). For much of the press and many of his peers, he was the consummate screen actor.

The Star System

By definition, stars are charismatic performers whose personae or versions of themselves connect to the historic moment (think of Shirley Temple and the Depression) and convey a cultural meaning that exceeds any single character they play. Sound produced a new breed of movie stars. Like silent film stars, who were gods and goddesses to be admired from afar, stars during the Golden Age embodied the daydreams of the movie-going public, who often saw them as idealized versions of themselves. At the same time, sound made stars more human and accessible, enabling moviegoers to experience a world of distinct vocal styles, such as Bette Davis's nervous, clipped delivery, Katharine Hepburn's pronounced Bryn Mawr accent, Henry Fonda's flat Midwestern inflections, and Judy Garland's quivering vibrato. Some critics, however, tended to dismiss stars as having little acting ability because they did not conform to long-held notions of acting that derived from the stage. To be sure, stars usually did not play a broad range of roles or possess the vocal equipment needed for projection. Nonetheless, many of them, like Muni, Crawford, and Tracy, were as committed to bringing their roles to life as any professional stage actor. Indeed, they not only mastered the medium in which they worked but developed a unique skill, playing variations of their persona, developing it, and fine-tuning it over time. In his early roles, for example, Humphrey Bogart, who had some theater experience, played heavies, his craggy looks and slightly paralyzed upper lip seemingly not the stuff that stars were made of. To individualize these heavies, he deployed certain gestures, such as "putting his tongue behind his lower lip, pushing it slightly forward while the mouth as a whole pouts."[30] When he made the transition to leading roles, such as Rick in *Casablanca* (Michael Curtiz, 1942) and Sam Spade in *The Maltese Falcon* (John Huston, 1941), Bogart refined these gestures to show that his corrupt, aloof tough guy was an act, and that he was on the side of good.[31] Later in his career, he continued to refine these gestures, as he played more psychologically complex roles in films such as *The Treasure of the Sierra Madre* (John Huston, 1948) and *In a Lonely Place* (Nicholas Ray, 1950). In Bogart's case, star and actor were synonymous. The same held true for many other gifted performers.

As it does today, stardom often had a downside: typecasting. Dick Powell, a box office favorite in the mid-1930s, was so strongly identified with Warner Bros.' backstage musicals that when he was cast as the private detective Philip Marlowe in RKO's adaptation of Raymond Chandler's *Farewell My Lovely*, the title of the film was changed to *Murder, My Sweet* (Edward Dmytryk, 1944) lest audiences mistake it for a musical. During this period, perhaps even more than today, stars invariably took a risk when they ventured too far from their image. One of Cary Grant's cherished projects was *None But the Lonely Heart* (Clifford Odets, 1944), in which he played a Cockney resident of the London slums. The role was a major departure from the sophisticated persona that had made him a star—apparently

FIGURE 14: Hattie McDaniel in her Oscar-winning performance in *Gone With the Wind*.

too much so. The film played to empty houses. Some stars, however, managed to overcome typecasting. For example, prior to *Double Indemnity* (1944), Fred MacMurray mostly played lightweight roles, but at director Billy Wilder's urging he took on the part of the film's amiable but amoral protagonist. It proved to be one of the highlights of his career.

That said, no stars or actors found it more difficult to escape typecasting than nonwhite performers. Given the racism of the day, the best they could hope for was to endow their stereotyped characters with some semblance of individuality and humanity. A notable example of an actor who did just that was Hattie McDaniel. Although she was restricted to playing domestic servants throughout her career, her acting choices made the wise, loving, and indomitable Mammy in *Gone with the Wind* (1939) less of a stereotype than she might have been (see figure 14).

The Production Code

As the film scholar Erica Carter has stated, the Production Code "moulded star images after 1930 to US moral, legal and aesthetic norms."[32] Fearful that censorship would "eventually find its way into legislative policy with disastrous effects on the moviemaking business,"[33] Hollywood adopted the Production Code Administration (PCA) in 1934 as a policy of self-regulation. The Code was a response to religious and other pressure groups, including the powerful Catholic Legion of Decency, which saw Hollywood as a modern Babylon. It established a strict set of guidelines that included such subjects as sex, profanity, homosexuality, miscegenation, and violence. Stars who traded in too much sexual frankness saw their careers flounder, none more so than Mae West for her double entendres, suggestive songs ("I Like a Man Who Takes His Time"), and spoofing of sex. In the pre-Code *I'm No Angel* (Wesley Ruggles, 1932), when a friend remarks, "Goodness, what beautiful diamonds," West rejoins, "Goodness had nothing to do with it." Swaying her hips, batting her eyelashes, and oohing-and-aahing breathlessly, West took pleasure in her sexuality and didn't care who knew it. Her many fans got the joke, but the bluenoses of the day had little sense of humor, and by the time she made the post-Code *My Little Chickadee* (Edward F. Cline) in 1940, she was but a shadow of her former uninhibited self.

West was by no means the only star to give pressure groups cause for alarm. Miriam Hopkins starred in a number of controversial films, especially *The Story of Temple Drake* (Stephen Roberts, 1933), which dealt openly with "the raw stuff of American culture"[34] and cast her in the role of a willful Southern belle who is raped and forced into prostitution by a gang of bootleggers. Barbara Stanwyck raised eyebrows on at least two occasions. In *The Bitter Tea of General Yen* (Frank Capra, 1933), which flirted with the theme of miscegenation, she was a young New England woman whose repressed sexual desires are awakened by a Chinese warlord who abducts her. And in *Baby Face* (Alfred E. Green, 1933) she played a hard-as-nails small-town girl who sleeps her way to the top of corporate America. The film "was so troubling to the censors that it was cut by five minutes even before the Code was enforced; the full-length pre-release version was only rediscovered by Mike Mashon in the Library of Congress archives in 2005."[35] Jean Harlow, the decade's reigning sex goddess, made it very clear in comedies such as *Red-Headed Woman* (Jack Conway, 1932) and melodramas such as the steamy *Red Dust* (Victor Fleming, 1932) that her "good bad girls" liked sex. However, after the Code crackdown, she did an about-face in *The Girl from Missouri*, aka *100% Pure* (Jack Conway, 1934), as a chorine who saves herself for marriage. For the remainder of her career—she died prematurely at the age of twenty-six in 1937—Harlow's brassy, tough-talking seductress was largely a thing of the past. Another actor that the Code had a major impact on was Marlene Dietrich. In *Desire* (Frank Borzage, 1936), the former femme fatale of Sternberg's films—who famously kissed a woman on the lips in his stylish *Morocco* (1930) and often dressed in male suits—played a high-class jewel thief who finds love and redemption, marries Gary Cooper, and settles down in Detroit to be a devoted housewife. In *Destry Rides Again* (George Marshall, 1939), Dietrich solidified her new image, playing a feisty, fun-loving entertainer in a frontier saloon.

However, what "provoked the greatest moral panic" among censors were the nearly seventy-five gangster films made before 1934,[36] which tended to glorify the criminal world. Of these films, the most influential were the seminal works starring Edward G. Robinson and James Cagney. Thanks to these actors' raw performances—Cagney was cocky, dapper, and pugnacious; Robinson was snarling, swaggering, and monomaniacal—their characters had a tragic stature that was magnified by a sudden and inevitable fall from fortune. Hence Robinson's stunned disbelief in *Little Caesar* when he is shot down on the street: "Mother of Mercy, is this the end of Rico?" or Cagney's realization in *The Public Enemy* (1931) after being mortally wounded, "I ain't so tough." To appease the censors, Hollywood made an effort to deglamorize crime. For example, in *Angels with Dirty Faces* (Michael Curtiz, 1938), Cagney's hoodlum pretends to break down into cowardly hysterics on his way to the electric chair to steer the neighborhood kids away from a life of crime. Cagney's enactment of noble sacrifice made his character even more heroic, in effect qualifying, if not actively undermining, the intention of the censors. Resourcefully, Hollywood often found ways to comply with the censors while at the same time circumventing them. In *Gilda* (Charles Vidor, 1946), for example, Rita Hayworth does a sizzling striptease to the tune of "Put the Blame on Mame," removing only her elbow-length satin gloves. Here less was definitely more, and Hollywood and its audience knew it.

Sophisticated Comedy: *Trouble in Paradise*

Ernst Lubitsch's sophisticated comedy *Trouble in Paradise* (1932) deals with two high-society jewel thieves, Gaston Monescu (Herbert Marshall) and his lover, Lily (Miriam Hopkins), who pose as servants in the household of wealthy widow Mariette Colet (Kay Francis) in order to rob her. Unfortunately, trouble finds its way into paradise when Madame Colet falls in love with Gaston, and he not only falls for her but considers going straight—much to Lily's displeasure. In the end, practicality wins the day, and he returns to Lily. As the couple hurries off in a taxi, they compare their spoils, courtesy of Madame Colet, and look forward to a life of stealing, swindling, and robbing.

Set during the Great Depression, *Trouble in Paradise* includes a scene that can be found in any number of realistic dramas of the period. A couple—in this case, Gaston and Lily—is having a quiet breakfast; she reads her paper; he reads his. They are down on their luck, but interrupt their reading to assure each other that "prosperity is just around the corner." This nod to contemporary reality notwithstanding, the film's real interest is in creating a sublime world of artifice. As was his custom, Lubitsch acted the parts himself for his cast.[37] Here he did so in order to demonstrate how the genre's highly self-conscious dialogue called for a specific kind of theatrical delivery—lilting and rhythmic, mannered, yet seemingly natural, and as light as gossamer. Hopkins had worked with Lubitsch before, and he allowed her "to do outlandish takes and inventively eccentric line readings as Lily flits and chatters away."[38] All three actors had stage experience. In fact, Marshall, who hailed from a theatrical family, was a celebrated leading man in London and New York, and already a mature star of forty-two when he made the film.

Like his co-stars, Marshall is ideally cast. His mellifluous voice, impeccable timing, and understated manner make Gaston the nonpareil of urbanity—his moments of unexpected behavior an added delight. For example, during a late night dinner, where he and Lily pose as aristocrats and quietly filch items from each other's person, Gaston ("the Baron") rises from the table, locks the door, returns to the table, takes Lily ("the Countess") by the shoulders, and shakes her until his wallet tumbles from inside her dress onto the floor. What appeared to be a prelude to sexual seduction turns out to be an unmasking: he knows she is a crook, and she knows he's one as well. They then continue their meal, as if nothing has happened, and politely return *most* of the items they stole. (Gaston, ever the gentleman, asks to keep the garter he took from her thigh as a keepsake.) It's a match made in heaven. The scene ends with the couple retiring to a chaise lounge to make love.

As Gaston's working-class partner in thievery, Miriam Hopkins's Lily is something of a chameleon. She can be shy and demure, or sexy or coy, or feisty and fast-talking, and when it comes to verbal dexterity she is Gaston's equal. In the dinner scene, for instance, she declares matter-of-factly, "Baron, you are a crook," then asks, without missing a beat, "May I have the salt?" Earlier in the same scene, dressed in a stunning lamé gown—her work clothes—she arrives at Gaston's hotel room in a feigned tizzy, protesting her fate as a long-suffering aristocrat ("One gets so tired of one's class"), pacing around the room nervously, then collapsing into an armchair and bringing her arm to her head in a gesture of weariness worthy of Delsarte, a nineteenth-century codifier of acting gestures. It's a performance-within-a-performance, and part of the fun comes from trying to figure out how seriously she means Gaston to take it. Lily's poses and affectations may be an act, but her love for Gaston is the real thing, and she won't let him forget it. Thus, when she suspects he is more interested in Madame Colet than in her money, Hopkins pulls out all the stops, reveling in the fuss that Lily makes. Never has Lily moved faster, talked faster, or been more mocking or combative. She cleans out Mariette's safe, pledges never to fall for another man, even "if he were the biggest crook on earth," and repeatedly insults Gaston ("Shut up, you liar, you!"). Dangling her loot in his face, she exclaims, "This is real! Money! Cash!" She refuses to be a woman scorned.

Kay Francis, on the other hand, makes sensuality the key to Mariette's character.[39] Living in a gilded cage, she yearns to break free. Enter Gaston, pretending to be a member of the "*nouveau* poor" to return her handbag (which he had stolen in the first place) and claim the reward. Francis makes it quite clear that Mariette's passions are stirred by his savoir-faire and take-charge manner. Her voice

FIGURE 15: Herbert Marshall and Kay Francis's sublime flirtation in *Trouble in Paradise*.

softens, her body assumes a relaxed stance, and when he flirts with her she flirts right back. Emboldened by the sexual chemistry she senses between them, she leans back on her couch provocatively, looks him over, smiles, and offers him a job as her personal secretary (see figure 15).

In his book on Lubitsch, William Paul notes that throughout the film Mariette lapses into frozen poses.[40] These poses, however, convey more than just languor and passivity; they constitute her chief weapon: presenting herself for admiring eyes. As she later tells Gaston, "You like me. In fact, you're crazy about me." And she's right. In one scene he tries to dissuade her from spending the evening out. Enjoying her power over him, she makes slipping on a glove a consummate act of coquetry. Why must she go? he asks. "Because," she answers, pausing before drawing out the rest of the sentence, "I want to make it *tough* for you." Clearly, Mariette matches Gaston in the game of domination and submission they play. Fittingly, Lubitsch photographs them in full figure, her face lifted toward his, their bodies so close that they seem about to kiss. Yet they both recognize that lovemaking demands a light touch and that her social status dictates that satisfaction must be postponed. Expecting that she and Gaston have "weeks, months, years" ahead of them, she luxuriates in the promise of romance. She is no simple victim. Nonetheless, when she learns he had planned to rob her, her sadness is so real, her melancholy so profound, that it hurts. "You wanted a hundred thousand francs, and I thought [she pauses slightly] you wanted me." Rather than call the police, she chooses to hold on to the memory of what-might-have-been. "It could have been marvelous," she says wistfully. "Divine," he replies. What ultimately distinguishes sophisticated comedy is "the tone of characters who pretend to be gay and carefree and free-spirited but in truth care passionately and mourn their losses with heavy hearts."[41] The leading actors in *Trouble in Paradise* clearly understand as much. This alone makes Lubitsch's comedy only superficially superficial.

The Musical: *Swing Time*

For many moviegoers, the 1930s musical reached its apogee in the series of nine films that Fred Astaire and Ginger Rogers made at RKO between 1933 and 1939. The plot of George Stevens's *Swing Time* (1936) is a staple of courtship romance: Lucky Garnett (Astaire), a hoofer with a yen for gambling, comes to the big city to earn $25,000 so that he can marry his fiancée back home. He meets Penny Carroll (Rogers), a dance instructor, and immediately falls in love with her, but their relationship is beset by misunderstandings and complications until the final, never-in-doubt happy ending.

For every film Rogers made with Astaire, she did three or four films without him.[42] During this time, Astaire and Hermes Pan worked out the choreography. Once she arrived on the set, she and Astaire typically practiced their dance numbers eight hours a day for six weeks prior to the actual shooting.[43] As she has said, *Swing Time* was her favorite of their musicals together, for besides allowing her to sing and dance, it extended her range by allowing her to play someone other than her usual, wide-eyed ingénue.[44]

As a genre, the musical constitutes a "double mode of presentation," in which song and dance (the theatrical/nonrealistic mode) express the emotional lives and deepest feelings of the characters, while the realistic/naturalistic mode "carries the story line forward."[45] In *Swing Time*, Ginger Rogers's ability to convey her character's feelings in both modes can be best seen in the sequences involving three musical numbers: "Pick Yourself Up," "A Fine Romance," and "Never Gonna Dance."

As Elizabeth Kendall has persuasively shown in her book on romantic comedy, Rogers does not play her scenes comically or tongue in check, but "aimed instinctively at quiet realism."[46] Indeed, in a scene that exemplifies the film's realistic mode and paves the way for the "Pick Yourself Up" number, Rogers quickly establishes Penny Carroll as a hard-working, self-respecting woman with a strong sense of decency.[47] In this scene Rogers meets Astaire's Lucky for the first time and, thinking he has pocketed her quarter, has no use for him. However, he is so smitten with her that he follows her to the dance studio where she works, pretending to want lessons. Irked by his unwanted attention, she nevertheless tries to teach him. But when he (deliberately) falls on the floor twice and takes her with him, she ends the lesson abruptly. Her boss, who has overheard everything, promptly fires her. Trying to undo the harm he has caused, Lucky insists on showing her boss how much she has taught him. He sweeps her up in his arms, and—presto!—they leave the world of realism behind and dance the exhilarating tap routine, "Pick Yourself Up." However, Rogers doesn't just execute the dance; she *acts* it, tracing each stage of Penny's feelings from bewilderment to astonishment to pure delight, as she gives herself over to the sheer fun of it. Experiencing a sense of what life and love can be, she sees Lucky's true character. However, she soon discovers that she is unable, as Edward Gallafent describes it in his book on Astaire and Rogers, "to move the Astaire figure except within the spell of the dance."[48]

In the duet "A Fine Romance," with its magical winter setting, alternation of dialogue and song, and seamless blend of realistic and musical modes, Rogers underplays; as Hannah Hyam observes in her book on the Astaire-Rogers partnership, she uses "a change of expression here, a different tone of voice there, a minimum of gestures."[49] Not wanting to seem too forward, Penny cuddles up to Lucky cautiously. Her voice soft and intimate, her expression one of yearning, she tells him she feels cold, hinting for him to put his arms around her. However, he rejects every overture she makes, since—unbeknownst to her—he has a fiancée back home. Repeatedly, Penny tries to draw him out. Close-ups of Rogers single out both Penny's growing frustration and her effort to conceal that frustration by biting her lip. Occasionally, Lucky forgets himself, as when he fondly refers to their being thrown together as "quite an experience." Taking advantage of the moment, Penny says quietly, "Sort of like a romance, isn't it?" And when he agrees, she snuggles up to him even closer. Just then he remembers himself and puts an end to the romantic mood, chastising her for not wearing galoshes. Exasperated, she says sullenly: "I think we better go home." Walking away, Rogers affects a deliberately exaggerated stride and swings her handbag to express Penny's irritation. However, Penny hasn't given up—far from it. Stopping abruptly, Rogers turns around to face Astaire and strikes a decidedly defiant pose, leaning against a tree with one arm, while placing the other arm on her hip. She then begins singing, "A fine romance with no kisses . . . ," and resumes walking. Astaire follows at a safe distance. Then in a medley of actions that express Penny's hurt and disappointment, Rogers sits, rises, moves toward him, then moves away from him.

Rogers's performance culminates in a series of crisply executed gestures and a pronounced emphasis on specific words and lyrics. Thus, at various points, she tosses Astaire sidelong glances (sad, sardonic, even self-pitying), dismisses him with a wave of her arm, and crosses her arms tightly in self-protection. At the same time she gives a sarcastic spin to the words "romance" and "good fellow." By the end of the song, Penny is on the verge of tears. Trying to console her, Lucky takes her in his arms and is just about to kiss her when he is abruptly called offstage. It is then that Penny accidentally learns about his engagement and is more deeply hurt than ever. No matter that Lucky has suddenly decided to ignore his engagement. When he rejoins Penny, he finds her ardor has turned to ice. As Astaire sings his part of the duet ("A fine romance with no clinches . . ."), Rogers ignores him and walks away.

In the "Never Gonna Dance" number, Penny and Lucky seem resigned to the fact that their dream of being together can never be. However, they find it impossible to part. In what film historian Arlene Croce calls "the dance of dances,"[50] Astaire and Rogers walk side by side forlorn, separating, coming back together until finally Rogers breaks away from Astaire, who remains behind, shattered. As Hyam rightly contends, "It is a fragmented dance, broken into several disparate pieces but unified by an emotional coherence and dramatic force that are utterly compelling."[51]

One of the most moving of these pieces is the short dialogue passage in which Penny asks Lucky if the girl he is in love with dances beautifully. When he has to be reminded that she is talking about his fiancée, he says, unable to think about anyone but her, "Oh, I don't know. I've danced with you. I'm never going to dance again." This conversation, however, says far less than the look of despair on their faces, or the fact that Rogers has Penny repeatedly touch her engagement ring unconsciously (she too is about to marry another), as if it were the source of all her pain (see figure 16). Rogers's command of unstated emotions is matched by Astaire's gravitas. Indeed, in this dance, the distinction between theatrical (nonrealistic) and realistic (naturalistic) performance

FIGURE 16: "Never gonna dance." Fred Astaire and Ginger Rogers in *Swing Time*.

melts away, supporting the contention of film historian Leo Braudy that these forms of presentation are not always absolutes but rather points on a slippery continuum.[52] For many critics, this six-minute dance is the most perfect in the Astaire-Rogers series. But perfection clearly came at a price—in this case, forty-seven takes and a ten-hour shooting schedule.

Family Melodrama: *Make Way for Tomorrow*

In Leo McCarey's family melodrama *Make Way for Tomorrow* (1937), Beulah Bondi and Victor Moore play Lucy and Barkley Cooper, an elderly retired couple who have lost their home in the Depression and are forced to live apart with different children in separate locations. Bondi, who specialized in playing older women, made her Broadway debut in 1929 in Elmer Rice's Pulitzer Prize–winning *Street Scene* as a malicious neighborhood gossip, a role she re-created in King Vidor's film version. Throughout her film career, she played supporting parts. The one exception was the starring role of Lucy Cooper. Bondi explained that she found it challenging,[53] but that she prepared for it in her usual way: "From the feet up . . . I must make the character play true from the foundation—in voice, body, imagination, interest in humanity."[54]

In his study of the genre, Richard de Cordova contends that melodrama "places an overriding emphasis on the inner emotional states of the characters" and that "certain melodramatic scenes are written as showcases for performance."[55] Beulah Bondi's performance offers proof of de Cordova's contention, especially in one deceptively simple scene that represents a unique synthesis of realistic (naturalistic) acting and theatricality—what one critic has rightly called "an amazing piece of theatre."[56] In this scene Lucy receives a long-distance phone call from Barkley, unintentionally disrupting her daughter-in-law's bridge class. McCarey initially presents Lucy with her back turned to the camera, but for most of the scene has her face to the camera with the class visible in the background, watching and listening. At the beginning of the phone call, Lucy speaks too loudly, irritating the class and embarrassing herself. However, when she expresses her love and concern for Barkley and her wish to be reunited with him, the expressions on the students' faces soften. She has brought them face to face with painful reality. As the film scholar Robin Wood points out, this scene is "at once funny, sad, and acutely embarrassing for both the characters and the audience: archetypal McCarey" (see figure 17).[57]

Apropos of melodrama, the phone conversation couldn't be more banal, the plaintive, choked tone of Lucy's voice and her repetition of words imbuing it with the feeling of ordinary colloquial speech. "I was worried about you," she says, at first gently scolding Bark. "Why didn't you write? You ought to write. You know I worry." Complementing Bondi's realistic acting is McCarey's staging

FIGURE 17: Beulah Bondi and the in-frame audience in *Make Way for Tomorrow*.

of the scene, which constitutes "a doubling of perspective." Here we, the movie audience, watch the characters in the narrative watch Lucy, and in this privileged position, see more than they do—their different points of view and feelings, and the dramatic action in a broader context. This alone makes the scene not only a rendering of quotidian reality but an example of self-reflexivity, foregrounding what Murray Pomerance calls in his essay on screen acting "performed performance."[58] Differing from straight performance, "performed performance" is "acting put up for display, even though the characters onscreen may or may not see it as acting, too."[59]

The result is a heightening of realism that gives a complex tone to the scene's inherent pathos. In this regard Bondi and McCarey make us keenly aware of the meaning of public versus private space. We never forget that although Lucy is caught up in a highly private moment, she occupies a space—her son and daughter-in-law's living room—that the presence of the class makes public. By and large she tries to ignore the class but remains aware of them, subtly glancing in their direction at one point, which they do not see. The fact that all eyes are on her—ours as the movie audience, as well as those of the class (the in-frame audience)—makes this a strongly marked scene of performance, one that requires Beulah Bondi to express her character's most personal feelings in a manner congruent with the setting and circumstance. Indeed, even though her body movements and vocal and facial expressions are necessarily restricted, she manages to delineate Lucy's character in full: her innocence, fragility, determination, and selfless radiance.

Throughout the scene, Bondi projects complex emotion with clarity and precision. Underplaying, she keeps her gestures to a minimum, her head slightly lowered, her eyes downcast. Only when she turns to the topic that is uppermost in Lucy's mind does she speak more deliberately and emphatically: "How are you, Bark? You know what I mean. How is everything?" Her words are in effect code, the language shared by a long-time married couple. As if in response to his reply (which we do not hear) Bondi punctuates her line delivery with unexpected pauses, her voice quavering slightly ("It must have cost you a lot to call me," she says at one point. "Well . . . that's a lot"). Here Bondi breaks and retards the rhythm to express how deeply touched Lucy is by Bark's sacrifice. She then makes a sacrifice of her own. (Indeed, the self-sacrificing woman is a recurring figure in 1930s melodrama.) Tending to Bark's needs, she first gives him this piece of advice: "It's getting cold. Don't go out without your coat. And if it rains, don't go out at all." Then, as Lucy brings the conversation to a close, she does what she has always done: she gives him strength and assurance: "We'll soon be together for always," she says. "And you won't worry, will you?" Then she says, "Goodbye." Bondi repeats the word three times, giving it a delicate shading and allowing her voice to rise, almost in a question, before fading into a whisper. As Lucy leaves the room, Bondi reveals the toll the conversation has taken on her. Physically and emotionally spent, she walks more slowly than before and seems older, feebler. Initially, Bondi's performance and McCarey's staging traced divergent meanings for the movie audience and the in-frame audience. However, when Lucy says goodnight to the class, they stand in respect. With this act, the once-divergent meanings are resolved.

In the final scene, following a poignant reunion, Lucy sees Barkley off on a train that will take him across the country to live with one of their daughters. (She, in turn, will go into a nursing home.) Although the couple pretends that the parting is only temporary, we know it is not. Trusting that the scene speaks for itself, Bondi does not play it as a big moment but simply stands in place on the station platform. As the train pulls away, Lucy looks away briefly, then allows herself one last look at Barkley. Bondi's facial expressions are so tiny and concentrated that they cannot help but compel our attention. A flicker of her eyelids clears away barely visible tears. She then turns and walks away.[60] It is a heartbreaking scene.

Even though this scene does not have the complex aesthetic structure of the phone conversation scene, it exemplifies the integral relationship between performance, theatricality, and realism. Indeed, Bondi and McCarey do not use theatricality so much to counter realism as to explore it. Bondi's performance is built not only on this premise but on the understanding that sometimes nothing more is needed in melodrama than the flicker of an eyelid. She has gone on record saying, "I never went out of my way to physically change my appearance.

You don't have to when you're dealing with the mind and the heart. Those are the two things that dictate my character."[61] To this must be added two other things: restraint and self-effacement. Astonishingly, she was only forty-five when she played the seventy-five-year-old Lucy.

Film Noir: *Double Indemnity*

In Billy Wilder's film noir *Double Indemnity* (1944), the insurance agent Walter Neff (Fred MacMurray) is seduced by the blonde *femme fatale* Phyllis Dietrichson (Barbara Stanwyck) into helping to kill her husband for an insurance payoff. They devise an ingenious plot to carry out the murder, but come to a bad end because of Phyllis's duplicity, Walter's discovery of her duplicity, and the tenacity of claims investigator Barton Keyes (Edward G. Robinson).[62]

Central to the film is the use of voiceover narration. As the film scholar Mary Ann Doane has observed, although voiceover as a major element of film "has been approached largely in terms of its narrational function, [it] plays a crucial role in structuring performance."[63] Indeed, "put forward as a performance for someone—implicitly, at least, the spectator,"[64] it is an example of theatricality, showcasing performance as performance and calling attention to its own artifice and rhetorical strategies. As such, it complements and serves as counterpoint to the realistic presentation of performance in the story proper, which in film noir is often structured as a flashback or series of flashbacks. In *Double Indemnity* this conjunction of theatricality and realism lies at the heart of Fred MacMurray's performance.

At its most basic level, Walter Neff's voiceover is a confession. Using Keyes's Dictaphone to address him, Walter recounts his tale of involvement with Phyllis Dietrichson, beginning with their first meeting and leading up to the present moment. All the while, he is slowly bleeding to death, having been shot by her. It is a performance-within-a-performance, in which MacMurray charts Walter's decline from slick, smarmy, talkative wise-guy (who isn't as tough or smart as he thinks) to a man who is weary of self-deception and determined to expunge his sordid past. Indeed, the longer he talks into the Dictaphone, the more he abjures his characteristically hard-boiled, snappy jargon, such as in this remark to Keyes: "You think you're such a hot potato as a claims manager, such a wolf on a phony claim." Here the Walter of the voiceover and the Walter of the flashbacks meet on common ground, what the film critic Richard Schickel calls his "somber self-awareness,"[65] in one last attempt to regain his sanity and reason. Interestingly, Walter never tells Phyllis he loves her. Rather, he declares: "I'm crazy about you, baby." As it happens, this is not far from the truth.

The motive usually ascribed to Walter for getting ensnared in Phyllis's plot is that he wants to "crook the house," that is, cheat the insurance company he works for, and that she provides the opportunity. However, as J. P. Telotte points out, Walter is also driven by "the lure of money, the attraction of Phyllis, a desire for an exciting alternative to his humdrum life."[66] To this end, MacMurray doesn't rely only on the intricate interplay between his line readings in the voiceover and those in the flashbacks, or on his physicality—his six-foot-plus frame, basso profundo speech, and baby-soft facial features. Instead he deploys a select number of gestures, tamping them down to make them all the more natural and realistic. One of MacMurray's signature gestures is his habit of keeping his hands tucked in his pockets. At first, this gesture reinforces his attitude that he has everything under control. However, after he and Phyllis have killed her husband, it takes on a more urgent meaning. As Walter explains in voiceover, "I put my hands in my pockets because I thought they were shaking."

Before the murder, Walter's gestures and movements are open, casual, and relaxed: hence the way he positions his body in relation to Keyes and Phyllis. He sits on the edge of Keyes's desk and Phyllis's couch not only to be near them but to judge his effect on them.[67] In fact, MacMurray is at his most relaxed in the film in his first scene with Robinson where he maintains eye contact, something he will not always do later. And when Keyes, who is ranting and raving about a client's phony claim, pauses to catch his breath, Walter says, playfully, "All right, turn the record over. Let's hear the other side." The two men's affection for each other is evident, and is perfectly expressed by Walter's frequent lighting of Keyes's cigars, followed by his catchphrase, "I love you, too." Of course, Walter and Keyes's relationship—that of father and son—is the film's real love story.

By contrast, Walter's first meeting with Phyllis sets the tone for an altogether different relationship. Shamelessly flirting with her (which she does not discourage), he leans so close that there is hardly any breathing room between them. Moreover, as he is about to leave, he engages her in badinage that is charged with sexual innuendo. When she feigns innocence, saying, "I wonder if I know what you mean," he has a ready comeback: "I wonder if you wonder." On his second visit, he is even more brazen. He rings the doorbell, then waits for her to answer, leaning against the doorway like a teenager trying to be cool. Wearing a perpetual smirk, he makes it clear that selling her husband insurance is the furthest thing from his mind. For the only time in the film, he sits back comfortably, and even props a pillow behind him to make himself at home—too much at home. As for Phyllis, she sits just close enough to him to make sure she is tantalizing. Playing for sympathy, she explains how her husband neglects her and how she spends many evenings knitting. Walter assures her that she wouldn't have to resort to knitting if he were around. If this scene crackles with excitement, it is in no small part because MacMurray is clearly having a grand time giving himself over to Walter's sleaziness. Even so, at this point Walter has not completely lost his reason. Seeing through her, he says bluntly: "You want to knock him off, don't you?" Later he adds in voiceover that he "let her have it straight between the eyes." Yet

FIGURE 18: Fred MacMurray scrutinizes Barbara Stanwyck in *Double Indemnity*.

that hardly matters, since MacMurray's performance never leaves any doubt that Walter has already taken the bait (see figure 18).

If MacMurray's gestures, body language, and line deliveries are appropriately casual before the murder, afterward they are understandably guarded and kept to a minimum. Avoiding eye contact as much as possible, he rarely faces the person he is talking to but stands off to the side or in the background, holding himself rigidly, bracing for any new piece of evidence that might incriminate him. Take, for example, the scene in which Lola, Dietrichson's daughter, confides to him that she knows Phyllis killed her father. Walter listens, poker-faced, his discomfort betrayed only by the occasional twitching of his thumb as he strokes the lapel of his jacket. However, when she reveals that Phyllis, who was her mother's nurse, coldly and calculatedly killed her as well, Walter is visibly shocked. Nevertheless, he manages to hide his reaction, except for a subtle shift of movement in his eyes and the slow removal of his hand from his lapel. As he later remarks in voiceover, he decided to spend some time with Lola to prevent her from telling her story to anyone else. Yet he also adds that she was the only person with whom he could relax. Schickel has suggested that the film "hints that Walter has fallen in love with Lola,"[68] but if so, he cannot, for obvious reasons, admit this even to himself.

As Walter grows more fearful, Wilder films MacMurray in long takes that require him to show Walter's sustained reactions in their entirety. The most important of these long takes occurs after Keyes informs him that he has discovered the identity of Phyllis's male accomplice. Sneaking into Keyes's office, Walter listens to the report he has filed. Here, in a sixty-five-second shot, Mac-Murray's face undergoes scarcely a change of expression, even when he learns that Keyes not only has named another man but has in fact vouched for Walter. Only the sweat on his hands and face, which he dutifully wipes away, hints at the panic he feels. And even when he says in voiceover that he sees a way to free himself from Phyllis and pin the murder on her, his face registers no sense of relief or even a modicum of joy. On the contrary, MacMurray shows us that Walter is numb. He speaks in a weary monotone, a far cry from his line delivery early in the film where his voice had sass, color, variety, and texture. In fact, MacMurray lets his voice go dry, as if his vocal cords have tightened up and he is choking. Walter may not as yet have descended to the level of Phyllis's icy monotone, but he has become the dead man whose footsteps he could no longer hear after killing Dietrichson. Still, he manages to rouse himself one last time, but barely, when he asks Keyes to gently break the news about him to Lola. This act may not redeem him, but it is an unexpected grace note.

As an implicit address to the moviegoer, and a direct address to Keyes, Walter's voiceover exemplifies the role that the theatrical mode plays in showcasing MacMurray's performance and in shaping the world of noir. As the film historian Gene D. Phillips has noted, the world of noir is harsh and the lives of its characters are bleak.[69] In *Double Indemnity* this world means not only the drab assortment of settings—Walter's bachelor flat, Phyllis's bungalow, the corner supermarket, and the snake pit–like cubicles of the insurance company—but more significantly the film's pervasive mood of darkness. In complete harmony with this mood, MacMurray's performance never veers from a through-line of paradoxically self-inflicted behavior and unavoidable fate.

Conclusion

One of the major achievements of Hollywood's Classical Period (1928–1946) was the creation and blossoming of a protean acting style that was especially conducive to genre films. This style took two primary forms: realism/naturalism and nonrealism/theatricality. Realistic acting was essentially characterized by a single goal: it required the actor to avoid ostentation and conform more or less to a recognizable, albeit selective form of everyday behavior. Theatrical acting, on the other hand, manifested itself in various forms. Hence, verbal artifice in *Trouble in Paradise*, song and dance in *Swing Time*, performed performance in *Make Way for Tomorrow*, and voiceover in *Double Indemnity*.

Since its heyday, the Hollywood studio acting style has continued to make its presence felt, even as it embraced other modes and was, in part, supplanted by them. In the late 1940s, a new style of acting was introduced by Italian neorealism and sociologically conscious American films, such as *The Best Years of Our Lives* (1946), *The Search* (Fred Zinnemann, 1948), and *Pinky* (Elia Kazan, 1949). This style was documentary-like in its presentation of realism and sought to express the lives and struggles of ordinary people. As in the 1928–1946 period, character-centered drama remained the norm of commercial cinema. But in the 1950s there emerged a more intense and bold acting style, one that privileged psychological interiority and introduced to the screen a generation of actors that included Marlon Brando and James Dean, among others. To be sure, films continued to evince a plurality of acting styles, and the Hollywood studio acting style certainly did not fade away. However, it had to share the spotlight with this highly influential and celebrated performance style, which is often referred to simply as the Method.

3

POSTWAR HOLLYWOOD, 1947-1967   David Sterritt

The years following World War II were a time of transition for American cinema, as for American culture in general. A prolonged economic boom joined with advances in consumer technology, the growing influence of corporate power, military and ideological competition with the Soviet bloc, the mushrooming youth market spawned by the Baby Boom, and other factors to shape a psychological climate that oscillated among hope for a bright future, fear of conquest or annihilation by hostile others, and anxiety over the ever-increasing speed of social change. These and related factors shaped a complex and conflicted psychological climate that encouraged new tendencies in film style and technique, very much including the field of movie acting.

In a society where long-held notions of individuality felt threatened by urban anonymity and corporate groupthink, acting based on traditional screen charisma (Joan Crawford, Cary Grant) gave way to Method-based performances (Marlon Brando, Shelley Winters) that submerged the star persona in the idiosyncratic character. At a time when city and suburb were supplanting hill and dale, the seeming "naturalness" of a James Dean or Julie Harris, hinting of androgyny and the tortured soul, gained ground on the graceful professionalism of a Grace Kelly or a Tyrone Power, whose talents came to seem excessively crafted and refined.

As younger Americans began to associate consistency and self-discipline with monotony and inhibition—a tendency that picked up speed as the 1950s gave way to the 1960s—actors took on a wider, edgier range of character types than most of their studio-era predecessors would have dared. Unlike classical Hollywood performers who played steady variations on reliable, recognizable personae, their postwar counterparts wanted to swing among divergent looks and styles with chameleon-like ease. They were helped and also pressured by modifications in the industry—from the easing of censorship to the expansion of color cinematography—that affected all aspects of film production. In an era when the verities of Frontierland were challenged by the uncertainties of Tomorrowland, screen acting was a sensitive barometer of shifting American moods.

The Method

A key influence on postwar movie acting was the growing American interest in psychological theories and therapies, which were lent extra momentum by the traumas of the recent war and the sociocultural uncertainties that followed in its wake. The 1950s were famously marked by conservative values and capitalist imperatives, but they were equally marked by unease about those values and imperatives; many artists and intellectuals (if not many politicians or business leaders) pondered and deplored consumerism, conformity, and groupthink, seeing them as threats to American democracy and individualism. Members of the intelligentsia and the middle class turned increasingly to psychoanalysis, or at least the vocabulary and general ethos of psychoanalysis, in their effort to understand and negotiate these trends. Movies plunged into the psychoanalytic waters as well; in simplified forms, the discipline's ideas worked their way into a wide range of postwar films.

In this cultural climate, it is not surprising that the psychologically oriented performance techniques collectively known as Method acting became ever more prominent in American theater and cinema. The germ of this approach came from the acting "system" devised by the Russian actor, theorist, and teacher Constantin Stanislavsky around the turn of the twentieth century. Developed and refined in Stanislavsky's work with the Moscow Art Theatre (MAT) until his death in 1938 and articulated in three books he wrote on the subject, this innovative approach was fiercely opposed to the conventionalized mimicry of traditional acting styles.[1] Describing the system's goal of achieving "psychological realism" on the stage, theater scholar Mel Gordon calls it "a spiritual and humane behaviorism that penetrated beneath the surface" of whatever text is being interpreted. "Attempting to consciously parallel the experiences and feelings of the characters with their own," Gordon writes, the actors seek to convey "feelings and thoughts that [arise] sequentially moment by moment, rather than in conscious dramatic flares," doing so in part through detailed facial expressions that audiences can "read" in ways more commonly associated with "motion-picture players in close-up than [with] stage perform-ers." By this account, Stanislavsky's approach manifested a cinematic impulse at a time when cinema itself was still in its early stages of development—a pos-sible reason why some senior members of the Moscow troupe met his system with resistance and hostility.[2]

The young American actor Lee Strasberg encountered Stanislavsky's ideas when the Moscow troupe visited the United States as part of the world tour it conducted from 1922 to 1924. Strasberg explored the techniques further at the American Laboratory Theatre, founded by MAT veterans Maria Ouspenskaya and Richard Boleslavsky, who stayed in New York after the tour to teach and pro-mote the Stanislavsky system. In the early 1930s Strasberg and two colleagues, director Harold Clurman and producer Cheryl Crawford, founded the Group Theatre, a permanent company *à la* the MAT that privileged group identity and ensemble acting over individual virtuosity and star charisma. As the primary director of Group productions from 1931 to 1937, Strasberg began assembling the Method, his own system based on selective application of Stanislavsky's prac-tices. After moving to Hollywood and supervising screen tests for several years, he returned to New York and joined the Actors Studio, founded in 1947 by Elia Kazan and Robert Lewis, who wanted a workshop and training ground that was physically near but artistically sheltered from New York's commercially geared theater industry. Lewis taught the advanced students, among whom were Brando, Montgomery Clift, Patricia Neal, Eli Wallach, Sidney Lumet, Jerome Robbins, Maureen Stapleton, E. G. Marshall, Karl Malden, Beatrice Straight, John For-sythe, Mildred Dunnock, Tom Ewell, Kevin McCarthy, and Herbert Berghof, while Kazan instructed the neophytes, including Kim Hunter, James Whitmore, Julie Harris, Martin Balsam, Cloris Leachman, Steven Hill, Nehemiah Persoff, and others. Strasberg became artistic director of the Actors Studio in 1951, using it to teach and promulgate the Method until his death in 1982. Its influence on American theater and film is difficult to overstate.

Broadly speaking, Stanislavsky's approach "relates character to situation, emphasizes an actor's imagination, and discovers meaning in physical activity," in theorist Rick Kemp's words.[3] Stanislavsky's view of actor training places strong emphasis on two broad categories of proficiency. One is the lifelike presentation of appearances and behaviors, which the actor learns to replicate by carefully observing people and situations in the real world. The other is the communica-tion of psychological qualities and emotional tones, which the actor cultivates through personal introspection and meditation on the nature of the character at hand.

Strasberg regarded the Method as a faithful translation of the Stanislavsky system into the idiom of twentieth-century American performance. In fact, though, he exercised a fair amount of poetic license. Strasberg recognized the importance of external traits but was more fascinated by the challenge of projecting internal traits in lucid and compelling ways. His techniques included improvisation to draw out the actor's personal creativity, relaxation exercises to free the actor from ingrained habits of movement, and intensive work on affective memory, whereby actors tap into experiences, emotions, and motivations from their own lives and substitute the resulting energies for the merely imagined feelings of the character. One way of understanding Method acting is to contrast it with the mode inherited from nineteenth-century stagecraft.[4] In that tradition the actor was expected to put on a fetching show—to look appealing, speak fluently, and move stylishly—even when playing a reprehensible villain or a family drunk. Laurence Olivier, Judith Anderson, Ralph Richardson, and John Gielgud exemplify this manner in British movies, and the likes of Clark Gable, Joan Fontaine, Ronald Colman, and Greer Garson follow similar paths in American pictures. This is the cultural given that the Method set about discarding. Strasberg maintained that actors properly schooled in the Method are able to seem "spontaneous, not as if they were reciting or 'speaking well.' They seem to be speaking like you and me, they don't seem to be acting. . . . Often our actors [i.e., Method actors] are confused with their parts." Equally important, he saw the Method as a route to consistent, dependable excellence night after night or scene after scene. In support of the Method he pointed to Actors Studio alumnae who became major stars not by impressing theorists and partisans but by winning over a broad and diverse public.[5]

On the other end of the spectrum, some highly popular performers rejected and even mocked Method acting. George C. Scott, for example, deemed it "despicable" for actors to "smear their own hang-ups over [a] role" and said that he could not conceive of "anyone paying money to go to the theatre to look at the inner soul of any actor who ever lived."[6] Erstwhile colleagues of Strasberg such as Lewis, Stella Adler, and Sanford Meisner developed competing versions of the Method, reacting against what some observers perceived as the egotism, emotionalism, and self-indulgence fostered by a system that had placed too much weight on inwardness and memory, too little on technical skills and free-ranging imagination. This notwithstanding, theater scholar Bruce McConachie correctly states that in the late 1940s and early 1950s, the Method, "substantially unchanged from its years in the American Laboratory and Group theatres, took Broadway and Hollywood by storm."[7] Drama theorist Michael L. Quinn declares that the various Method studios produced "virtually all of the revolutionary screen performers of the post-war era," from Brando and Monroe to Geraldine Page and James Earl Jones, and adds that such celebrated younger stars as Dustin Hoffman, Robert De Niro, Jack Nicholson, and Meryl Streep reached dominant positions "largely by virtue of the extent to which they imitate Method technical standards."[8]

Italian Neorealism and the French New Wave

Two branches of modern European cinema also had notable influence on postwar Hollywood acting: Italian neorealism in the immediate postwar years and the French New Wave soon afterward. Neorealism was conceived and propelled by a group of filmmakers—primarily Roberto Rossellini, Vittorio De Sica, Luchino Visconti, and Cesare Zavattini—with shared political, sociological, and aesthetic concerns. Like the Americans associated with the Group Theatre and the Method, they wanted to anchor their work in the quest for psychological authenticity. Their goal was to replace the artificiality and superficiality of studio-made "white telephone movies" with the tough-minded immediacy of pictures shot in actual locations and telling real-as-life stories set in the here and now. Their movies featured actors who looked like everyday people and sometimes *were* everyday people, coached by the director one scene at a time, as when De Sica guided factory worker Lamberto Maggiorani and seven-year-old Enzo Staiola through central roles in his masterpiece *Bicycle Thieves* (*Ladri di biciclette*, 1948).

Themes and techniques imported from neorealist films appear in numerous Hollywood productions of the era; film noir, for instance, made extensive use of location shooting and nonprofessional extras, as in *The Naked City* (Jules Dassin, 1948) and *Panic in the Streets* (Elia Kazan, 1950). Nonactors created memorable characters in *Little Fugitive* (Morris Engel, Ray Ashley, and Ruth Orkin, 1953), about an eight-year-old boy lost in the Coney Island amusement park; directed in the purposefully unpolished neorealist spirit, it earned an Oscar nomination for its screenplay. Anna Magnani was an Italian star, but she is distinctly unglamorous in *The Rose Tattoo* (Daniel Mann, 1955) and *The Fugitive Kind* (Sidney Lumet, 1956). Ernest Borgnine was also a seasoned actor, but it was his unrefined screen persona that helped him win an Academy Award for his plainspoken performance in *Marty* (Delbert Mann, 1955), a no-frills drama about a butcher and a schoolteacher leading drab, lonely lives; the neorealist-style production also won Oscars for its director, for screenwriter Paddy Chayefsky, and for Best Picture.

The waning of Italian neorealism was followed by the advent of the French New Wave, which influenced American actors and directors from the second half of the 1950s until well into the 1970s. The filmmakers of the *Nouvelle Vague* were profoundly inspired by their neorealist forerunners (especially Rossellini) as well as selected French predecessors (especially Jean Renoir) and some Americans, including the makers of *Little Fugitive*. A prime innovation of the New Wave, exemplified most vividly by Jean-Luc Godard's films with cinematographer Raoul Coutard, was to replace Hollywood's penchant for three-point or single-source (chiaroscuro) lighting with the practice of spreading more or less uniform light over sizeable areas so that the camera—and, crucially, the actors— are freed from the requirement to hit specific marks at specific moments, and can instead move spontaneously within the space allotted to the scene. The radically independent actor-director-screenwriter John Cassavetes hit upon a similar technique when making his debut film, *Shadows* (1959), and although he did not follow up on its full implications until almost a decade later, the indelible performances by Gena Rowlands, Seymour Cassel, Ben Gazzara, Peter Falk, and assorted nonprofessionals in all of his movies from *Faces* (1968) to *Love Streams* (1984) were deeply influenced by the results he had achieved in *Shadows* as well as his own experiences as a theater actor, acting teacher, and Hollywood star.[9] Among the many 1960s performances bearing signs of New Wave spontaneity and unpredictability are those of Victor Buono in *What Ever Happened to Baby Jane?* (Robert Aldrich, 1962); Bobby Darin in *Captain Newman, M.D.* (David Miller, 1963); Warren Beatty in *Mickey One* (Arthur Penn, 1965); Michael J. Pollard and Estelle Parsons in *Bonnie and Clyde* (Arthur Penn, 1967); Salome Jens in *Seconds* (John Frankenheimer, 1966); Peter Kastner in *You're a Big Boy Now* (Francis Ford Coppola, 1966); and Harvey Keitel in *Who's That Knocking at My Door* (Martin Scorsese, 1967).

Femininities: Monroe, Winters, Taylor

Among the female stars who rose in Hollywood after World War II, none is more intriguing than Marilyn Monroe, arguably the most luminous and popular of them all. She skillfully crafted a comic "dumb blonde" persona, then fought against that objectifying stereotype for the rest of her career. She cultivated an acting style all her own, yet she could experience near-paralyzing spells of stage and camera fright. She profoundly doubted her own talent, but Strasberg profoundly believed in it, coaching her in private lessons at his home and then in regular Actors Studio classes. She stands out to this day as an uncommonly influential star and an indispensable icon of postwar popular culture.

Monroe's first year atop the list of female box-office draws was 1953, when her first three films as star had their premieres—*Niagara* (Henry Hathaway) in January, *Gentlemen Prefer Blondes* (Howard Hawks) in August, and *How to Marry a Millionaire* (Jean Negulesco) in November—and when her photo graced the cover of *Look*. December brought the first issue of *Playboy*, featuring a nude centerfold photo of Monroe, chosen because she suited Hugh Hefner's idea that girl-next-door types would have particular magic for the middle-class male readership he sought. Monroe's persona both mirrored and complemented the yen for natural sexuality that characterized the period. "In marked contrast to the venality of the film noir sexpot," cultural scholar Gaile McGregor accurately argues, "Marilyn represented desire in its most beneficent, unthreatening, *animal* form. As articulated by Marilyn . . . sex was no longer deforming but natural."[10]

Hollywood treated Monroe shabbily in many ways, and even in 1953 she had good reason to resent its handling of her steadily evolving and maturing talents.

By the end of the year her three latest pictures had pulled in some $25 million for Twentieth Century–Fox, but her studio salary remained less than $1,000 a week, whereas Jane Russell had earned $100,000 for starring with her in *Gentlemen Prefer Blondes*. "Remember, you're not a star," the studio explained to the star.[11] She went on to rank fourth among box office draws (male and female) in 1954, sixth in 1955, and seventh in 1956, and three years later she helped *Some Like It Hot* (Billy Wilder, 1959) earn a phenomenal $25 million, against a production budget of less than $3 million.[12] Why did the studio treat her so callously? One explanation comes from Shelley Winters, who was her roommate at one time. "Traditionally, the studios have cultivated a feeling of insecurity in their actors," Winters said in 1980. "That's what destroyed Marilyn Monroe. They wanted you to think it wasn't really you the public loved—it was the hair and eyelashes and clothes and publicity."[13]

The comedy *The Seven Year Itch* (Billy Wilder, 1955) epitomized the Monroe persona that reached its full flowering in the middle 1950s, according to Carl E. Rollyson Jr., who offers a concise summation of Monroe's movie trajectory. At first she played a mistress, as in *All About Eve* (Joseph L. Mankiewicz, 1950), or a secretary, as in *Monkey Business* (Howard Hawks, 1952), or a significant other in a bedeviled relationship, as in *Niagara*. Her range broadened in 1953 and 1954: she has an assortment of male scene partners in *Gentlemen Prefer Blondes*, including a froggy-voiced little boy (George Winslow), a tubby old tycoon (Charles Coburn), and a vacillating private eye (Elliott Reid); and her swain in *There's No Business Like Show Business* (Walter Lang, 1954) is a wisecracking vaudevillian (Donald O'Connor) with a weakness for booze. And in *The Seven Year Itch*, where she plays a frisky actress whose charms transfix a hitherto monogamous neighbor, "she fills in the middle ground of her democratic attractiveness," Rollyson writes, "by becoming the object of the middle-aged, middle-class male's sexual fantasies."[14]

Monroe jolted the film industry when she announced in 1954 that she would soon relocate from Hollywood to New York, a move precipitated by both personal and professional considerations. There she allied herself with Strasberg, building on her earlier studies with Michael Chekhov, another Stanislavsky devotee. She also deepened her reliance on medications to ease her chronic physical and psychological pains. Some of her friends felt that using the Method subjected her fragile sense of self to dangerous amounts of stress. Be that as it may, her anxieties grew more intense, and her husband (Arthur Miller) counseled her to take more movie roles, hoping that the discipline and concentration would offer some escape from her inner hurts. She gave two of her cleverest and liveliest performances in *Some Like It Hot* and the musical romance *Let's Make Love* (George Cukor, 1960), and her portrayal of Roslyn Taber in *The Misfits* (John Huston, 1961), written by Miller expressly for her, is arguably her most fully realized achievement as a dramatic actress. Her death in 1962, from acute barbiturate poisoning at age thirty-six, ended an acting career that was at once artistically ripe and full of promise.

Shelley Winters labored in Hollywood for almost five years before receiving her first important screen credit in *A Double Life* (George Cukor, 1947), where she plays a waitress endangered by an actor (Ronald Colman) whose long run as Othello has driven him insane. Around the same time she had a stage success in *Oklahoma!* on Broadway, and she also met Kazan, who introduced her to the Actors Studio, where she became a leading member. Her first exposure to the Method came when she saw Kazan's staging of a minor play with Julie Harris in the lead. "The acting was a revelation," Winters recalled later. "I had never seen ensemble acting before." While studying the Method she was especially drawn to affective-memory exercises, which she saw as a means of uniting a playwright's words with her own experience. "When I finally learned to use this correctly," she wrote, "it became the most powerful tool I ever learned to use in acting."[15] It is interesting to note that Winters's espousal of Method acting put her at odds with her second husband, Vittorio Gassman, a renowned Italian film and theater actor. When she asked him about his "preparation" before going onstage as Hamlet, he accused her of using "Actors Studio jargon" and retorted, "I don't need help from anybody. Especially from old-fashioned Stanislavskyites." When she then watched the performance in question, Winters squirmed with embarrassment at a posturing, exaggerated style that *she* found old-fashioned. But she also noted that the Italian audience was enthralled.[16]

One of Winters's most productive years was 1955, when she appeared in five features (plus a feature-length TV show) that demonstrate her energy and range, stretching as they do from the crime drama *I Died a Thousand Times* (Stuart Heisler) and the western *The Treasure of Pancho Villa* (George Sherman) to the more meaningful challenges of the film-industry drama *The Big Knife* (Robert Aldrich), the neo-gothic thriller *The Night of the Hunter* (Charles Laughton), and the urbane comedy-drama *I Am a Camera* (Henry Cornelius). Her best-known performance here is in *The Night of the Hunter*, where her character begins as a lonely, well-intentioned widow and ends as an emotionally blind victim reduced to passivity, immobility, and ultimately death. But it is *The Big Knife* that best displays the gift for fine psychological detail that Winters polished with Method techniques; although she plays a decidedly secondary character, she expresses some of the film's most nuanced emotional tones, through imaginative line readings and even more through the fluidity and inventiveness of her facial expressions.

The acting in *The Big Knife* is of interest for other reasons as well. The film is based on Clifford Odets's play about a successful Hollywood actor (Jack Palance) being pressured by a studio boss (Rod Steiger) to sign a contract he detests; succumbing to blackmail for the sake of his career, he betrays his wife (Ida Lupino), abandons his principles, and meets a sorry end. James Poe has ably adapted

Odets's drama for the screen, but the movie's theatrical origins remain visible in its structure, its circumscribed setting, and its tendency to tell rather than show what is going on inside and between the characters. Standard critical theory holds that a stage production's primary mission is to interpret and project the playwright's text, whereas a movie's primary mission is to translate the text into a specifically cinematic experience, more audiovisual than literary. Aldrich's version of *The Big Knife* breaks this rule in two ways: by retaining the kind of florid dialogue that normally seems most at home in a legitimate theater, where verbal density helps to span the physical and psychological distance between actor and audience; and by allowing (or requiring) the actors to declaim many of their lines in a manner that is recognizably theatrical and sometimes downright stagy. Remarkably and memorably, the extraordinarily skillful cast—those mentioned plus Wendell Corey, Wesley Addy, Jean Hagen, Everett Sloane, and Ilka Chase— plays into this design with aplomb, integrating the theatrical tenor of the script with the visual qualities instilled by Aldrich's artful camerawork and editing. The net result, paradoxically enough, is an intimate drama with a larger-than-life aura. *The Big Knife* is also an evergreen instance of the ensemble acting that Winters found so inspiring early in her career.

Elizabeth Taylor was a superstar, eliciting near-reverential devotion from legions of fans who easily outnumbered those of her fifth husband, Richard Burton—himself the highest-paid actor in Hollywood at one point—even during the years when their names were inextricably linked by avidly consumed reports of romance, scandal, and various combinations thereof. It is safe to say that Taylor's acting skills were neither as disciplined nor as versatile as those of Burton, Brando, Katharine Hepburn, Paul Newman, Eva Marie Saint, or many other top-flight actors with whom she shared the screen. This notwithstanding, she fared better in the Academy Awards sweepstakes than such contemporaries as Burton, Winters, and Monroe, winning twice as Best Actress—for *BUtterfield 8* (Daniel Mann, 1960) and *Who's Afraid of Virginia Woolf?* (Mike Nichols, 1966)— and being nominated three additional times.[17] Her high price tag reflected her popularity. Her portrayal of the title character in the epic *Cleopatra* (Joseph L. Mankiewicz, 1963) cost Twentieth Century–Fox a million dollars (she was the first woman to earn this figure for a role) plus 10 percent of the gross; although the picture lost a fortune on release—production problems had driven its budget preposterously high—it still became the highest-grossing picture of 1963. Taylor's vocal tones and line readings compare poorly with the modulated speech and imaginative interpretations of Burton as Mark Antony and Rex Harrison as Julius Caesar, but the film's box office success derived in no small measure from her celebrity charisma, immeasurably enhanced on this occasion by perfervid press accounts of her on-set love affair with Burton.

Taylor has given some of her most enduring performances in films based on plays; examples include *Cat on a Hot Tin Roof* (Richard Brooks, 1958), *Suddenly,*

Last Summer (Joseph L. Mankiewicz, 1959), and *Boom!* (Joseph Losey, 1968), all from stage works by Tennessee Williams; *The Taming of the Shrew* (Franco Zeffirelli, 1967), from William Shakespeare; and the Edward Albee adaptation *Who's Afraid of Virginia Woolf?*[18] Most of those pictures benefited from gifted directors and excellent casts. Yet it is also significant that in each of them, as in Aldrich's adaptation of *The Big Knife*, the theatrical origins of the project remain visible in the palimpsest of the finished film, bringing with them elements of theatricality: a slightly heightened degree of artifice, a leaning toward flamboyant speech and gesture. While the expertly assembled actors in *The Big Knife* used its theatrical qualities to augment and enrich the electricity of their performances, Taylor takes a more conventional approach, treating emphatic (or overemphatic) moments as opportunities for emphatic (or overemphatic) vocal and gestural display. *Who's Afraid of Virginia Woolf?* is a particularly good example since, as media scholar Harry M. Benshoff points out, director Nichols "took pains to preserve . . . the film's theatrical flavor." In keeping with this strategy, not only Taylor but the other actors as well—Burton, George Segal, and Method-trained Sandy Dennis—give performances that are "firmly grounded in camp" and seek the "fullest release of irony and sarcasm" from every scathingly sardonic line. "'I don't br-a-a-ay!' Taylor-as-Martha brays," preparing for the sadomasochistic pleasure of humiliating her husband before guests, and Taylor finds one of her greatest roles in a film that is informed thoroughly (although not exclusively) by the predominantly gay tradition of camp role-playing (see figure 19).[19]

If the movie version of *Who's Afraid of Virginia Woolf?* had not been made, Taylor would probably be best remembered for her work in *A Place in the Sun* (George Stevens, 1951) and *Giant* (George Stevens, 1956), and in two of her Williams adaptations, *Cat on a Hot Tin Roof* (which Williams liked best among

FIGURE 19: "I don't br-a-a-ay!" Elizabeth Taylor and Richard Burton in *Who's Afraid of Virginia Woolf?*

adaptations of his plays) and *Suddenly, Last Summer*, although in the latter film she is eclipsed by Katharine Hepburn's astonishing portrayal of Violet Venable, the dowager of the story. Taylor did not have the analytic self-awareness of a Method-style actor, but her best performances show an energy and straightforwardness that contrast interestingly with the more nuanced acting frequently found in Method circles.

Masculinities: Clift, Brando, Dean

In a subtle reading of screen masculinity during the early 1950s, film historian Kristen Hatch observes that two of the era's boldest and most successful innovators, Marlon Brando and Montgomery Clift, were brought to Hollywood by brokers who felt that the industry should produce more serious dramatic films to compete with newly popular foreign releases such as *Miracle in Milan* (Vittorio De Sica, 1951) and *Rashômon* (Akira Kurosawa, 1950), which reached American screens in 1951. "Associated with the psychological realism that had begun to change the tenor of Broadway," Hatch writes, "these actors immersed themselves in their roles" with unprecedented intensity. Equally important, they "refused the glamour of Hollywood stardom, exhibiting instead a rebellious iconoclasm that would inspire a new generation of American actors . . . and point to a new direction in the iconography of masculinity."[20]

Clift, an early member of the Actors Studio, made his Broadway debut as a teenager and entered movies with two 1948 releases. *The Search* (Fred Zinnemann), a well-received drama about an American soldier trying to reunite a Czech mother and son in postwar Berlin, earned Clift the first of four Academy Award nominations. The ambitious western *Red River* (Howard Hawks) opened six months later, teaming Clift with John Wayne and John Ireland in a cattle-drive story that has the Clift and Ireland characters, Matt Garth and Cherry Valance, comparing pistols in one of Hollywood's all-time-uproarious scenes of thinly encrypted homosexual desire:

CHERRY: That's a good-looking gun. . . . Can I see it?

MATT [handing it over]: And you'd like to see mine?

CHERRY [admiring it]: Nice, awful nice. You know, there are only two things more beautiful than a good gun: a Swiss watch or a woman from anywhere. You ever had a good Swiss watch?

When the two prove evenly matched in a shooting competition, sidekick Nadine Groot (Walter Brennan) sums up the contest in similar terms: "They was having some fun—peculiar kind of fun, sizing each other up for the future." And when young Matt charges cattle boss Tom Dunson (Wayne) with wanting to put his brand on "every rump in the state of Texas except mine," the older man retorts, "Ya don't think I'd do it, do ya?"

Hewing to Hollywood tradition, Hawks claimed that gay behavior was the furthest thing from his mind, saying it was a "goddam silly" notion.[21] Yet when token female character Tess Millay (Joanne Dru) intervenes in the climactic fistfight between Tom and Matt, she shoots a gun into the air and cries, "Stop fighting! You know you two love each other!" The evident nature of that love dared not speak its name in 1948, but the sparseness of its disguise spoke to the pluck of all three male stars in uttering the double entendres embedded in their dialogue. Clift, himself a bisexual man ensconced in Hollywood's celluloid closet, took the biggest risk—especially as a brand-new face in movies—and reaped the biggest reward, meeting a notoriously male-centered genre on his own terms and giving an enormous boost to a fresh kind of acting that indicated psychological complexity by blending distinct modes (masculinity and coyness, toughness and "peculiar fun") hitherto considered incompatible and perhaps contradictory.

Paramount Pictures played up the novelty of Clift and his style, promoting him as a "rogue personality which sincerely and honestly disdains the pedestrian point of view."[22] Perhaps because his primary Actors Studio teacher had been Lewis rather than Strasberg or Kazan, however, Clift paid as much attention to the externalities of his characters—their movements, gestures, gaits, and manners of speech—as to the interiorities emphasized by Method acting as Strasberg understood it. He was therefore an assiduous researcher when preparing for his roles. To ready himself for *The Search* he spent two weeks with soldiers in Germany, and not just any soldiers, only soldiers who were engineers, like his character. "He was totally obsessed with being specific," Zinnemann said. Five years later, as an established star, Clift spent countless hours in boxing rings before appearing in *From Here to Eternity* (Fred Zinnemann, 1953), where he plays Robert E. Lee Prewitt, a career soldier and skilled prizefighter who enrages an officer by refusing to compete in a boxing tournament for reasons of conscience. Clift also learned to play bugle calls, despite knowing that Prewitt's playing would be post-dubbed by a professional musician. Zinnemann cast Clift in *From Here to Eternity* over the powerful objections of Columbia Pictures president Harry Cohn, who was clearly not in tune with new currents in acting and felt that Clift lacked credibility as a soldier, a boxer, and even a heterosexual. Clift's preparations paid off—he received his third Academy Award nomination for the film—and Zinnemann, who took the Oscar for Best Director, was vindicated. ("[Cohn] thought the film was about boxing," Zinnemann said later, "and I thought it was about the human spirit.")[23] Vindicated as well was Zinnemann's faith in the unorthodox kind of screen manliness that Clift so distinctively projected.

Warner Bros. described Brando in similar ways, hailing the "colorful uncon-ventionality" of an actor who is "a non-conformist in everything he says and does."[24] Not everyone regarded this as an unalloyed plus, however. Williams, whose play *A Streetcar Named Desire* made Brando a Broadway star when he created the role of rude, sensual Stanley Kowalski in the original 1947–1949 pro-duction, called the actor a "genius" who deserved a lot of slack. Yet the savvy and experienced actress Vivien Leigh, who played vulnerable, self-deluded Blanche DuBois opposite Brando in the 1951 movie version, complained that "you never know what he's going to do next, where he's going or what he's going to say." Kazan, who directed both the stage production and the film, said Brando had "mannerisms that would have annoyed the hell out of me if I'd been playing with him. He'd not respond directly when spoken to, make his own time lapses, sometimes leaving the other actors hung up." Jessica Tandy, who played Blanche DuBois in the stage production, went a tad further, calling Brando "an impossi-ble, psychopathic bastard."[25]

All of this said, Brando's most fully realized performances had the force of revelation when he arrived on the scene. Seven years before writing *On the Waterfront* (Elia Kazan, 1954), which brought Brando his first Academy Award, novelist and screenwriter Budd Schulberg said that his acting in *A Streetcar Named Desire* was "beyond a performance. It was so raw, so real," with a climax "like a hard punch to the belly of the audience."[26] Similarly, dramatist Arthur Miller called Brando "a tiger on the loose, a sexual terrorist. . . . He roared out Williams' celebratory terror of sex. . . . Brando was a brute but he bore the truth."[27] The language of these testimonials demonstrates how fully Brando captured the striking transformations under way in American culture. Where traditional act-ing had emphasized the control, charisma, and dependability of alluring stars, Brando shot forth qualities that were not just new but thrilling, even electrifying in their effects: animality, sexuality, terror, the celebration of terror, and a raging sense of freedom. Brando was at once a volcano of unbridled human energies and an avatar of the ordinary guy writ very, very large.

Brando made his movie debut in a well-intentioned but commercially unsuc-cessful vehicle produced by Stanley Kramer, a Hollywood liberal who rarely lost an opportunity for sending messages through his movies. *The Men* (Fred Zinnemann, 1950) focuses on a group of paraplegic army veterans undergoing medical treatment and rehabilitation in a military hospital. Brando's character, Ken, is typical of the others in the ward—bitter and resentful at first, then hope-ful and determined to regain his strength, and finally at peace with his condition and his limitations. What sets him apart from his companions is Brando's phys-ical magnetism, which effortlessly eclipses all the other characters, some played by actors (Jack Webb, Richard Erdman) and others, in the neorealist manner, by real paraplegics. *The Men* testified to Brando's cinematic gifts and consolidated his newfound fame as the sexy headliner of Broadway; but just as important, it gave early evidence of his skill at underplaying dramatic incidents that less confident actors might have used for conspicuous displays. At some of Ken's key emotional moments—when he almost falls while getting married to Ellen (Teresa Wright), for instance, and when he hears a dedicated physician tell about his own paraplegic wife—Brando assumes a blank expression, as if nothing were going on behind his dully gazing eyes. This bespeaks Adler's sway over her star pupil; her revised version of the Method aimed at countering any action or gesture that might be called a cliché. "If an actor needs to emphasize a key line," Quinn writes, "the technical vocal choice . . . is not the usual shout, but an intense whisper." This variety of Method acting calls for "a cancellation of coded [stage] behavior . . . that incorporates understatement as a novel, consistently authentic device."[28]

Not all of Brando's films provided effective showcases for the undemonstrative side of his talent, but restraint remained an important and under-recognized resource for him. A good example comes in the political drama *The Ugly American* (George Englund, 1963) when American envoy Harrison MacWhite (Brando) cradles his cherished Asian friend Deong (Eiji Okada) as the latter dies in his arms; although Brando has played many agitated moments in the film, here the character's grief takes the form of a plain, almost vacant expression that is all the more potent for being so quiet and unexpected. As if to foreground his capacity for strategic underplaying, Englund contrasts Brando's disciplined diplomat with the lower-level envoy played by Pat Hingle, a character actor with a loose, vernacular style. From an acting point of view, their interactions are among the movie's main points of interest. Brando strikes a somewhat similar contrast with Brian Keith in the underrated *Reflections in a Golden Eye* (John Huston, 1967), where he also presents a hugely entertaining satire of the Method's alleged excesses, playing a desperately repressed gay army officer who manages to lecture, mumble, command, and fidget—sometimes all at once—in a bravura exhibition of acting skills that demonstrate and deconstruct themselves before the audience's very eyes.

Brando gave dull or misconceived performances long before his escalating girth and growing disregard for his profession put irreversible crimps in his career.[29] He does not succeed in enlivening the wooden *Viva Zapata!* (Elia Kazan, 1952), for instance, and the erstwhile tiger on the loose makes drifter Val Xavier in *The Fugitive Kind*, based on Williams's 1957 play *Orpheus Descending*, into a tiger who rarely seems very awake, much less prowling the territory for prey. His talent could erupt with startling force when good opportunities arose, however, and the best of these in the 1950s and 1960s—including his Mark Antony in *Julius Caesar* (Joseph L. Mankiewicz, 1953) and above all his Terry Malloy in *On the Waterfront*—deserve their lofty reputations.

One of Brando's finest artistic successes is his first and only film as a director: *One-Eyed Jacks*, an ambitious 1961 western wherein he excels on both sides of the camera.[30] He plays a gunfighter named Rio who has just emerged from five years in a Mexican lockup, where he landed because his partner, Dad Longworth (Karl Malden), betrayed him after a bank robbery they pulled together. Now he is panting for revenge. He tracks Dad down in Monterey, where the dissembling villain is now a respectable sheriff and the stepfather of lovely Louisa (Pina Pellicer), with whom Rio falls in love.

The story and themes of *One-Eyed Jacks* seem deliberately tied to the sort of psychoanalytic ideas associated with Method acting, and critics have taken particular notice of the film's sadomasochistic overtones. Pauline Kael called it a "particularly masochistic revenge fantasy," and Raymond Durgnat wrote that the oedipal relationship between Rio and the interestingly named Dad exemplifies an "underlying 'Freudian' pattern" that is far from rare in postwar films.[31] Pointed out less frequently are the interconnected themes of posing, acting, and performing that Brando weaves into the movie. We first see Rio striking a lazy pose while his henchmen carry out a robbery behind him, and soon afterward we watch him romance a woman by improvising a fictional self-aggrandizing monologue. His ad-hoc performances continue in scene after scene, revealing him as a pretender, poseur, and con artist—but a gifted one, played by Brando with a self-aware enthusiasm that often blurs the line between the character's acting and his own acting. In this way he tempers the supposed realism and authenticity of Method acting with the "theatricalized realism" and "near-naturalism" also found in Method-based productions.[32]

Taking an expansive view of Method technique allows Brando to play Rio's coolness and detachment with a broadness that purposefully mocks the "good manners" of traditional acting, as film scholar James Naremore has observed.[33] As we watch Rio talk with his mouth full, drink with a matchstick between his teeth, and clean his ear with a finger while seducing a woman, we see Brando serving up three coextensive showpieces: the sight of Rio's behavior, the sight of Rio's performances for other characters, and the sight of Brando uniting those spectacles while maintaining the differences that distinguish them from each other.

Dad is an actor too—a thoroughgoing bad guy playing the role of a reformed criminal and honest sheriff—and a subtext of the relationship between him and Rio arises from the awareness of film-savvy audiences (or almost any audiences in 1961) that the cat-and-mouse games between the characters indirectly mirror the competition between Brando and Malden as actors—a competition with quite a history, since they had also appeared together in *On the Waterfront* just eight years earlier. The theme of performance in *One-Eyed Jacks* reaches a climax when Dad inflicts awful punishment on Rio by whipping and maiming him in the town's public square. Here as elsewhere in the film, director Brando sought to enhance the feeling of spontaneous reality by using the risky (and expensive) technique of improvisation while the camera rolled. "As he worked with his actors," biographer Peter Manso reports, "it was straight Method improv."

FIGURE 20: The whipping. Marlon Brando and Karl Malden in *One-Eyed Jacks*.

Malden started the flogging scene cautiously, handling his twelve-foot-long bull-whip with care (see figure 20).

The script called for Rio to collapse when Dad said, "Have you had enough?" But after several takes, Brando did things differently, abruptly wheeling and spitting voluminously in Malden's face (see figure 21). "I mean, he put a real glob there," Malden said later. "I wiped it off and ad-libbed, 'Guess you haven't had enough,' and went back to the whipping." Malden's shocked surprise lends an authentic jolt to the superbly executed scene, and he acknowledged afterward that Brando achieved "exactly what he wanted."[34] Perhaps for that reason, Brando's

FIGURE 21: The glob. Brando and Malden in *One-Eyed Jacks*.

FIGURE 22: The swagger. Brando and Malden in *One-Eyed Jacks.*

own comportment takes on a touch of edgy swagger for a few fleeting seconds, suggesting that the actor and his character are bound together with particular intimacy at this moment of brazen, impetuous display (see figure 22).

A few years after Tandy called Brando a psychopathic bastard, Kazan described James Dean as self-absorbed, undisciplined, and "a far, far sicker kid" than Brando, who had acted in three Kazan pictures between 1951 and 1954. "He was very twisted," Kazan said of Dean's bodily demeanor, "almost like a cripple or a spastic of some kind. He couldn't do anything straight. He even walked like a crab, as if he were cringing all the time. . . . Dean was a cripple, anyway, inside— he was not like Brando. People compared them, but there was no similarity. . . . Brando's not sick, he's just troubled." The director further complained that Dean "could not play a part outside his range," that his "intelligence [was not] of a high order," that his "imagination was limited," and that his "considerable innocence" was not "an adjunct of strength or courage" but rather of "hatred and a kind of despair." The process of obtaining Dean's cooperation depended so heavily on rewards, threats, and psychological games, Kazan concluded, that directing him was "somewhat like directing Lassie the dog."[35]

Fresh from directing Dean in *East of Eden* (1955), Kazan shared his low opinion with Nicholas Ray when Ray was wooing the young actor for *Rebel Without a Cause.* Perhaps buoyed by the discovery that he and Dean consulted the same Beverly Hills psychiatrist, Ray pressed on with his courtship.[36] Indeed, if anyone was hesitant about this proposition it was Dean, who felt "unsure about Ray's ability to pull off the kind of top-line movie" that he wanted to have in his résumé.[37] Dean's doubts and Kazan's caveats notwithstanding, Ray's most celebrated (and most personal) film became the second of the three major motion pictures upon which Dean's reputation will forever rest.[38] He died four days after finishing

Giant, in which his character—Jett Rink, a Texas ranch hand who becomes an oil baron—goes from youth to middle age, taking Dean considerably beyond the teenage characters of his preceding movies.

Brando was Dean's favorite actor; when Brando visited the *East of Eden* set, Kazan recalled, "Jimmy was awestruck and nearly shriveled with respect." Dean too had attended the Actors Studio, and the limitations of that institution emerge when one notes that in the estimation of Kazan, one of its founders and early leaders, Dean "lacked technique" and "had no proper training."[39] Then again, Dean was hardly a model student; he was "devastated" when Strasberg responded to his first solo class performance with a "harsh critique," according to cultural critic Claudia Springer, and afterward "he rarely attended classes, spending his time soaking up the vibrant urban scene and frequenting diners, bars, and all-night dives."[40] Dean belonged to the same nonconformist camp where Brando and Clift pitched their tents, and he outdid them when it came to personal demeanor. "He was physically dirty," one acquaintance said. "He hated to bathe, have his hair cut, shave, or put on clean clothes. He smelled so rankly that actresses working in close contact with him found him unbearable."[41] Springer wryly quotes Dean's own view of these matters: "I wouldn't like me if I had to be around me."

Moviegoers had nary an inkling of particulars like these, thanks to studio publicity departments that circulated sanitized, scandal-free star biographies that could be almost as fictional as the films they were designed to promote. Dean's private personality was thorny at best. So the crafters of his public image employed the technique known today as spin, pitching him as a soulful, individualistic artist who would rather be an iconoclast than an icon. The ploy worked very well. Dean's offscreen scorn for conventional decency and decorum became evidence of a poignantly complex, compulsively inner-directed nature that the public could safely and comfortably admire. And the ramifications extended far beyond Dean's bankability for producers. He was "celebrated for his rebellious otherness at the same time that his persona was rendered acceptably mainstream," Springer observes. "The figure of the young rebel thus emerged as a forceful but empty style, the antithesis of effective political resistance," demonstrating corporate capitalism's flair for "marketing oppositional forms after draining them of their subversive power."[42] Thus did the rebel without a cause become an early instance of postmodern iconicity in a clearly manufactured and manipulative form.

As an actor with a certain amount of Method training, Dean presumably wanted his own personality to be overshadowed by the personality of the character he was playing. But it is not clear that he was prepared to sacrifice his own idiosyncrasies in the process.[43] Film scholar Matthew Sewell notes the busy rush of details that Dean embeds in the much-analyzed moment of *Rebel Without a Cause* when Jim Stark cries out to his parents, "You're tearing me apart!" In just half a minute, the actor "contorts his face, strains his voice, twists his hands,

FIGURE 23: "You're tearing me apart!" James Dean as Jim Stark in *Rebel Without a Cause*.

swings his arms, grabs his tie, and clutches his coat like a security blanket, all in the service of communicating . . . anguished adolescent turmoil" (see figure 23).[44] Sewell regards this and other fraught moments as evidence of "exceptional . . . physical inventiveness" on Dean's part, which is a fair reading; but an alternative reading might find that Dean habitually relies on a limited repertoire of very similar histrionics. Kazan lends support to the latter view when he points out how weak Dean is in the last portion of *Giant* when playing a character much older than himself: "He looked like what he was: a beginner."[45] Further evidence lies in the many shared tics and traits that make his Jim Stark in *Rebel Without a Cause* and his Cal Trask in *East of Eden* even more alike than their anagrammatic last names suggest. Both let their arms flap to suggest flyaway teenage feelings, for instance, and both crinkle their brows and eyes to connote mischievous charm. And during the hyperemotional scene in *East of Eden* where Cal's father (Raymond Massey) rejects his son's birthday gift of laboriously earned money, Dean offers a display of face contorting, hand twisting, voice straining, and other behaviors closely resembling Jim's and the young Jett Rink's in Dean's subsequent films (see figure 24).

FIGURE 24: The birthday gift. James Dean as Cal Trask in *East of Eden*.

Any analysis of Dean's acting must of course take the brevity of his career into account. In the course of a longer life he might have become as subtly expressive as Brando at his peak, or declined as sadly as Brando did after *Apocalypse Now* (Francis Ford Coppola, 1979), or settled into a respectable mid-level career as Brando did between the high points of *On the Waterfront* and *The Godfather* (Francis Ford Coppola, 1972).[46] Judging from the three feature films that made him a star, Dean was a gifted but unpolished actor whose affinities with the Method were a matter of intuition rather than intellect. His limitations notwithstanding, he remains a quintessential icon of postwar pop culture. "The single factor most responsible for the popularity of the Method in the Eisenhower years," cultural historian Steve Vineberg writes, "was that the rebel without a cause was the exclusive turf of Method actors."[47]

Crosby and Company

Central though it is to the evolution of Hollywood acting, the Method accounts for only part of the story, as one quickly gathers by noting which particular actors ranked highest with moviegoers according to such standard criteria as box office appeal and Academy Award recognition. On the list of top box-office draws in the early postwar era, Bing Crosby took first place in 1947 and 1948, second place in 1949, third place in 1950, and fifth place in 1951. Betty Grable was close behind him in each of those years except the last, when she came in two notches above him. Bob Hope also made the top ten in all five years. Others on the list between 1947 and 1951 included Bud Abbott and Lou Costello four times, Gary Cooper four times, Humphrey Bogart three, and John Wayne three. None of these worthies could be called a Method actor.

Nor could Edie Sedgwick, Ed Hood, Ondine, or Nico in *Chelsea Girls*, the inimitable epic of avant-garde cinema created by Andy Warhol and Paul Morrissey in 1966. Although it was seen by relatively few viewers even when "underground movies" were fleetingly in vogue, this and other experimental films that incorporated acting in some way, shape, or form—as did works by Ken Jacobs, Jack Smith, George Kuchar, Kenneth Anger, and Ron R
in subtle but genuine ways with the era's mainstre

The years right after World War II did not brin
ditions, conventions, and practices of prewar mo
of Crosby and company attests. What those yea
dissolve in which the end of one era, identified v
world war, blurred into the beginning of another,
ity, ideological uncertainty, and cultural restlessr
in the late 1960s to an epoch more adventurous
Warhol, Dennis Hopper, Jane Fonda, Jack Nichols

children of the 1950s. The postwar decades are unique. No twenty-year period in film history has wrought more momentous transformations in acting styles, methods, and techniques.

4

THE AUTEUR RENAISSANCE, 1968-1980   Julie Levinson

The years between 1968 and 1980 comprised a singular period in the history of American movies, not to mention in the culture at large. A perfect storm of social, economic, industrial, and ideological factors conspired to throw the film industry into upheaval. One of the upshots of that upheaval was a fleeting cultural moment variously known as the Auteur Renaissance, the New Hollywood, or, nostalgically, Hollywood's last golden age. The recent demise of the studio system and the ensuing rise of independent producers, young auteurist directors, and free-agent actors opened the door for new expressive possibilities and new synergies among those involved in film production and resulted in a remarkable, if short-lived, creative efflorescence. In that brief period, while Hollywood transitioned from the studio-era star system and mode of production to an era of film personnel as independent contractors, a host of swashbuckling young directors and actors shook up and reinvigorated American film practice.

While many of the actors prominently featured in movies during those years were old stalwarts who were familiar to audiences from previous decades, a slew of new acting talent burst upon the screen, bringing fresh approaches to the craft and a diverse array of artistic influences. It would be facile to claim a consistency of creative vision or performance technique in the cinema of that period. After all, the Auteur Renaissance refers not only to the artistically adventurous movies of such directors as Martin Scorsese, Frances Ford Coppola, Robert Altman, Bob Rafelson, Hal Ashby, Stanley Kubrick, and John Cassavetes but also to the cannily commercial work of Steven Spielberg, George Lucas, and the other auteurs whose high-concept blockbusters boosted Hollywood's bottom line beginning in the mid-1970s.[1] Indeed, the period is characterized by its very lack of consistency, as film historian David A. Cook makes clear in *Lost Illusions: American Cinema in the Shadow of Watergate and Vietnam, 1970–79*, his authoritative film history of the period: "That an aesthetically experimental, socially conscious *cinéma d'auteur* could exist simultaneously with a burgeoning and rapacious blockbuster mentality was extraordinary, but it became the defining mark of 1970s cinema."[2] Both the small-scale personal films of this period and the blockbusters of the latter half of the decade have had lingering influence on, respectively, the art and business of American film, but it is the former that is invoked with wistfulness for a lost golden age of the movies. The creative ferment that characterized the Auteur Renaissance was a heady brew, distilled from concurrent—and sometimes contradictory—impulses and characterized by a mix of performance styles and approaches.

In the annals of Hollywood, there is an oft-told story about screen acting in that period. During the shooting of *Marathon Man* (John Schlesinger, 1976), Dustin Hoffman, so the story goes, stayed up for several nights in order to convincingly play a scene in which his character was meant to appear exhausted. When he arrived on the set and told co-star Laurence Olivier what he had done, the older actor's supposed rejoinder was, "My dear boy, why don't you just try acting?" Various versions of this story have been bandied about by journalists, scholars, Hollywood types, and Hoffman himself for many years.[3] Like a lot of widely repeated, pithily amusing stories, this one is perhaps apocryphal but nonetheless telling (see figure 25).

FIGURE 25: Dustin Hoffman's Method-induced exhaustion in *Marathon Man*.

The story has legs primarily because it points up the stark difference in approach between Hoffman's Method-derived focus on living a role and Olivier's rigorous craft that built character from the outside in. In this fable of artistic folly, Olivier gets the better of Hoffman since the younger actor's reliance on a dubious route to emotional truth is presumably trumped by the practiced old thespian's ability to conjure up the called-for feeling by dint of skill and will. Moreover, the anecdote endures because it spotlights the strange bedfellows who sometimes cohabited in movies of the time and it speaks to a sea change during which old approaches to film performance existed alongside new experiments and techniques.

While the putative exchange between Hoffman and Olivier makes for a good story, it makes for simplistic history. The 1970s was not the first time that Method-trained actors crossed paths—or crossed swords—with old-school performers.[4] By all accounts, Hoffman's focus on internal feeling and intensive, body- and mind-challenging preparation was already the ascendant method for film actors of the period, whereas Olivier's more contrived performance style felt somewhat outmoded by mid-1970s standards. By the time *Marathon Man* was made, acting that seemed to access and reveal the inner self had taken precedence over acting that adorned the outer self with mannerisms and expressions donned like a costume. The performances considered most in tune with prevailing notions about authenticity and believability in screen acting were a far cry from Olivier's repertoire of strategically selected gestures, vocal tricks, and false noses: what he once called "one or two extraneous externals" that he used to build a character.[5]

This story's encounter between an actor who worked from the inside out and one who created character from the outside in represents only a small part of the larger story of Hollywood acting during the Auteur Renaissance. The stylistic contrast that it draws attention to is one among many commingled creative stimuli that characterize the period. Those years were defined by a clash of cultures both on and off the screen. As the common wisdom began to seem not so wise, orthodoxies of all sorts were challenged. Particularly from 1968 to the mid-1970s, an onscreen ethos of experimentation and edginess took place against the backdrop of a country divided culturally as well as politically and an industry in flux between old and new modes of production. The era's juxtaposition of performance styles parallels and, in some cases, reflects the collisions and confusions that were taking place in many arenas of American life.

In their introduction to *More Than a Method: Trends and Traditions in Contemporary Film Performance*, editors Cynthia Baron, Diane Carson, and Frank P. Tomasulo maintain that "acting is best understood as a form of *mediated performance* that lies at the intersection of art, technology and culture," and they go on to discuss how extra-cinematic factors shape expressivity.[6] Surely every cultural artifact is mediated and informed by its historical moment as well as by institutional and social conditions and suppositions, but the 1970s had an espe-cially robust back-and-forth between social currents and artistic expression. In crafting their onscreen personae, young actors, in particular, were influenced not just by the history of their craft and the tenets of their training, but also by the highly charged zeitgeist. Since a confluence of intersecting factors—aes-thetic, industrial, technological, social, ideological—affected the nature of film performance at that time, any analysis of film acting during Hollywood's Auteur Renaissance requires a concomitant exploration of the tensions that defined the era and the complex ways in which cultural production addresses and assimilates its milieu. Performance codes and conventions need to be understood in the con-text of not just the history of film acting but also the particularities of their time and context. The forthcoming analysis will untangle some of the intertwined industrial practices, artistic impulses, and sociocultural factors that shaped screen performances between 1968 and 1980 and that contributed to the variety and richness of acting styles in that period. Along the way, illustrative examples from a range of movies will speak to the sundry influences on and approaches to some of the most memorable performances in American film history.

The Shifting Screen

The large number of books devoted to 1970s cinema all view the period as a watershed in film history: a decisive shift in the production, distribution, exhi-bition, and popular perception of movies. As the country was grappling with a late-1960s economic recession, the film industry was reeling from a series of large-scale, big-budget flops, among them *Dr. Dolittle* (Richard Fleischer, 1967), *Star!* (Robert Wise, 1968), and *Hello, Dolly!* (Gene Kelly, 1969).[7] Box office receipts declined precipitously, triggering a crisis of confidence in Hollywood's established business structures as well as in the formal and thematic paradigms that characterized the American commercial cinema.[8] The industrial changes that resulted from the turmoil in the film business of the late 1960s and early 1970s transformed the existing model for movie production and, consequently, the working methods of directors and actors.

The old studio system, in which actors were employees with long-term con-tracts, had been eroding for many years. As early as 1947, Burt Lancaster led the way for actors to become independent contractors who could pick and package their own movie roles.[9] By the 1970s, many actors were, in effect, their own brand: more cultural capital than cultural labor. Aligned with the creative agencies that arose in the middle of that decade, they could peddle themselves or, in the case of the big stars, assemble their own movie projects. Unlike during the classical film era, when producers and powerful directors would cast stars for their mov-ies simply by selecting from their studio's stable of show horses, now directors sometimes had to audition for stars as much as vice versa. So-called package deals, in which talent was pulled together on a film-by-film basis, became the norm. Many actors and directors began to see themselves—and to be seen by the public—as expressive artists rather than simply as hired hands. The decade's most creatively ambitious movies were, in turn, presented and promoted as not just industrial products but as personal artistic statements.

In discussing the increased agency that stars attained once they became free agents, Barry King writes, "Stars are no longer employees . . . but stakeholders in the enterprise that manages their career. Within any product cycle the star has a direct commercial interest in claiming a deep existential commitment to a given role."[10] During the studio era, stars and journeyman actors alike, who all were under contract to their studios, were assigned multiple roles in a given year. The new model saw actors playing fewer parts but preparing for and inhabiting them with a greater sense of ownership over the role and the film. By the 1970s, actors' hand-picked roles, along with their self-promotion, defined their public image. Since established stars were often granted a percentage of their movies' profits in addition to their salaries, it literally paid to be strategic in selecting one's roles. Hence, in this period, many actors' devotion to developing a character seemed to emanate both from that "deep existential commitment" and savvy careerism.

Ellen Burstyn, for example, had a large part in shaping the script (and in selecting the director) of *Alice Doesn't Live Here Anymore* (Martin Scorsese, 1974). Burstyn was intent on ensuring that Alice rang true to her sense of the character and to her desire to make a movie that tapped into second-wave feminism. As she told *Newsweek* several months before the movie's release, "We collaborated between [Scorsese's] sense of the dramatic line and my representation of the woman's point of view. We'd write in the margin of the script: 'No, a woman wouldn't do this.' 'Yes, she'd say that.' 'That's not the way.'"[11] New Hollywood's new collaborative spirit, in which stars often possessed a role from the development of the script and the selection of the talent package through the promotion of the film, was already being analyzed and applauded by film writers at the time. In *The New Hollywood*, his breezy, state-of-the-movies romp through the first half of the 1970s, Axel Madsen proclaimed that then-contemporary trends "allow today's actors a freer, more honest, and more amplified self-projection than was possible for Golden Era stars. . . . For actors it has meant a new sense of complicity in the creative process."[12]

That self-projection and sense of complicity encouraged actors to identify with the character and, indeed, sometimes *become* the character for the duration of the process from pre- through post-production, rather than just competently preparing for and playing a role and then moving on. For the prison movie *Straight Time* (Ulu Grosbard, 1978), Dustin Hoffman spent eight months visiting jails to interact with inmates and soak up the atmosphere. He may be the only person ever to break *in* to San Quentin prison where, having managed to finesse his way through the gates without being identified, he spent several hours researching his role behind the penitentiary walls.[13] In advance of shooting *Taxi Driver* (Martin Scorsese, 1976), Harvey Keitel worked on his impersonation of his pimp character by recording role-playing exercises with an actual pimp that he had brought to the Actors Studio to improvise with him.[14] For *Raging Bull* (Martin Scorsese, 1980), Robert De Niro, who was already celebrated for his *ne plus ultra* dedication to his art, famously transformed his body by gaining sixty pounds to play boxer Jake La Motta in his later years. He also spent several months learning to box and even took part in three professional bouts to assure that his boxing moves would look bona fide. The actor tape-recorded the actual La Motta for a full year and even lived with the ex-boxer and his wife, who came to consider his fixation on getting the real La Motta down pat as obsessive burrowing into their lives. Once production began, De Niro insisted on staying in character around the clock.[15]

That sort of all-out commitment to a role became fetishized in the 1970s by actors as well as by the press and the moviegoing public. In the public mind, actors' intensive preparations for a role—particularly in the case of biographical films—were equated with veracity. In an article in *Vanity Fair*, film critic Richard Schickel commented on De Niro's bodily transformation in pursuit of verisimilitude in acting: "Of course this devotion to the cause of realism was all the press wanted to talk about when the film was in pre-release. The art of acting, for all the words expended upon it, remains a mystery to the public. But something like weight gain—any sort of physical contortions an actor submits to for his art— that's something the public can relate to with headshaking amazement." Schickel concludes, "It's possible, and wildly unfair, that De Niro won his Oscar for his

FIGURE 26: Robert De Niro shows off his weight gain in *Raging Bull.*

prodigious eating."[16] The willingness of an actor to transform his body for a role became tantamount to commitment to one's craft; it was authenticity in material form—in the flesh, as it were (see figure 26).

For his role in *New York, New York* (Martin Scorsese, 1977), De Niro spent months learning to play the tenor saxophone even though he would only be miming his character's musicianship while a professional sax player supplied the music for the sound track. His doggedness in mastering the instrument irritated his music teacher's wife so much that she complained, "We thought he was going to climb in bed with us with the horn."[17] Along with his co-star, Liza Minnelli, De Niro improvised many of the scenes in the movie during the lengthy rehearsal phase while Scorsese recorded their improvisations so he could then incorporate portions of them into the screenplay, which was still being written.[18] Scorsese described his back-and-forth telepathy with De Niro: "Well, Bob De Niro, when he shows me something, or when he has an idea, when something comes right from that visceral part of him, it just comes out of his soul. You know, I'm surprised that it's always extremely valid and quite good—I usually find it to be pretty much according to what I feel. We're always finishing each other's sentences creatively. . . . If we're struggling for words, creatively, he can find them."[19]

Scorsese's spirit of collaboration with his actors affected not just the film's script but its cinematic style as well. Because Scorsese had De Niro and Minnelli do so much improvisation for *New York, New York*, he needed to use a lot of long takes, since otherwise the movie's editor would have had a hard time matching shots.[20] De Niro's, Minnelli's, and Burstyn's status as co-creators with Scorsese was a distinct departure from the working methods of even the most powerful stars in studio-era Hollywood. Since many of the auteur directors of the 1970s worked repeatedly with the same actors from film to film (e.g., Scorsese with De Niro, Woody Allen with Diane Keaton, Robert Altman and John Cassavetes with their repertory companies of actors), they had ample opportunity to develop and hone a collaborative creative process.

There are many more instances of actors in the 1970s not only embracing and shaping their roles with fervor but also participating in elaborate preparatory exercises, often in partnership with their directors. As part of his preproduction process for his role in *Coming Home* (Hal Ashby, 1978), Jon Voight lived in a wheelchair for hours each day and hung out with paraplegic men as he prepared to play the role of a returning Vietnam veteran.[21] His intensive immersion in the community of paraplegic vets lends credence to the largely improvised speech that his character makes to a high school assembly at the end of the movie. Along with co-stars Jane Fonda and Bruce Dern and director Ashby, he also engaged in several multi-hour sessions, referred to as behavioral rehearsals, in which the four together intensively analyzed character psychology, devised backstories for their roles, delved into the political situation that informed the movie, and discussed their own feelings.[22]

Such a process of shared discovery meant that scripts were not so much sacred texts but scrims through which to project directors' and actors' on-the-spot improvisations and inspirations. The accounts of actor-collaborators on Ashby's, Altman's, and Cassavetes's movies, among others, are legion. In one, Warren Beatty claims that Altman wanted the actors simply to improvise the story of *McCabe and Mrs. Miller* (Robert Altman, 1971), so the actor took it upon himself to pull together the script. "I watched [the rushes] on *McCabe and Mrs. Miller* because Robert Altman wanted me to participate very heavily in the writing and construction of the film. I watched the rushes to see what the hell we should do next. . . . We kind of discarded the original script and I found myself writing most of the scenes. I wrote all my dialogue. . . . Bob works in such a way that he wants a high level of participation from people."[23]

These creative partnerships complicate the designation "Auteur Renaissance" and raise the question of the extent to which an actor can be considered an auteur.[24] To be sure, this period saw the rise of a director-driven cinema in which, rather than being assigned movies by production companies, many directors devised their own projects and infused them with their ongoing thematic preoccupations and stylistic signatures.[25] But over time, as the notion of film authorship has become more vexed, film scholars have dismantled the mystique of the director as the lone creator of a movie.[26] Even Andrew Sarris, whose writings established auteurism as the lingua franca of American film criticism, wrote an article in 1977 entitled "The Actor as Auteur," in which he admitted that auteur criticism tends to slight the actors' contributions. He went on to say, "Though I still believe in a cinema of directors, I have come to believe also that the actor constitutes much of the language of the cinema, and that directors, writers, and technicians have always had to cope with that language as one of the conditions of creation."[27] Sarris's article continued to see the performers' contributions as subordinate to those of the director (who has to "cope" with the actor's craft) and it did not discuss the then-contemporary actors whose portfolio of performances announced them as a new breed and whose personae were imprinted like insignia from one film to the next. Nonetheless, the article's timing and its proposal that actors might also be considered auteurs of a sort are indicative of a heightened awareness of and respect for actors' creative contributions during the 1970s.[28]

Of course, particular actor/director combinations of the period displayed varying models of power-sharing in the creation of the movie. In her article "Screen Performance and Directors' Visions," Sharon Marie Carnicke distinguishes between directors whose working method and creative vision privileges visual design and those who are more oriented toward performance. She goes on to analyze how individual actors adjust their performances to different directors' visions. In writing about how Shelley Duvall interacted with Robert Altman on *Nashville* (1975) and with Stanley Kubrick on *The Shining* (1980), she explores the extent to which different directors consider their actors as valued collaborators.

Whereas Altman prodded Duvall and the movie's other actors to bring their own perspectives and experiences to the creation of their roles, Kubrick withheld information about the movie from Duvall and played on her emotions to achieve the performance that he wanted. As Carnicke puts it, "While Altman had included her in the collaborative team, Kubrick controlled her work by psychologically beating her into a frenzied emotional performance."[29] Directors such as Altman, Scorsese, and, notably, Cassavetes may have, in essence, shared the generative process with their actors but, as Carnicke shows, directors on the other end of the spectrum, such as Kubrick and Antonioni, maintained a tight grip on creative control. Such counterexamples as the latter two are a reminder not to overstate the extent to which actors during the Auteur Renaissance may themselves be considered auteurs. Nonetheless, there is no denying that the new structural model for film personnel—which in at least some cases was more horizontal than hierarchical—had a major effect on how several movies of the era were crafted and how actors arrived at their interpretations and personifications of their characters.

The increased power and collaborative opportunities for actors of the 1970s were not the only industrial changes that shaped film performances and allowed for liberation from past practices. Technological inventions and predilections—among them the Steadicam that facilitated long takes and the wireless microphone that could capture dialogue on the run—also affected the ways that actors worked onscreen. In some cases, the easy mobility of the Steadicam as it wandered about surveying the action rendered the actor as just another element of the mise-en-scène. But because the camera could now keep step fluently like a dancer following a partner's lead, it might also enhance the spontaneity and perceived veracity of a performance by freeing the actor to move about on the set with less need to think about hitting one's mark or hewing to a preset path. The lengthy shots that the Steadicam enabled also gave actors the opportunity to reveal character gradually and subtly within a single shot.[30]

The famous (and the first ever) Steadicam shot in *Bound for Glory* (Hal Ashby, 1976), which lasts over two minutes, follows David Carradine as folk singer Woody Guthrie ambling through a migrant camp. The pace of his walk, his shambling gait, and his small gestures such as tucking in his shirt as he moseys around combine to create a vivid sense of character and setting. As the kinetic camera varies its distance and angle vis-à-vis the character, Carradine's understated facial expressions, postures, and gestures gradually delineate Guthrie's response to what he is seeing. This is a long way from the sorts of performances that are fine-tuned in the editing room through shot juxtapositions. Here, the vivid "you are there" quality is enhanced by the shot's duration, its maintenance of actual space and time, and the consequent ability of the actor to limn character in a leisurely, seemingly spontaneous manner (see figure 27).

FIGURE 27: The Steadicam follows Woody Guthrie (David Carradine) as he ambles through a crowd of migrant workers in *Bound for Glory*.

The array of contemporary technological capabilities and proclivities could cut both ways, sometimes increasing and sometimes lessening the actor's jurisdiction over his or her performance. Cultural critic Peter Biskind commented about Robert Altman's fondness for the zoom lens and its shifting focal point: "Actors don't like it much either. They regulate their performance according to how far they are from the camera, but the director would stage a master shot packed with people, and then would reach through the crowd with the zoom for close-ups so that the actors were unsure if they were one face among twenty, or all alone."[31] Similarly, Altman's well-known penchant for overlapping dialogue, in which characters step on one another's lines rather than declaiming them in turn, robbed actors of the certainty that their words would be heard, let alone understood, in the finished film. Directorial tendencies such as these made elocutionary excellence and careful enunciation—skills in which Olivier and his ilk excelled—seem like vestiges of the past. Stylistic propensities such as overlapping dialogue or the liberal use of zooms or open-frame shots meant that the actors were kept off-balance about which of the tools in their toolkit would actually be operable—or audible—onscreen. But some actors thrived on that uncertainty and used it to their advantage. As Karen Black explained, "In his films, [Altman] radio mikes you and you're not aware of where the camera is, and then you invent things. . . . Most of the things I said in *Nashville* were totally improvised. . . . He doesn't pounce on you and you don't feel crowded or feel that he is watching you critically. He never says you play the line wrong; he lets you makes your choices. He believes in what is true for you and that's all he's interested in."[32]

Since technical devices including zooms and radio mikes and Steadicams could thwart an actor's awareness of how his or her work in a scene might figure in the final film, their prevalence in this period altered the way in which performers interacted with the visual and aural components of the production.

Cultural Conversations and Crosscurrents

In addition to structural and technological changes in the film industry, eclectic influences from a variety of other expressive forms also had a bearing on the range of performance styles appearing on screens. Many of the highly lauded actors of the time had begun their careers in the theater. A second generation of Method-trained actors absorbed not only the philosophies of Stanislavsky by way of Lee Strasberg or Stella Adler; they also came of age artistically during a time when experimental theater was thriving. Casting directors in that era were mostly based in New York and they trolled the downtown, off-Broadway theaters and beyond for new talent.[33] The regional theater movement, too, was gathering steam in the late 1960s and early 1970s and was stretching actors beyond the performance conventions of commercial productions. Prominent New Hollywood actors Robert De Niro, Al Pacino, Dustin Hoffman, Jon Voight, Stockard Channing, Blythe Danner, Jon Cazale, and Robert Duvall were each, at one time, members of the Boston Theater Company, which was known as a laboratory of theatrical derring-do that presented the works of such playwrights as Harold Pinter, Samuel Beckett, Sam Shepard, Edward Albee, Bertolt Brecht, and Jean Genet. Alan Arkin and Peter Boyle, one-time members of Chicago's Second City troupe, brought to Hollywood that company's grounding in improvisational technique and seat-of-the-pants creativity. Such actors' exposure to avant-garde plays and experimental performance practices expanded their acting repertoire well beyond the naturalism espoused by the Method gurus. By cutting their teeth on theatrical innovation, these actors came to the movies endowed with an array of techniques and tricks of the trade, enabling them to elaborate character using both their Method training and their acquaintance with experimental modes of performance such as Brechtian distanciation or self-reflexive pastiche.

The general broadening of film culture in America from the 1960s into the 1970s also contributed to how films were created, consumed, and talked about. So-called art house cinemas proliferated, exposing American audiences to foreign cinemas, documentaries, and the occasional American independent feature or avant-garde film.[34] Some of the stylistic inventiveness of those forms worked its way into Hollywood fare.[35] Several directors, some of whom were among the first generation to come out of film schools where they were taught to consider cinema as an art form, acknowledged their debt to foreign directors and film movements.[36] European art cinema, and the French New Wave in particular, imparted to certain movies of the Hollywood renaissance a freewheeling style of narrative and characterization. In those American movies, the hallmarks of the classical style—among them its realist presumptions, continuity editing, and definitive sense of closure—were superseded by a more aleatory, incidental approach. Stylistic tendencies including jump cuts, lack of establishing shots, and off-center compositions made for a different sort of character exposition and presentation.

In some New Hollywood movies of the period, this modernist (and, in some cases, postmodernist) tilt meant that psychologically coherent and logically motivated characters with individual agency were replaced by characters whose identity and quiddity were more indeterminate. Acting choices followed suit. In a film such as *The King of Marvin Gardens* (Bob Rafelson, 1972), the episodic structure and cryptic visual compositions are accompanied by performances that are intentionally hard to read. Since the characters' emotions and actions are often logically unmotivated, the acting is, at turns, deadpan, maudlin, and scenery-chewing. The ambiguous temperament of the character played by Jack Nicholson, in particular, is rendered with a hodgepodge of sometimes incongruous acting styles, complicating spectators' engagement with him.[37] Nicholson's self-consciously opaque performance, in which he alternates between low-key impassivity and overwrought angst, is in keeping with a film that refuses to anchor its characters in behavioral consistency or plausible motivation. The movie opens and closes with extended close-up monologues from Nicholson that seem like a parody of overwrought Method acting; these scenes bookend a performance that sometimes veers toward catatonia in its inexpressiveness. As

FIGURE 28: Jack Nicholson's Method angst in *The King of Marvin Gardens*.

Nicholson and the other actors toggle between acting styles, willfully refusing to commit to any one, the audience goes back and forth between identifying with the characters and being utterly baffled by their actions and expressions. In the destabilized universe of such films, the actors' voices and bodies become sites of impenetrability and their performances are purposely not legible in conventional terms (see figure 28).[38]

Alongside French New Wave films, *cinéma vérité* documentaries, with their raw and ragged hand-held aesthetic and their fly-on-the-wall detachment, likewise informed both the cinematic style and the approach to character in several narrative movies of the period. That strain of film aimed for a seemingly unscripted, documentary-like impression of spontaneity and a subtle performance style. In movies such as *Husbands* (John Cassavetes, 1970) or *The Last Detail* (Hal Ashby, 1973) or *Days of Heaven* (Terence Malick, 1978), the characters seem not so much performed for the audience as happened upon by them, and the camera seems merely to be catching the action rather than creating it. The presentation of character in another Malick movie, *Badlands* (Terence Malick, 1973), is very much in line with the *cinéma vérité* aesthetic: observational and dispassionate. The affectless, matter-of-fact quality of the performances is more allusive than evocative in explaining the characters' personalities and motivations.

In her book on film dialogue, Sarah Kozloff suggests how this loose, observational aesthetic shaped the vocal delivery of many actors in the late 1960s and early 1970s: "American films appeared in which the dialogue was noticeably more colloquial, less careful about rhythm, less polished, more risqué, and marked by an improvisational air. The accompanying acting style was less declamatory, faster, and more throwaway; the recording of lines allowed much more overlapping and a higher degree of inaudibility."[39]

Good diction was no longer a criterion of good acting: perhaps just the opposite. Swallowing one's words or mangling syntax or trailing off at the ends of sentences were vocal mannerisms akin to ordinary conversation, in which people tend not to talk in well-crafted sentences. However affected it may be as a mode of characterization, the stammering delivery of Diane Keaton's locutions in *Annie Hall* (Woody Allen, 1977) came across as less perform-y and, therefore, more organic than the careful enunciation of actors with a more declamatory style. Casual-seeming dialogue *à la* the French New Wave and camera techniques in the *cinéma vérité* mode encouraged the impression of such a thing as film truth and the creation of characters that seemed more authentic and less stagey than those in more conventionally crafted movies. The period's valorization of authenticity made such techniques timely and appropriate to the overriding sensibility of the New Hollywood.[40]

Also contributing to a broader interest in film culture was an upsurge of widely read and discussed film criticism and a proliferation of celebrity-centered publications and television broadcasts. Post-studio era actors now had their own publicists who, in turn, had a veritable maw of celebrity-hungry publications and programs to which they fed stories. *People* magazine published its first issue in 1974 and *Us Weekly* followed suit in 1977; along with other fan magazines and talk shows, they gave their consumers the illusion of access to the private lives of public figures. The regular focus not just on actors' offscreen doings but also on their preparation for film roles meant a greater public awareness of how actors worked and a greater—if specious—sense of access to their personal and professional lives. In a culture saturated with stories about movies and movie stars, actors were not just commodified but fetishized to an extent that went beyond the studio system's well-oiled publicity campaigns.

Since the late 1960s into the 1970s were glory days for not just film production but film criticism as well, reviews by such high-profile critics as Sarris or Pauline Kael or Rex Reed became part of the discourse of the chattering classes.[41] All this increased focus on actors and acting created an endless feedback loop among Hollywood, the promotional machinery of the popular press, the critics, and audiences. Sometimes, the boundary between those who made movies and those who wrote about movies was porous. Like the young critics-turned-directors of the French New Wave, Paul Schrader and Peter Bogdanovich began their professional lives as film critics before eventually turning to writing and directing in Hollywood. Perhaps the oddest melding of those two worlds was when, at the behest of Warren Beatty, Kael took a leave from her reviewing job at *The New Yorker* in 1979 to work for Paramount Pictures, advising on scripting and casting. Although her foray in Hollywood was a short-lived disaster, it points to the prospect, in that era, of critical feedback contributing to an actor's approach to his profession.[42]

The convergence of film performance and entertainment journalism tended to conflate actors' star personae and their roles. In his groundbreaking work on film stardom, Richard Dyer posits movie stars as complex cultural sign systems whose onscreen images are inevitably colored by the public's knowledge of and interest in their offscreen lives.[43] The ramped-up celebrity apparatus and the glut of information about stars of this period elided the distinction between actor and character even further than before, giving audiences a sort of double vision in which the character channeled the actor as much as vice versa. Seemingly, both onscreen and off, Jack Nicholson played the rebel, Warren Beatty was the lothario, Jane Fonda took on the part of a fire-breathing radical, and Diane Keaton and Woody Allen performed the ditz and the neurotic, respectively. This elision of actor and role encouraged the assumption that the actors were simply playing heightened versions of themselves. As Barry King explains:

> In general, the public is invited to suppose that what is seen on screen, if aided cinematically, is nonetheless the 'natural' fruit of the star's personal agency—creative vision, personality, etc.—that inheres before and

after filming. . . . The melding of the onscreen performance and offscreen publicity—both *kinds* of performance—imparts an *existential* portability to a fictional character which is wrapped around the *being in public* of the star.[44]

On the occasions when actors broke out of the public's perception of who they were, such as when post–*Annie Hall* Diane Keaton appeared in *Looking for Mr. Goodbar* (Richard Brooks, 1977) and *Interiors* (Woody Allen, 1978), audiences and critics sometimes responded with dismay, as if a shadow self had emerged from behind the familiar public persona. In reviewing *Goodbar* on its release, Kael pointed out that Keaton's line delivery "sounds just like Annie Hall" and then spent part of her review invoking the Woody Allen film as a touchstone for Keaton's performance.[45]

Certainly, the public's extra-filmic awareness of actors' lives and their fore-knowledge of performers' preparations for a role—losing or gaining weight, interviewing people on whom to base their characters, turning activist on issues related to their upcoming film—molded audience expectations and affected how they responded to characters onscreen. But it is trickier to gauge how the interconnection among actor, character, and celebrity may have affected the actors' actual performance choices. One can only speculate about whether such recurring actorly signatures as Nicholson's cat-that-swallowed-the-canary grin or Al Pacino's bug-eyed stare grew out of conscious acting decisions aimed at character definition or whether they were simply *de rigueur* to promote those actors' performative brands. They and other actors sometimes seemed to be quoting—or at least paraphrasing—their own earlier performances. Actors have a vested career interest in perpetuating a durable branded persona, but they also have an interest in demonstrating range and making sure that their well-worn offscreen image does not interfere with audience identification with their successive characters or absorption in the movies' narratives. Although it may be hard to pinpoint the extent to which conflating the actor with the celebrity affects performance style (not to mention the extent to which performance style may be separated from directorial intention), the question of how acting strategies relate to ongoing audience associations with specific actors is nonetheless crucial in reading the particularities of a given performance.[46]

Beyond the Screen

There has been a good deal of scholarly discussion about the interplay between social, political, and ideological forces in the years between 1968 and 1980 and the movies that overtly or subtextually responded to those forces.[47] Determining the reciprocal impact of sociohistorical happenings and the symbolic

realm of the cinema is inevitably a speculative exercise, since it is rarely possible to prove causality or direct influence. Still, several shifts in the prevailing
culture seemed to find expression on the screen and, more specifically, on how
actors approached their craft. Among other cultural developments that were
in progress, the changing demographics, the so-called sexual revolution, and
the rise of ethnic pride movements were, to varying degrees, manifest in the
narrative focus and the intended audience for movies of the period. The spirit
of the times also found expression in the kinds of characters and characterizations—and, for that matter, in the kinds of actors—that appeared during the
Auteur Renaissance.

The coming-of-age of the baby boomers as a force both behind the camera and
at the box office led to a general drift toward stories centered around young protagonists. This was, first of all, good business, given that a 1968 survey revealed
that the sixteen-to-twenty-four-year-old age cohort accounted for 48 percent
of movie tickets.[48] Among the opening salvos of the New Hollywood were such
youth-oriented films as *The Graduate* (Mike Nichols, 1967) and *Easy Rider* (Dennis Hopper, 1968). The return on investment of these and other movies aimed
at young audiences was both surprising and impressive, prompting the studios
to reorient their production strategies toward the growing youth market and to
exploit its heft as a ticket-buying cohort.[49] Young protagonists required young
actors, so a rash of newly discovered talent appeared in movies in those years. The
roles that they inhabited—renegades, hippies, antiheroes, social outcasts—were
very much in tune with the youth culture and its anti-authority stance.

The demise of the censorship system, enforced by the Motion Picture Production Code, had been in the works for a while, with its death knell definitively rung
in 1968 when the Motion Picture Association of America (MPAA) rating system
was put into place. The loosening of cinematic taboos afforded actors more creative latitude in the characters they played and gave directors and screenwriters
more options in the stories they told.[50] The frank portrayals of Ratso Rizzo and
Joe Buck in *Midnight Cowboy* (John Schlesinger, 1969) would have been unimag-
inable—or, at least, unfilmable—a mere two years earlier. Relaxed restrictions
against graphic violence and profanity onscreen gave actors playing such antiso-
cial types as Travis Bickle in *Taxi Driver* or Jack Torrance in *The Shining*—Robert
De Niro and Jack Nicholson, respectively—full rein to cut loose and convey their
characters' ferocity without restraint. Under the new system, actors no longer
had to tiptoe around formerly forbidden subjects or use innuendo in place of
candidness or profanity. Elliott Gould, who once claimed for himself the moni-
ker "the first American jazz actor,"[51] celebrated what the new freedom meant for
his improvisatory process:

> I love to use colloquial words to color my performances. . . . Not because
> I'm trying for any sensational effect but simply because that's the way

people really talk. In *Little Murders* [Alan Arkin, 1971], I was able to ad-lib a colloquialism that I think makes an important scene work. . . . Without telling Alan or [screenwriter] Jules [Feiffer], I screamed out of the window, "Cocksucker!" My character had gone mad by this time, and for it to be reduced to that kind of shock language was an inspiration.[52]

Along with the era's focus on youth and the "anything goes" spirit of the post-censorship movie landscape, the rise of identity politics and pride movements, with their embrace of ethnicity and their scorn for knee-jerk assimilation, reverberated onscreen. This influenced not only how actors approached their parts but also who got to play what roles. Performers who in previous generations would most likely have remained character actors or would have been consigned to broad ethnic caricatures (e.g., Hoffman, De Niro, Gould, Pacino, Richard Pryor, Richard Benjamin, George Segal, Woody Allen, Barbra Streisand, Richard Dreyfuss) were now among the biggest stars in Hollywood. There were still pretty-boy actors in the movies of that era (e.g., Robert Redford, Paul Newman, Warren Beatty) as well as conventionally beautiful women (e.g., Faye Dunaway, Julie Christie, Jane Fonda), but the new breed of rough-hewn types seemed to be more in line with the prevailing spirit of flaunting, rather than effacing, both the actors' and the characters' ethnicity. Although "acting ethnic" and ethnically inflected vocal patterns were present from the earliest days of sound film with its dialect comedians, this period saw an increase in overtly ethnic actors and characters and their associated repertoire of gesture and speech.

Sometimes these performances confronted well-worn ethnic and racial signifiers head on, not only embracing but also exploding their representational conventions. This is particularly evident in comedies, which offer actors the leeway to create characters who exhibit a sort of double consciousness—existing within the narrative while also commenting on it. As Woody Allen wallows in his echt–New York–Jewish shtick, he both exemplifies the stereotype and pokes fun at those who buy into it. Several performances by African American actors of the period go further by crafting what amount to ironic meta-performances aimed at undermining the hackneyed racial caricatures of Hollywood's past. In portrayals that are both witty and pointed, Cleavon Little's western sheriff in *Blazing Saddles* (Mel Brooks, 1974), Godfrey Cambridge's *Watermelon Man* (Melvin Van Peebles, 1970), and Richard Pryor's many comic characters of the 1970s make sly digs at the shucking and jiving mannerisms and inflections that, per American movie history, exemplified the race. By exaggerating the vocal and gestural performance styles that defined so many earlier movie depictions of black characters, they manage simultaneously to evoke and excoriate those demeaning emblems of racial identity.

In the period's films, ethnicity was often correlated with authenticity and raw emotion, giving the performances of such actors as De Niro and Pacino an air

of gritty naturalism.[53] Sometimes, as in many of Streisand's movies, the performances involved brandishing a sort of stylized ethnicity: an in-your-face display
of coded vocal and gestural markers that might, in earlier eras, have been either
downplayed or played strictly for laughs. Either way, such expressions of ethnicity were generally read as tokens of genuineness. In the steak scene of *Raging
Bull*, De Niro as the *déclassé* La Motta talks with food hanging out of his mouth
and gestures broadly while bellowing at his hapless wife, "Waddya doin'?" In
conveying a character whose hands are far more expressive than his words, De
Niro relies on a familiar trope of Italian manhood. It is a performance that veers
toward ethnic caricature, and yet it was roundly acclaimed as a convincing,
biographically apt impersonation. That equation of ethnicity with authenticity
was parodied by Woody Allen in the split-screen dinner scene in *Annie Hall*. The
actors playing Annie's family use erect posture and modulated tones to convey
those characters' buttoned-up WASP rectitude while Alvy's Jewish family members, crammed into a tight frame, talk with food in their mouths, reach over and
interrupt one another, and gesture effusively. The joke derives partly from the
implication that overt ethnicity, devoid of culturally prescribed decorum, is an
authentic expression of self—a premise that was much in evidence in the social
discourse of the time (see figure 29).

It was not just ethnically identified types who took center stage in this era.
The decade's devotion to the aura of authenticity opened the doors to a new breed
of actor: unglamorous, ordinary looking, and seemingly more attuned to New
Hollywood's proclivity for less burnished, artificial-seeming narratives and pro-
duction values. The young turk directors intentionally turned their backs on old
Hollywood with its gods and goddesses of the silver screen. The presence of such
unlikely leading players as Robert Duvall, Lee Marvin, Glenda Jackson, Bruce
Dern, Karen Black, and Gene Hackman, among many others, prompted director

FIGURE 29: Split-screen ethnicity in *Annie Hall*.

Sydney Pollack to remark, "They were not like the old-fashioned movie stars. . . . They were dark, they were imperfect, they weren't completely god-like. . . . A whole different kind of movie star emerged. They almost looked like they could be your neighbor."[54] There was something self-consciously Oedipal about the embrace of this new kind of star. Some actors and moviegoers saw it as a youthful usurpation of power and presence. Bruce Dern talks about it as a generational thing: "Brando, McQueen, Paul Newman . . . They were movie stars when we were in high school. . . . Why should they have a corner on the market? We can act. Yeah, we don't look like they do. We aren't handsome like they were, but we're fucking interesting. And we were interesting because we were honest."[55]

Although all these factors—the ascension of youth culture, the relaxation of prohibitions against sex and violence in movies, the validation of ethnicity and ordinariness in the name of truthfulness—had a part in shaping film performances in the late 1960s and 1970s, arguably the most significant cultural influence on actors' conceptualization of and preparation for their roles was the self-actualization movements that proliferated during the years in question. The cultural imperative to explore and develop the self was promoted by an explosion of self-help books, magazine pieces, and television segments premised on guiding those who consumed them toward their true inner being. The ideology of the self as an autonomous entity that, with enough effort, could be understood, worked on, and improved upon was certainly not new. The 1970s version offered up an old recipe with some fresh ingredients: good old American individualism with a dollop of therapeutic self-help, a dash of Freud by way of pop psychology, and a seasoning of spirituality for extra flavor. In *Self-Help Inc.*, her book on the commodification of the self-help ethic, Mickey McGee describes one conception of the authentic self as "the quest for some kind of original ur-self unsullied by the impact of socialization. Such a self has to be 'discovered,' 'uncovered,' or 'recovered' and figures prominently in the literatures of self-improvement, where one is urged to 'excavate' and unearth' one's true self or true desires."[56]

This sounds a lot like the techniques of Method acting: discovering and excavating the essence of a character by probing one's inner self and unblocking repressed emotions or memories. The quest for personal authenticity and the popularizing of therapeutic culture in the 1970s did not catalyze Method-style performances, which had already been visible in and influential on American movies for a few decades. But the notion of a genuine self waiting to be uncovered did redound on Method acting's privileging of interiority and its approach to character development and delineation. The culture of self-actualization added to the Method's insistence on emotional truth and psychological believability of gesture, expression, tone, posture, and movement. As Steve Vineberg, in his history of Method acting, points out, "The Method's rhetoric appeared to make large moral and mystical claims for 'the power of truth in acting.'"[57] Likewise, 1970s self-actualization discourse made equally large claims that deep knowledge and development of one's true self was the route to fulfillment and achievement—a sort of ethic of authenticity.

There was always a psychotherapeutic aspect to Method acting, which saw performance as a sort of vision quest in which exhaustive probing of the actor's inner life would lead to self-discovery that, in turn, would purportedly enrich the creation of psychologically believable characters. James Naremore describes Lee Strasberg's "extreme form" of naturalism as "lead[ing] to quasi-psychoanalytic rehearsal techniques, inviting the actor to delve into the unconscious, searching out 'truthful' behavior."[58] Method-trained actors participated in exercises—not unlike some of the processes of therapy—designed to access their own motivations and memories. Acting talent and the ability (as well as the willingness) to plumb one's emotional depths were not always easily distinguishable from one another. Vineberg quotes actor Estelle Parsons saying that Lee Strasberg "sometimes confuses a disturbance with a gift."[59] Many writers on acting have commented on how Method acting, in effect, elevated neurosis and edgy intensity to an acting style.[60] Since Method techniques and therapeutic practices were both premised on rummaging around one's psyche to confront subconscious emotions and unresolved issues, they made for a neat fit.

In the 1970s, when the cult of the Method met the creed of the self-actualization movements, the boundary between preparing one's role and probing one's inner being became even more permeable. *No Acting Please: A Revolutionary Approach to Acting and Living*, a widely read book of acting exercises with a foreword by Jack Nicholson, first published in 1977, was part actor's manual, part self-help guide.[61] In such an approach, acting was viewed as self-discovery as much as craft. Accounts of the preparations and interactions of actors on films including *Apocalypse Now* (Frances Ford Coppola, 1979) and *Coming Home* sound like the 1970s encounter groups where participants sought to develop self-awareness and emotional expressiveness through group prodding and confrontation.[62] Such interactions among actors held self-knowledge and deep knowledge of their characters as intertwined prerequisites for a truthful, fully realized performance.

Awash in the spirit of the know-thyself culture, performers went to great lengths to scrutinize and individuate their characters. Bits of business, the use of significant objects, and the development of backstories for one's character had long been cornerstones of realist acting methods; those small nuances and granular details lent credibility to a role and contributed to the naturalistic acting style dominant in American movies after the silent era. Although the standard technique of devising backstories for characters was practiced by Hollywood actors well before this period, the pre-production research process, in which actors investigated their characters as if they were analysands, was now paramount.[63] This was the case not only for biographical and dramatic roles but even for more lighthearted fare. Before filming the romantic comedy *Starting Over* (Alan Pakula, 1979), Jill Clayburgh fleshed out her character, Marilyn, by supplying her (as well as her parents, who were not even in the script) with extensive backstories and psychological motivations. In a letter that she sent to director Pakula before filming began, she wrote:

> Her family I feel is poor—ethnic—maybe immigrants—intellectuals who left another country to find something here and were disappointed. For instance if her father were a doctor or a professor in Poland or Yugoslavia, maybe he teaches high school here. Her mother is maybe professional too. A nurse, a lab technician and I definately [sic] feel she is an only child. But whereas Jessica's struggle is not to be a pampered, middle class, spoiled sheltered *wife*, Marilyn comes by her independence with an ease which is rare but beautiful. Jessica takes photographs with a Nikon, Marilyn draws pictures with colored felt *pens*. (I have some specific ones in mind that I could probably get hold of.)[64]

While emotionally charged objects were always important signifiers for Method performances, the overkill of those specific felt pens as an essential delineator of character is indicative of the period's fixation on delving into the deep recesses of a role. Even actors untrained in or skeptical of bedrock Method verities often gave performances that were intent on psychological depth. Richard Maltby points out that "by the 1970s, the Method had been absorbed into mainstream acting practice to such an extent that audiences watching *The Godfather Part II* (1974) were offered no visible stylistic grounds for distinguishing between the performance of Actors Studio devotee Al Pacino and that of Robert Duvall, who had distanced himself from the particular techniques of Strasberg's Method."[65]

This fealty to reality and to the creation of characters who evinced emotional truth was, increasingly, the measure of a good performance. By the 1970s, the ability to transform oneself—to seemingly become rather than simply create a character—was, for actors as well as for the public who watched them onscreen and read about their preparations, the *sine qua non* of good acting. From film reviews to actor interviews to awards ceremonies, there was consensus about what constituted laudable acting: psychologically convincing, all-out performances in which the audience could intuit the characters' depths.

The realist predisposition of several decades of American sound film may have flattened the range of acting styles that Hollywood trafficked in, but the Method was far from the only approach drawn upon by actors of the 1970s to foster the illusion of unmediated access to the soul of their characters. In addition to a focus on depth psychology, actors used an array of stylistic idioms to fashion effective affective portrayals. So-called inner work was augmented by other forms of preparation for a role, including actors' physical transformations and their immersion in the social and political circumstances of characters. Even among actors trained by Strasberg or Adler, there was a broader sense of what they might pull out of their bag of tricks. In an interview, De Niro, who had been trained in the Method, explained, "[Acting] is like anything else. In the beginning you learn the rules, and then you realize that the rules are there to use or not use and that there are millions of different ways of doing something."[66] Dustin Hoffman said much the same thing: "You study acting until you're blue in the face and you go out there and it's got nothing to do with what you studied."[67] Both actors gave credit to their Method training but did not slavishly adhere to its principles; the Method was merely a springboard from which to dive into a variety of techniques. External characterizations, such as De Niro's weight fluctuations or Meryl Streep's accents, were as much a part of the actor's arsenal as were such Method-associated conventions as inarticulateness and deep sensibility.

The coinage neonaturalism is sometimes used to differentiate the sorts of realist performances that began appearing in this period. Diane Carson suggests that neonaturalism is both an extension and reinterpretation of the conventions of studio-era realist acting.[68] In their breadth and ambiguity, terms such as realism and neonaturalism are somewhat slippery but, in general, neonaturalism has been framed by scholars as acting that seems spontaneous and artless, in the service of characters that are multidimensional and, in many cases, socially determined. Neonaturalism further implies that other film stylistics, along with extra-cinematic factors, collude to affect how a performance is situated and perceived. The term is useful in moving the discussion about realist performance styles beyond the looming mystique of the Method and in acknowledging that perceptions of the relative truthfulness of performances are historically as well as culturally contingent. The markers and measures of authenticity change with time. For instance, stylistic idioms that are coded as naturalist are different in the 1950s and the 1970s; Brando's performances in *A Streetcar Named Desire* (Elia Kazan, 1951) and *On the Waterfront* (Elia Kazan, 1954), much admired in their day for their immediacy and genuineness, seem more flagrantly actorish than many of the performances that were singled out for their verisimilitude during the Auteur Renaissance.

Barry King has distinguished between impersonation, in which performers fully inhabit a role with the intent of subsuming their own identity in that of their characters, and personification, in which a performer's public persona is readily discernible across roles.[69] Movie actors in the 1970s tended to privilege impersonation, although the widespread commodification of stars and the public's fascination with their methods sometimes blurred those categories. As psychologically complex and compelling as Vito Corleone is in *The Godfather* and as much as the actor is immersed in the role, the legend of Brando and the mystique of his Method training are like a palimpsest, always discernible beneath the veneer of the character. For all of its naturalist delineation of character, a performance such as Brando's is bravura, look-at-me acting; due to the 1970s abundance of celebrity journalism, the actor's presence shows through his skilled construction of the character. This is the paradox of realist acting in the age of celebrity idolatry and entertainment journalism; it is often accomplished and convincing but the spectator, plied with foreknowledge such as how Brando's jutting jaw was created, cannot help but think about the performance technique behind the character. As Andrew Higson has written, "The institution of the star-system means that Hollywood constantly runs the risk of foregrounding the actor's persona, potentially against the grain of the narrative." He goes on to say that although a performance may aim for the quintessence of naturalism, the intention and the effect may be different since, due to extra-textual factors, would-be naturalist acting can have an anti-naturalist outcome.[70]

Although naturalism and interiority were the predominant performance conventions of the Auteur Renaissance, alternative styles of acting were visible in certain movies of the era. The self-actualization movements with their enshrinement of authenticity were one cultural impulse among many to have an effect on performance styles. A nascent postmodern sensibility, informed by a notion of selfhood that challenged realist precepts and practices, yielded some examples of anti-naturalist performances. Erving Goffman's *The Presentation of Self in Everyday Life*, first published in 1959, had, by the 1970s, worked its way into the discourse on acting. In claiming that all interpersonal dealings involve playing carefully crafted versions of ourselves, Goffman's book smudged the distinction between self-expression and artful presentation. Naremore explains what such an approach means to the development of a character: "Instead of treating performance as an outgrowth of an essential self, it implies that the self is an outgrowth of performance."[71] The notion of selfhood as incoherent—as a succession of strategically selected self-projections—pointed the way to a reflexive performance style that appeared in some movies of the time. Such films tended to trumpet their awareness of their own aesthetic form and history through self-referentiality or irony, and the performances followed suit.

These anti-naturalist performances disrupted realist posturing about access to psychological truths. They also complicated the relative positioning of actor, character, and audience. Jerzy Growtowski was an experimental theater practitioner in Poland and author of the 1968 manifesto *Towards a Poor Theater*, which was a mainstay of university acting curricula and performance experiments in that era. Among other challenges to conventional, fourth-wall theater, Growtowski advocated the erasure of the traditional boundary between audience and performers.[72] That and other challenges to the realist conventions of classic cinema made their indirect way to some of the movies constituting the Auteur Renaissance. Although there is not a straight line between Hollywood movies and the thinking of Goffman, Growtowski, and other theorists of modernist and postmodernist performativity, there are ample examples of performances that were self-aware imitations of life rather than would-be illusions of life.[73]

Performances that willfully defied the orthodoxies of naturalist acting were often found in the many genre films of the time that riffed on earlier conventions and characterizations. Genre transformations, including *McCabe and Mrs. Miller*; *New York, New York*; *The Long Goodbye* (Robert Altman, 1973); *Chinatown* (Roman Polanski, 1974); *Cabaret* (Bob Fosse, 1972); *The Friends of Eddie Coyle* (Peter Yates, 1973); the blaxploitation cycle; and the entire oeuvre of Mel Brooks, showcased performances that indulged in a knowing wink at the audience. Naremore distinguishes such performances as more presentational than representational, and he uses the term "ostensiveness" to elucidate the extent to which a performance (or, in some of these cases, a meta-performance) acknowledges itself as such.[74] The acting styles in these films range from minimalist to over the top; either way, they are poles apart from naturalist performances that purport to reveal character psychology and to be true to life.

Such performances do not court audience identification with the characters or aim at an understanding of their psychological makeup; instead, they encourage distanciation. Robert Mitchum's laconic characterization in *The Friends of Eddie Coyle* or Elliott Gould's self-consciously hip take on the private eye figure in *The Long Goodbye* are styles of surfaces, not depths. Pam Grier's larger-than-life presence in *Coffy* (Jack Hill, 1973) and *Foxy Brown* (Jack Hill, 1974) does not try to get under the skin of her characters; instead, she steps into a persona as if it were a costume and acknowledges it as such. In an analysis of Julie Christie's often opaque performances, Nick Davis writes, "Her wry, riffy style of acting works against the grain of realist, holistic characterization, instead emphasizing ironic line readings, prismatic facial expressions, and wistful, translucent postures and gestures."[75] He goes on to suggest how her acting in *McCabe and Mrs. Miller* is of a piece with that film's presentational style: "Christie's performative mode of sketched, improvisatory suggestion rather than Method subjectivity or generic typology resonates perfectly with the film's own penchant for oblique historiography and reverse discourse."[76]

Sometimes, Method-influenced, inner-oriented acting and ironic, nonnaturalistic approaches existed side by side within the same movie. A single film or, sometimes, a single role could encompass both methodologies. In the genre-bending musical *Cabaret*, Michael York gives a performance aimed at plumbing the depths of his character, while Liza Minnelli's rendition of Sally Bowles is more of an atomized abstraction than a fully realized, psychologically lucid person. Joel Grey, meanwhile, gleefully gnaws on the scenery and aggressively breaks the fourth wall; his highly expressionist acting yields a character who is all self-mocking spectacle, with no implication of an interior life. Although the film's discordant performances do not mesh into a cohesive whole, this is not a failure of acting skill or directorial vision. The three characters serve different functions in the narrative; each of their performance styles acknowledges, in its own way, the power of artifice and the difficulty of self-knowledge, which, as it happens, are among the thematic threads of the film (see figure 30).

FIGURE 30: Joel Grey's expressionist rictus in *Cabaret*.

As film historians have worked to codify a common lexicon for analyzing screen acting, the standard distinctions between naturalist and anti-naturalist acting or inside-out and outside-in performance approaches have come to be viewed as reductive polarities. In any given era, eclectic styles of acting exist on a spectrum. The Method focus on psychic probing in the name of emotional truth and the Brechtian antirealist stance aimed at political praxis both found their place in the polyphonic refrain of movies produced between 1968 and 1980. The supposed antipodes represented by Dustin Hoffman's and Laurence Olivier's respective techniques indicate, above all, the performative hybridity of the period's films. It would be overly schematic to claim any consistency or ubiquity of acting technique across those twelve years or even, in some cases, within individual movies. The splayed sensibilities of the era, with its welter of cultural, industrial, social, ideological, and artistic inclinations, defy neat demarcations both onscreen and off. If acting during the Auteur Renaissance can be characterized at all, it would be as a mixed bag filled with a vibrant variety of performance styles, techniques, and influences.

5

THE NEW HOLLYWOOD, 1981–1999 Donna Peberdy

In both popular perception and box office earnings, the American cinema of the 1980s and 1990s was dominated by the size, strength, and spectacle of the block-buster. Spanning 1981 to 1999, a "new new Hollywood" saw the beginning of a new multinational, corporate Hollywood, defined by the rise of the conglomer-ates and by the "high concept" filmmaking best epitomized by Don Simpson/Jerry Bruckheimer popcorn movies. "With increased conglomeration," Jon Lewis notes, "came an abandonment of the auteur theory and a growing emphasis on formulaic blockbusters—thrill-ride movies that deliver on a simple promise to entertain."[1] By the end of the 1990s, "the whammy theory" had taken over and "films became more spectacular than ever before."[2] The box office was also dom-inated by sequels and franchises, leading Stephen Prince to only half-joke that "it seemed as if the industry had been taken over by mathematicians" on account of the use of numbers in titles to indicate a follow-up to a successful film.[3] Critics of the high-concept style of filmmaking acknowledged that the stars, spectacular visuals, and synergistic tie-in products were often prioritized, in the pursuit of profit, over story and character. As Barry Langford succinctly puts it, "The story was not told, rather the film was sold."[4]

The blockbuster came to represent the antithesis of the personal cinema of the preceding decade, which had enabled not just directors, but actors, to emerge as auteurs. The blockbuster's excesses were encapsulated in the critical and box office flop *Heaven's Gate* (Michael Cimino, 1980), which, for many, signaled the end of the director-led cinema of the 1970s. Indeed, in popular and critical discourse, the period has often been overshadowed by, and unfavorably compared to, the cultural richness of the 1970s, what David Thomson has referred to as "the decade when movies mattered."[5] According to James Kendrick, the 1980s are "frequently dismissed as a period of artistic and ideological retreat in which movies became simplified and empty."[6] Similarly, Linda Ruth Williams and Michael Hammond note, "The image of the [1990s] is that of a Hollywood dominated by spectacle machines, making extravagant, formulaic movies that play well in non-English-speaking foreign markets, at the expense of innovative development in character and style."[7] The simplified and empty spectacle machine was personified in the excessive "musculinity" of its hard-bodied action heroes who became synonymous with the Hollywood blockbuster.[8] Arnold Schwarzenegger and Sylvester Stallone were two of the highest earning stars of the 1980s, and their action-packed, high-budget films, such as *The Terminator* (James Cameron, 1984), *The Terminator 2: Judgment Day* (James Cameron, 1991), and the three *Rambo* films (1982, 1985, 1988), capitalized on the literal and metaphorical strength of their stars, emphasizing the brand and the "glossy surface" of the star body over depth of character and acting ability.[9]

However, as Stephen Prince has argued, such claims about a shift toward a more conservative cinema that reflected American politics, along with a "general lowering and coarsening of the quality of filmmaking" as a result of the blockbuster, oversimplify a period that was much more complex, often contradictory, and characterized by significant transformations in both the film industry and wider culture.[10] Star power rapidly increased during the period as stars demanded, and received, higher salaries and more control over the filmmaking process. At the same time, many actors embraced the chance to move between large- and small-budget films, waiving their fees for a share of the film profits or just for the chance to work with an up-and-coming director. When *Toy Story* (John Lasseter, 1995) became the first feature-length, entirely computer-animated film to receive a theatrical release and went on to become the year's biggest earner, questions were asked about the necessity of stars at all, along with the long-term currency of live actors. Such anxieties about technology were brought to the screen in the cinematic cyborgs and techno-bodies of *Blade Runner* (Ridley Scott, 1982), *RoboCop* (Paul Verhoeven, 1987), and *The Lawnmower Man* (Brett Leonard, 1992), displaying developments in visual effects and computer-generated imaging and tapping into fears around computer viruses and bugs. Almost one hundred years after the birth of film, historians and cultural critics started to wonder if this was "the end of cinema as we know it."[11]

These indicative events carve out a time period that was far from stable and was characterized by transformation and change as much as the decades that straddled it. Many of these transformations were manifested in social groups and collectives—the gay community, Reaganite yuppies, independent filmmakers—that gained increasing cultural and creative visibility during the era. Those transformations that bordered on and sometimes tipped over into excess posed challenges to established social norms and acting conventions and led to anxieties over identity that had far-reaching implications. The star as brand and celebrity overshadowed considerations of the actor's labor, but this overview already indicates some of the ways sociocultural and technological developments had an impact on screen acting during the period, affecting acting choices, the relationship of actors to the screen, and how audiences interact with performances. For the remainder of the chapter, I focus on three modes of acting—transformation, excess, and the ensemble—that were particularly prominent across the 1980s and 1990s. Transformation in performance brings together the bodily transformations of actors physically adapting for roles, dual-role performances, body mutation, gender alteration, the Cinderella makeover, and physical and mental adaption. Excess reveals itself when transformations go too far beyond the boundaries of the norm, evident in the pronounced musculature of the 1980s hard body. It can also be identified in the performances of addiction and obsession that littered the period and in the exaggerated, histrionic performances of actors recurrently associated with "bad acting." Finally, the ensemble offers a rich space in which to showcase a variety of actors and acting styles, bringing together excess and transformation as indicators of social and cultural concerns of the period. While they are by no means exclusive to the 1980s and 1990s, transformation, excess, and the ensemble not only are key to deciphering acting in the period but were significant features in defining the sociocultural, political, technological, and cinematic landscape.

Transformation

Experimentation was rife on the screen in this period, evident in developments in special effects and digital technology but also in the ways that actors transformed into characters by incorporating and responding to technological advancements, moving between genres, working with multiple directors and actors, and experimenting with acting styles and their own bodies. In acting, transformation refers to the process of becoming a character and embodying the role by adopting the appropriate mannerisms and expressions to convincingly blur the boundaries between actor and character. What might at first appear to be straightforward is revealed as a complex system composed of actions and movements that manipulate the performing body until it reaches the intended state. The popularization of Method acting reached new levels as actors went to extreme lengths in the pursuit of authenticity, "becoming" their characters psychologically and physically. For

Kevin Esch, "actorly transformation" refers to a trend that emerged in the 1980s that "evoked the Method's behavioral extremes at the same time that it fetishized discipline."[12] Esch considers examples such as Robert De Niro's sixty-pound weight gain for *Raging Bull* (Martin Scorsese, 1980), Sylvester Stallone's weight gain for *Cop Land* (James Mangold, 1997), or Edward Norton's pronounced musculature in *American History X* (Tony Kaye, 1998) as examples of "strategic" actorly transformation that signal "dedication to the craft of acting" and a "new Method" involving extreme behavior on the part of the actor. Responding to the aesthetic demands of the genre, the actor's body is "transformed through concentrated, film-specific self-imposed body alteration" in order to achieve "greater fidelity of performance."[13]

Discussing his thirty-pound weight gain for the role of an imposing neo-Nazi in *American History X*, Norton described the importance of embodying the right physicality in order to become his character: "Derek needed to be as physically intimidating as he was on every other level. He needed to be larger than life. . . . The physicality was the part I was the least sure of being able to pull off. But I shaved my head, grew a beard, bulked myself up . . . to stretch my elasticity over the role and encompass it."[14] For Norton, the body transformation was not just about looking the part. Putting on weight and muscle mass inevitably affected the physicality of his performance: "I found you do carry yourself differently when you have that much power in your upper body; you start to feel that right away."[15] The fidelity of performance achieved by bodily transformation thus requires the actors to adapt their movements, postures, and sense of presence to their new physique. Norton's Oscar nomination for his performance, along with a number of other bodily transformations that resulted in Oscar nominations, suggest that the 1980s and 1990s were instrumental in establishing extreme actorly transformation as a legitimate acting technique. This perception would continue into the 2000s and beyond with the morphing bodies of actors such as Christian Bale, Charlize Theron, and Matthew McConaughey, whose extreme weight loss or weight gain was rewarded with widespread acclaim and acting accolades.

While all performances are, to varying degrees, transformations, an abundance of films in this period foregrounded transformation both as a part of the performance repertoire and as a part of the diegesis. The dual or multiple role was a popular cross-generic narrative device that necessitated actors taking on more than one role in a single film. The act of playing multiple roles, which dates back to a long vaudevillian comic tradition, is seen in a number of film comedies, including *Spaceballs* (Mel Brooks, 1987), *Coming to America* (John Landis, 1988), *The Nutty Professor* (Tom Shadyac, 1996), and the *Austin Powers* films (Jay Roach, 1997–2002) in which Mike Myers progressively extended his list of characters from two to three to four roles in each subsequent contribution to the franchise. The device is also employed in horror and thrillers with common tropes including films about twins (*Dead Ringers* [David Cronenberg, 1988]; *Jack's Back* [Rowdy

Herrington, 1988]; *The Parent Trap* [Nancy Meyers, 1998]); split personalities, bipolar disorder, and alter-egos (*Raising Cain* [Brian De Palma, 1992]; *The Dark Half* [George A. Romero, 1993]; *Lost Highway* [David Lynch, 1997]), and "body swap" films (*Vice Versa* [Brian Gilbert, 1988]; *Big* [Penny Marshall, 1988]; *Face/ Off* [John Woo, 1997]) where two characters exchange places within the narrative, causing the actors involved to play two roles. In *The French Lieutenant's Woman* (Karel Reisz, 1981), Meryl Streep and Jeremy Irons each play two roles in a film within the film; this transformation of actors is a key plot device in John Fowles's novel on which the film is based. Similarly, in the Kenneth Branagh–directed thriller *Dead Again* (1991), both leads, Branagh and Emma Thompson, take on two roles. A number of films also featured triple role performances, such as *Sunshine* (István Szabó, 1999), in which Ralph Fiennes plays three characters who are blood relatives across different decades; *Joe Versus the Volcano* (John Patrick Shanley, 1990), in which Meg Ryan plays three women who each serendipitously cross paths with Tom Hanks's character; and *Dead of Winter* (Arthur Penn, 1987), in which Mary Steenburgen plays an actor hired to replace another actor who has gone missing (also played by Steenburgen) as well as the missing actor's sister.

The challenge for the actor taking on multiple roles in a realist drama is to perform each role as authentically and coherently as possible so that the transformation is believable. Indeed, "seamlessness" is often invoked as a measure of achievement by reviewers.[16] Conversely, failure to achieve seamlessness leads to critical derision: Sean Young, for example, won two Razzie awards for *A Kiss Before Dying* (James Dearden, 1991) for Worst Actress ("for the twin who survives") and Worst Supporting Actress ("for the twin who is murdered"), while Arnold Schwarzenegger divided critics for playing both a character and himself in *Last Action Hero* (John McTiernan, 1993), receiving both a Saturn award nomination for Best Actor in a Science Fiction Film and a Razzie nomination for the year's worst actor.

Transformative authenticity and seamlessness are equally important in comedy. Appropriating anthropologist Erving Goffman's term, James Naremore uses "expressive coherence" to refer to maintaining "coherence of manner but also a fit between setting, costume, and behavior." Often, a comic effect comes when the actor does not sustain "expressive coherence."[17] In *Vice Versa*, for example, when Charlie (Fred Savage) swaps bodies with his father, Marshall (Judge Reinhold), the narrative requires Savage to convincingly play both an eleven-year-old and an older man trapped inside his body. Moments of comedy are produced when Savage allows the father to break out. Similarly in *Big*, released three months later, Hanks plays a twelve-year-old boy trapped inside the body of his thirty-year-old future self. Hanks, thirty-one at the time of filming, convincingly portrays an adolescent trying to pass as a thirty-year-old to his new colleagues and love interest, resulting in frequent opportunities for physical comedy. Hanks performs adolescence with youthful, wide-eyed facial expressions and a

FIGURE 31: Performing adolescence. Tom Hanks plays a twelve-year-old trapped in a thirty-year-old's body in *Big*.

physicality comprising pronounced, agile movements, including swinging arms and a bouncing walk (see figure 31).

According to Cynthia Baron and Sharon Carnicke, films in which actors perform more than one role "make performance eminently visible," calling attention to performance *as* performance, offering a challenge to the "opacity of performance elements."[18] As the authors note, the realist mode of performance renders acting choices invisible, whereas such instances of multiple roles make what is often hidden more transparent. Multiple roles offer a clear opportunity to read shifts in performance and to determine the acting process in a way that is less possible without such a contrast. According to Baron and Carnicke, personality shifts across dual characters rely on the actors' "virtuosity to morph from one personality to the other."[19]

Edward Norton's shift from stuttering adolescent to menacing bully for his debut film performance in *Primal Fear* (Gregory Hoblit, 1996) is a clear case in point. Speaking about the specific difficulties of playing a dual character in film, Norton noted, "Anything that involves a specific evolution of a character on film is tough because the shooting is broken up over many days. Having moved from stage to film, one of the things I've had to accept is that most days on the making of a film are not big acting days. There are days where you almost have to just go through the motions because if you don't all your moments would be too large. You have to trust minimalism through the bulk of the shooting process, and just pick the moments that need to be bigger." The actor also described charting his character's development on chronologically ordered index cards that he pinned to the wall of his hotel room and consulted when shooting out of sequence to "make sure I didn't overdo it or show too much."[20]

Norton's dual performance in *Primal Fear* has much in common with Will

Smith's performance in *Six Degrees of Separation* (Fred Schepisi, 1993), another narrative of duplicity and deception. In the film, Smith plays a character who passes himself off as the charming and charismatic son of Sidney Poitier but turns out to be a con artist and imposter. Much of the narrative involves the other characters retrospectively analyzing the imposter's performance to understand how they were duped. Smith's transformative performance was noticed by director Roland Emmerich, who cast him in a career-defining role in *Independence Day* (Roland Emmerich, 1996), despite the role not being originally written for an African American: "We were so blown away by what he did in [*Six Degrees of Separation*]. . . . He can be very serious and dramatic in a part, but at the same time, in the switch of a second, very funny, which is what heroes are made of."[21]

His comment points to a confluence between transformations on screen and a wider necessity to be versatile and adaptable as an actor. Barry Sonnenfeld, who directed Smith in the hit science fiction comedy *Men in Black* (1997) and the less successful comedy western *Wild Wild West* (1999), has said Smith has an "innate ability, to be natural for whatever medium he's working in."[22] This assessment, along with Edward Norton's earlier comment about the importance of stretching his "elasticity," evoke Barry King's argument about how the "elastic self" in stardom applies to the star persona and extends to performance. "As demands compete and have to be managed, persona work involves stretching an apparent core of personal qualities to cover all contingencies," he states. "In this process, persona is elastic rather than plastic, closer to a procedure for surviving."[23] With an incredibly successful performance repertoire that encompasses rap music, television comedy (*The Fresh Prince of Bel Air*, 1990–1996), film comedy, and dramatic performance, Smith is an exemplar of the contemporary elastic persona.[24] Smith's dual role performance in *Six Degrees of Separation* reveals a diversity of skill that is indicative of the actor's apparently seamless movement between genres and formats.[25]

While Smith did not have any formal acting training, his career points to a need for actors to be adept in performing a wide range of characterizations. Actors such as Meryl Streep and Robin Williams, who produced some of their best work in the period, also exemplify the notion of elasticity in performance with their shape-shifting embodiments and vocal acrobatics across comedy and serious drama. In a 1985 article on the growth of actor conservatories, Michael Hofferber suggests a "renaissance" in actor training was taking place, which was responding to a "growing desire to play a broad range of roles rather than settle for a single, successful 'type.'"[26] He cites the indicative example of finding the lead actor for David Lynch's *Dune* (1984), a role that eventually went to twenty-five-year-old screen newcomer Kyle McLachlan, whose prior acting experience was in regional theater and a season at the Oregon Shakespeare Festival. "Greater emphasis is now being placed on tutoring actors in the craft of acting and the related disciplines of voice, movement, and stage fighting," Hofferber notes.

Prosthetics and Physiognomies

A critical distinction can be made between those films where the multiple role device is seen as a novelty, largely achieved as a result of prosthetics and caricature, and those where the dual role device calls attention to the dramatic choices originating with the actor. *The Nutty Professor*, for example, won an Oscar for Best Makeup, but Eddie Murphy's multiple performances in the film went unacknowledged. The prosthetics dominate in *The Nutty Professor*, obscuring or restricting the actor so that his agency is more difficult to determine. With developments in makeup and visual effects in the 1980s and 1990s, physical transformations became more convincing, adding to the seamlessness of the transformational moments, but such a seamlessness sometimes made it difficult to ascertain the extent of the actor's contribution. While those contributions may be more difficult to locate and measure underneath the changes to the actor's appearance, transformative performances that incorporate prosthetics require skill. Prosthetics often place restrictions on the range of movement and require actors to adapt their performances accordingly. This is very much the case with films that foreground body modification and mutation, using makeup and prosthetics to assist the transformation of the actor's body from one state to another. David Cronenberg's films are a case in point. As with Esch's "actorly transformation," what the body looks like has tended to overwhelm what the body does, yet transformation is as evident on the body as it is in the performance of it.

In Cronenberg's *The Fly* (1986), scientist Seth Brundle's (Jeff Goldblum) experiment to teleport himself from one telepod to another backfires when his genes are spliced with those of a fly. At first, the experiment is considered a success; Goldblum's slim, gangly frame transforms into a honed and defined musculature; his energy levels surge, leading to much darting around and an impressively enhanced sexual stamina. Then, with the help of extremely convincing and Oscar-winning prosthetics and pre-CGI visual effects, Brundle's flesh rapidly decays until he becomes more diptera than human; he becomes "Brundlefly." Goldblum's idiosyncratic stutter, fast-paced delivery, and "twitchy bug eyes" contribute to a performance that is convincingly and increasingly insectlike, with erratic jolting and angular distortions of his limbs.[27] For the journalist Vic Ziegel, Goldblum's "comic, stutter-step delivery and the almost mime-like use of his rangy body make his performances jump off the screen," and his performance is largely in keeping with the "agitated, witty, and horny" character he played in the ensemble film *The Big Chill* (Lawrence Kasdan, 1983) three years earlier, as well as in later performances in *Jurassic Park* (Steven Spielberg, 1993), *Independence Day*, and a series of Holsten Pils advertisements in the 1990s.[28] Yet Goldblum, who had mostly supporting roles prior to *The Fly*, plays the role with frantic yet controlled aplomb, avoiding the exaggeration that might be expected given the darkly comic nature of the story.

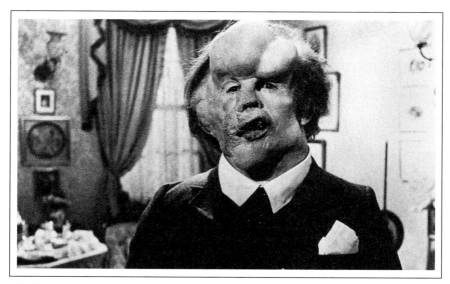

FIGURE 32: John Hurt responding to the restrictions of prosthetics in *The Elephant Man*.

If *The Fly* provides an example whereby the actor's idiosyncratic tics and expressions can be drawn on to enhance the effect of the makeup and prosthetics, locating the actor's contribution to performance is much more difficult in *The Elephant Man* (David Lynch, 1980). The film's approach offered a contrast to the 1979 Broadway production in which, in a bid to represent the character's inner beauty on his exterior, the actor playing the genetically disfigured John Merrick did not wear prosthetics or disfiguring makeup. To become Merrick for the film, however, John Hurt spent eight hours a day having the sixteen-piece mask applied. Hurt was nominated for an Oscar for his performance and the film was nominated for another seven (although, controversially, the makeup did not receive a nomination).[29] For *New York Times* critic Vincent Canby, it was "to the credit of Christopher Tucker's makeup and to Mr. Hurt's extraordinary performance deep inside it, that John Merrick doesn't look absurd, like something out of a low-budget science-fiction film." Canby went on to note, "Mr. Hurt is truly remarkable. It can't be easy to act under such a heavy mask."[30] The difficulty in locating the actor's contribution to the performance "deep inside" the makeup is something Hurt himself observed. The actor noted that he only went to see the dailies once: "There was no point. With all that makeup on I couldn't be sure what I was doing. I had to rely totally on our director. . . . At one point I became very depressed and felt nothing I was doing was coming through on screen. It seemed to me my stand-in could do it just as well as I. . . . To be quite honest, the film was misery to make."[31] Hurt's performance in *The Elephant Man* was very well received, however, and critics called attention to the "expressive"[32] and "virtuoso performance [which] gradually reveals suppressed depths of humanity."[33] Even Roger Ebert, who gave the film only two

FIGURE 33: Billy Bob Thornton transforming physiognomy in *Sling Blade*.

stars and struggled with what he saw as its "pure sentimentalism," acknowledged Hurt's skill at "projecting a humanity past the disfigured makeup".[34]

Yet it is difficult to determine the actor's contribution; given the size, weight, and shape of the mask, only Hurt's eyes and the inside of his mouth are visible. A mouthpiece was worn to give the impression of enlarged gums and a distorted jaw. Hurt's performance is very much a composite, affected by the demands of the mask and costume that were made from a cast of the real Merrick's body. The mask and costume were incorporated into the performance as opposed to being separate from it, and the actor reacted to the restrictions placed upon him. The vocal performance required the actor to adapt to the mouthpiece and speak through one side of his mouth, resulting in a muffled and often indistinct voice, punctuated by repeated slurping sounds where the actor inhales his saliva. Hurt adjusts his posture to respond to the weight of the mask that sits disproportionally in relation to his frame. He adapts his body by tilting, toppling, and awkwardly balancing, his right arm hanging limply by his side as he awkwardly shuffles his feet. The body in this instance becomes all the more important as a site for performance due to the constraints of the mask and costume.

Billy Bob Thornton's Oscar-nominated transformative performance in *Sling Blade* (Billy Bob Thornton, 1996) provides quite the counterpoint to Hurt's masked depiction. Thornton both directed and took the lead role in the low-budget feature about the social reintegration of a mentally disabled man after a twenty-five-year hospitalization for killing his mother and her lover. As Karl Childers, Thornton is unrecognizable, which is even more impressive for being a wholly physical performance that did not use special effects or prosthetics. In the opening scene, the camera pans around the back of his head to reveal his side profile and display his distorted physiognomy, which remains in the foreground for three minutes. As he juts out his jaw, pulls in his upper lip, and pushes up his lower lip, Thornton's face appears swollen. His hair is a closely shorn bowl-cut, receding and balding on top, and his eyes are narrowly pinched. When he finally makes a noise, he grunts gravelly and monotone "uh-hmms." The scene is followed by a seven-minute monologue where Childers explains his motivation for murder. Thornton's voice has a synthesized sound akin to a digital voice generator, and the actor has noted that he used Chloraseptic spray to numb his throat and achieve the extremely low pitch.[35] Every now and then his head twitches from side to side, a nervous tic that draws attention to the character's discomfort in telling his story, and he compulsively rubs his hands together for the duration of the monologue. Asked by James Lipton on *Inside the Actor's Studio* if he could reproduce his performance in front of the live audience, Thornton proceeded to lower his head, metamorphose into Childers, and raise his head "in character." His shifting physiognomy clearly demonstrated the transformative potential of the face and how acting can be an exercise in bodily contortion (see figure 33).

Gender Transformation

During this period, the Julliard-trained actor William Hurt took on a number of roles that necessitated a distinct transformation. In an illuminating interview with *American Film* in 1986, Hurt spoke candidly about his acting philosophy and the importance of transforming into a role.[36] The actor considers acting a sacred ritual that involves putting on a metaphorical mask: "You take your body and you shape it and you change it. You treat it just like you would putty or paint, with the same underlying principle as putty or paint or clay or stone—you adapt the body to the theme of the piece in an atmosphere that is trusting and enlightened, and hopefully, eventually—if you work hard enough and sincerely enough—transcending."[37] Hurt sees his job as an actor to adapt to, rather than impose himself on, the character. His film career started in the 1980s with Ken Russell's psychotropic fantasy *Altered States* (1980). Hurt plays a Harvard scientist who conducts experiments on himself, subjecting himself to sensory deprivation in order to induce a regressive state. Like *The Fly*, the bizarre plot could invite an over-the-top and extravagant performance, yet Hurt was generally acclaimed for his understated acting.

Critics were divided over Hurt's flamboyant performance of a transsexual in *Kiss of the Spider Woman* (Hector Babenco, 1985), which won him an Oscar. For Roger Ebert, Hurt played "a frankly theatrical character, exaggerated and mannered—and yet he never seems to be reaching for effects," while Susan Linfield was more ambivalent, noting that the performance was "on the verge of being either really great or really terrible."[38] The film also includes a purposefully overblown performance by Sonia Braga as the eponymous spider woman, an approach that acts as a bracketing device that has the effect of making Hurt's performance seem more subtle by comparison. In another interview, Hurt observed: "The line between the feminine and the masculine parts of ourselves moves around all the time. It's not hard for me to identify with a woman."[39] *Kiss of the Spider Woman* is just one example of performative transformation in films about gender and sexuality alteration released during the 1980s and 1990s. These films offer up gender as a construction, suggesting gender is something that is performed via codes and conventions. "Performance" in these films refers to identity as a social performance but also to the techniques used to perform gender, both of which question the presumed naturalness of gender and sexuality and thereby confront the viewer with questions about identity and normativity.

In another Oscar-winning role, Hilary Swank's transformation from female to male in *Boys Don't Cry* (Kimberly Peirce, 1999) foregrounds transgender Brandon Teena's method of passing. The performance of gender is clearly visible. Swank is shown tightly binding her breasts and putting socks in her jockey shorts; she combs her hair forward and then sweeps her palms over the sides of her head to create a boyish hair-style before looking in the mirror to take in the overall effect. Repeatedly clenching her teeth, she creates the effect of a strong jawline, an action Swank employs and the camera focuses on a number of times throughout the film. The ability to convincingly pass as male was crucial to the casting process and acting preparation. Kimberly Peirce spent three years holding auditions for the role of Brandon and said it was crucial he was played by an unknown, "someone the public didn't recognize." The director was drawn to Swank's androgynous look in the auditions but needed further convincing: "I said, 'Look, you can have the role if you do a Robert De Niro and do a full transformation into a boy. And that means psychologically and physically.' I got her a voice trainer and a physical trainer, because the voice is the thing that gives them away. And I made her live as a boy for four weeks" (see figure 34).[40]

In 1983 both Dustin Hoffman and Julie Andrews were nominated for Oscars

FIGURE 34: Performing gender and sexuality in *Boys Don't Cry*.

for playing characters who pass for the opposite sex in order to get jobs, respectively a male actor who disguises himself as a woman to get a role in a soap opera in *Tootsie* (Sydney Pollack, 1982) and a female singer who performs as a male female impersonator in *Victor Victoria* (Blake Edwards, 1982). Tom Hanks's Oscar-winning portrayal of a gay man with AIDS in *Philadelphia* (Jonathan Demme, 1993), along with other examples of straight actors "playing gay," such as Ewan McGregor and Jonathan Rhys Meyers in *Velvet Goldmine* (Todd Haynes, 1998) and Matt Damon in *The Talented Mr. Ripley* (Anthony Minghella, 1999), paved the way for a number of award-winning performances in the 2000s, including Heath Ledger in *Brokeback Mountain* (Ang Lee, 2005), Sean Penn in *Milk* (Gus Van Sant, 2008), and Colin Firth in *A Single Man* (Tom Ford, 2009). In these examples, gender and sexuality become something to put on or wear—a costume, a wig, a rolled-up sock—as well as something to perform in an affectation or an accent. Even in those examples that deploy exaggeration as a performance mode, gender and sexual identity are also performed in subtle and nuanced ways so that the end result is far from a two-dimensional stereotype.

The performances considered here reveal a thematic preoccupation with the boundaries of the body and of cultural norms, played out on the (often excessively) transformed bodies of actors. The examples of bodily modification and mutation test the limits of the body through the actor's expressive contortions and manipulations, either amplified with prosthetics, accentuated by weight gain or loss, or solely constructed by acting choices. The transformations that engage with gender and sexuality as performance reveal the confines of normative culture, posing a challenge to established conventions and audience expectations. Many reveal a fascination with transgressing the boundaries of the body, what Elizabeth Bronfen has referred to as a "mutable corporeality," characterized by a "blurring of the boundary between internal and external body spaces."[41] Linda Badley, who outlines a shift in perceptions from the 1970s to the 1980s where "image was everything," notes, "By the 1980s, the body was no longer a temple or receptacle for the spirit. . . . The site of the self had shifted to the body—albeit manipulated, technologized, and transformed."[42] We might put such performances on a sliding scale of how much the actor's technique is "visible" or to what extent the actor's performance is a composite, as much affected by prosthetics or other visual effects as it is the actor's own skill, and yet all the performances originate with the actor who is the site of the transformation. The examples show actors making creative decisions to modulate their performances and demonstrate their self-awareness of the processes of transformation, as evidenced in John Hurt's frustration at his inability to recognize his performance in *The Elephant Man* and Billy Bob Thornton's metamorphosis in front of a live audience. Many of the aforementioned performances were acknowledged with award nominations and critical acclaim, although an actor's failure to strike a balance and convincingly transform oneself can result in critical disdain or dismissal. Such imbalances often become associated with excess and an overabundance of emotion, resulting in characters that lack expressive coherence.

Excess

A number of transformative narratives directly commented on the association of excess with the contemporary period. Michael Douglas's Oscar-winning performance as Gordon Gekko in *Wall Street* (Oliver Stone, 1987) provides a fitting icon for 1980s excesses with his "greed is good" bravado encapsulating both the heights of the individual pursuit of wealth and its failures. Films such as *Trading Places* (John Landis, 1983), *Secret of My Succe$s* (Herbert Ross, 1987), *Dirty Dancing* (Emile Ardolino, 1987), and *Pretty Woman* (Garry Marshall, 1990) also depicted success in terms of performance. Focusing on the ability of characters to project a convincing image of success, such films suggested success and prosperity were achievable for those who did not have immediate access to wealth and power as long as they could act the right way. These "Cinderella" narratives can be read as the epitome of Reaganism; with the right clothes, elocution lessons, vocabulary, and swagger, even the poorest person could project an image of success. A common narrative device in these films is the use of a music-video-like sequence, compressing a character's transition from nobody to somebody in the space of a few minutes and often set to a pop sound track. These montages chart the actor's performance of transformation from awkwardness, ineptness, and ordinariness to poised elegance (*Pretty Woman*), effortless self-confidence (*Secret of My Succe$s*), and graceful agility (*Dirty Dancing*). At the same time, these morality tales were cautious about having their characters going too far in a bid to be successful and losing sight of the authentic self. In such works, excess, including transformation that goes too far, is to be avoided. Modulation within moderation is the ideal. However, a number of transformations in the period dabbled with or even embraced excess as a performance mode.

As is clear from the reviews already cited, the line between performance realism and excess is not straightforwardly determined and it is certainly not fixed. What one reviewer may perceive as honed theatricality necessary for convincing character portrayal, another reviewer might consider over the top. Conceptions of excess are historically determined; for example, Marlon Brando's performances were praised for their dedication to realism in the 1950s but appear theatrical to today's audiences. In popular usage, excess refers to unconventional indulgence and extravagance that exceeds the defined parameters of normative behavior. The term has been theorized by some critics as something more complex, even subversive. Writing in 1977, Kristin Thompson saw excess in film as a disruption to the viewer's engagement. Instead of dismissing excess as a mistake that detracts from narrative unity, Thompson saw excess as something with the potential to break what she called the viewer's "total absorption in the narrative." It invites the viewer to ask questions about the narrative in a way that would not be possible without such disruptions.[43] Excess, Thompson argues, invites a "perceptual play" resulting in heightened viewer awareness of the structures and conventions of film narrative.[44] Building on Thompson's work in 1993, Carole Zucker explores excess specifically in relation to film acting. Challenging critics who dismissed excess as unskilled overacting and citing Jack Nicholson's performance in *The Shining* (Stanley Kubrick, 1980) as a "prototype" for excessive performance, Zucker calls for excess to be recognized as "extreme and courageous . . . a challenging, exploratory style of acting."[45]

While Nicholson's performance in the Stephen King adaptation is now widely celebrated, then-contemporary critics were unsure how to make sense of it. *Variety*, for example, called him "jumpy," noting, "The crazier Nicholson gets, the more idiotic he looks."[46] Pauline Kael disliked the film and his performance, describing the acting as "cramped, slightly robotized," the actor as "borderline funny—which he isn't meant to be" and "tiresome, a mixture of Richard III and the Big Bad Wolf huffing and puffing."[47] His performances of excess are mostly restricted to roles in fantasy or horror films such *The Shining* or *Wolf* (Mike Nichols, 1994), and in roles including The Joker in *Batman* (Tim Burton, 1989) and the devil in *The Witches of Eastwick* (George Miller, 1987). Although the actor's repertoire includes a larger number of more modulated, restrained performances such as in *Reds* (Warren Beatty, 1981), *Terms of Endearment* (James L. Brooks, 1983), *Prizzi's Honor* (John Huston, 1985), *Ironweed* (Hector Babenco, 1987), and *As Good as It Gets* (James L. Brooks, 1997), for which he received Oscar nominations, Nicholson's restrained performances are generally overshadowed by his more exaggerated ones. Out of the twenty-one films the actor made in the 1980s and 1990s, he distinctly employed excess as a performance mode in five (two horror and three fantasy films), suggesting that his approach to performance is more about genre specificity than an idiosyncratic method or style.

Zucker notes that excessive performances result in "an unequivocal cleavage between the act and the actor. And in that gap, there is a declaration of acting as an instrument of reflection, an arena of play and experimentation, and a forum for commentary."[48] Such performances call attention to themselves as performance and invite the viewer to ponder the acting choices. It is not coincidental that three out of the four performances she mentions are from 1980s films, with the other two being Nicolas Cage's "acting set off in quotation marks" in *Vampire's Kiss* (Robert Bierman, 1989) and Crispin Glover's "disturbing" performance in *Twister* (Jan De Bont, 1988). Such performances can be read as speaking to an interest in excess evident in the wider culture during the period.

Cage's performance of a New York executive who believes he is turning into a vampire was not positively received, and critics struggled to make sense of the actor's histrionics. For *Variety*, "Cage's over-the-top performance generates little

FIGURE 35: Nicolas Cage rupturing the diegesis in *Vampire's Kiss*.

sympathy for the character."[49] For Caryn James of the *New York Times*, "the film is dominated and destroyed by Mr. Cage's chaotic, self-indulgent performance."[50] Hal Hinson called it "scorched-earth acting—the most flagrant scenery chewing I've ever seen," and noted that "no amount of description can prepare you for these mad excesses. They have to be seen to be believed."[51] Cage intended his performance to be read as an homage to German Expressionism and expressionist acting in particular, speaking in interviews about his intention to acknowledge the histrionic mode of acting: "It's all about that memory of *Nosferatu*," the actor noted, "that Germanic, expressionistic acting style."[52] While in expressionist acting exterior emotionalism is used to project social unrest and discontent, functioning as a dynamic counterpart to the distorted sets, in *Vampire's Kiss* (and indeed in other excessive performances in the 1980s and 1990s) there are no distorted sets; the acting is not a counterpart to anything but instead stands out by rupturing the diegesis, clashing with the larger film aesthetic and isolating itself, which may explain the negative criticism of Cage's performance (see figure 35).[53] Far from being an isolated example, such excess became a key part of Cage's screen performance repertoire in the 1980s and beyond. Mockery and derision leveled at the actor escalated in the 2000s: he was nominated for six Razzies for nine films made between 2006 and 2011.

Excess as a performance mode also features in three of his most critically acclaimed performances: *Moonstruck* (Norman Jewison, 1987), *Leaving Las Vegas* (Mike Figgis, 1995), and *Face/Off*. In the Mike Figgis-directed drama *Leaving Las Vegas*, Cage plays Ben, an alcoholic screenwriter, who is sacked from his job and moves to the land of casinos with the self-proclaimed intention to drink himself to death. The film opens with him wearing aviator shades and dancing down a supermarket aisle, whistling and pirouetting while filling his trolley with bottles of alcohol. Playing an alcoholic affords the actor countless opportunities for exaggerated gestures, wide-eyed, bulging expressions, and spitting out his words with emphatic, explosive pronouncements. His laughter is shrill and jarring like a bird call. At one point, while under the influence, he bares his teeth and hysterically shouts, "I'm like a prickly pear!" waving his arms around until falling over. Elizabeth Shue's performance as Sera, Ben's love interest and a prostitute, is, by comparison, understated and pained, masking her character's vulnerability with a tough front and offering another example of a bracketing performance. Brian Johnson called the film Cage's "most powerful performance to date."[54] Janet Maslin considered his performance "improbably exhilarating."[55] David Thomson observed that his "way with words and wooing when he's drunk [is] beyond acting," which turned out to be accurate given Cage's later admission that he drank during filming to help him get a better sense of the character's motivations and emotions.[56] The general critical consensus was that Cage's performance in the film was more muted than previous performances. However, rather than solely being indicative of a more restrained acting style (and there are numerous instances of a more subdued Cage as the film progresses), Cage's performance in *Leaving Las Vegas* is carefully tempered and regulated by directorial and editing choices. For example, in one sequence that calls for him to shout and frantically wave his arms around in a drunken stupor, a sound track of classical music plays over the scene, giving it operatic qualities and filtering Cage's performance through music that modulates his extravagant gesticulation.

Giving an unusual amount of attention to acting for a film review, *Sight & Sound*'s Philip Kemp suggests another rationale for why Cage's performance in *Leaving Las Vegas* was successful: "Nicolas Cage was surely made to portray a terminal alcoholic on self-destruct. Deploying a fearsome battery of gulps, twitches and off-the-wall gestures, Cage turns in a performance of . . . nailing physicality. . . . At moments of stress—which are frequent—his whole body goes into spasm, and he even seems able to make his eyeballs pulsate."[57] Kemp sees the role as a perfect fit for Cage's performance repertoire but also suggests that his excessive style, rather than being more toned down or restrained, is more in keeping with the wider narrative focus on alcoholism and addiction.

Excess as an acting mode lends itself well to performances of compulsion and obsession. Performances of drug addiction during the period, such as Robert Downey Jr. in *Less Than Zero* (Marek Kanievska, 1987), Demi Moore in *St. Elmo's Fire* (Joel Schumacher, 1985), and Leonardo DiCaprio in *The Basketball Diaries* (Scott Kalvert, 1995), afford the actors space to indulge in excessive acting methods. In performances of alcoholism by such actors as Jack Nicholson and Meryl Streep in *Ironweed*, Mickey Rourke in *Barfly* (Barbet Schroeder, 1987), Meg Ryan in *When a Man Loves a Woman* (Luis Mandoki, 1994), and Nick Nolte in *Affliction* (Paul Schrader, 1997), the actors depict inebriation by moving between the extremes of explosive outbursts and sluggish, degenerative inertia. Since these performances aim to capture non-normative behaviors, their excessive realization is in keeping with thematic expectations.

While alcoholism and drug addiction have often been the terrain of male actors, women dominate in narratives of crazed obsession, with Glenn Close's "bunny boiler" Alex Forrest in *Fatal Attraction* (Adrian Lyne, 1987) and Kathy Bates's passive-aggressive fan Annie Wilkes in *Misery* (Rob Reiner, 1990) being two prominent examples. Although a number of feminist critics viewed these characters and the actors' performances as misogynistic, fueling negative perceptions of women as irrational, there is a complexity to both performances that distinguishes them from two-dimensional portrayals. Despite three Oscar-nominated performances in films such as *The World According to Garp* (George Roy Hill, 1982), *The Big Chill*, and *The Natural* (Barry Levinson, 1984), Close was still required to test for the role of Alex Forrest. Producer Stanley Jaffe was concerned the actor was too old and too cold to play the "other woman." Adrian Lyne, the director, admitted she was "not obviously erotic" but he was convinced by Close's "mesmerizing" screen test.[58] Close consulted with three psychoanalysts to understand her character's state of mind, which helped to give depth to what could have been a caricature and led to the fourth of five Oscar nominations she would receive during the period. Bates similarly constructed a character biography, deciding with director Rob Reiner that Annie had been molested as a child by her father, thus providing a rationale for her psychosis.[59] Theatrically trained, Bates relied on extensive rehearsal to create her Oscar-winning performance, in contrast to her co-star, acting veteran James Caan, who worked by the principle of "the less I feel I act, the better job I feel I do." Bates apparently used her frustration with such an acting style to inform her character's wrath. However, she also acknowledged that her steps to understand the depths of her character led her to feel "dislocated," pointing to the psychological dangers of transformative performances that move toward excess.[60]

Consistent with the transformative performances discussed earlier, excess calls attention to bodily and cultural boundaries, yet it also offers a direct affront to the existence of those boundaries, testing both the body and the audience with its rejection of realism. As with performance of dual characters, there are spaces where excess sits more comfortably and is less likely to raise objections. Whereas many transformative performances are concerned with striking a balance in a bid to achieve seamless transformations, excess as a performance mode revels in its disproportionality and distinctiveness from the more realist performances around it. Finally, a third performance mode that became popular in the 1980s and 1990s offered a space where both transformative performance and excess often came together and were negotiated and managed via the interplay of actors.

The Ensemble

In the conventional ensemble, screen significance and/or screen time are fairly evenly weighted across the cast, as the actors interact around a central theme or event. There is generally no principal player or single protagonist; all the actors take supporting roles, which perhaps explains why the Academy has struggled with what to do with ensemble acting.[61] The ultimate goal of the ensemble is actors working together for a unified effect, although the various ensemble films of the period achieved their effect very differently, showcasing a diversity of acting styles and methods.

The Brat Pack is probably the ensemble most associated with the 1980s, although who or what was included in the Brat Pack is often debated, and considerations of their work have predominantly emphasized celebrity over acting talent. Journalist David Blum, who first wrote about the Brat Pack in a rather condescending article for *New York Magazine* in 1985, bemoaned the actors' lack of formal training and formal education, which distinguished them from their technically trained predecessors such as Marlon Brando, James Dean, Robert De Niro, and Al Pacino: "Young actors used to spend years at the knee of such respected teachers as Lee Strasberg and Stella Adler," Blum noted. "Today, that step isn't considered so necessary."[62] The article defined the central "Brat Packers"—Emilio Estevez, Judd Nelson, and Rob Lowe—by their excessive partying and flirtatious behavior, sidelining their film outputs, dismissing their acting ability, and altogether ignoring the key female actors often associated with the group: Molly Ringwald, Ally Sheedy, and Demi Moore.

Ensembles were also a prominent feature of Lawrence Kasdan's output during the period; the performances in his films were generally taken more seriously than those of the Brat Pack. The writer-director received three Oscar nominations for Best Screenplay for the ensemble films *The Big Chill, The Accidental Tourist* (1988), and *Grand Canyon* (1991). Glenn Close was nominated for her "supporting" performance in *The Big Chill* while Geena Davis won for *The Accidental Tourist*. Other ensemble films were recognized by the Academy for writing, but acting was largely overlooked. Robert Altman's *The Player* (1992) and *Short Cuts* (1993), John Sayles's *Lone Star* (1996), Quentin Tarantino's *Pulp Fiction* (1994), and Paul Thomas Anderson's *Boogie Nights* (1997) and *Magnolia* (1999) all received Best Screenplay and/or Best Director nominations, but only in the latter film was acting recognized, with a Best Supporting Actor nomination for Tom Cruise. Other examples such as Sayles's *Matewan* (1987), Anderson's *Hard Eight* (1996), and, bookending the period, Robert Altman's *Come Back to the Five and Dime, Jimmy Dean, Jimmy Dean* (1982) and *Cookie's Fortune* (1999) demonstrate that the ensemble was an important output for these writer-directors during the period and show how the ensemble privileges the interplay of actors, seeking to construct a naturalness of interactions that often passes itself off as improvised.

Writing about the ensemble in theater in *Film Technique and Film Acting* (1958), V. I. Pudovkin saw the ensemble as "that general composition which embraces the work of all the actors collaborating in the play."[63] By comparison, he argued that the film ensemble was more determined by the director and editor than it was a product of the actors. Many ensembles in the 1980s and 1990s, however, employ a longer than average shot length to allow the ensemble performance to unfold in front of the camera, with action sometimes continuing off camera but still audible or in deep focus. Of course, actors may still be juxtaposed via careful editing, as is the case with *Magnolia* where not all the central actors interact with each other, but the actors' interactions are the driving force in terms of narrative organization. Through its emphasis on questions of personal and collective identity, the 1980s and 1990s ensemble film provides a rich space for transformative performance. In comparison to ensemble films in the 2000s such as *Babel* (Alejandro González Iñárritu, 2006) and *Crash* (Paul Haggis, 2004), the 1980s and 1990s ensembles are more concerned with the local and personal, rather than global, connections. Many ensemble films from the period focus on notions of self-discovery and individual identity, yet this is done within a communal context whereby multiple personalities engage and interact during the course of the journey.

In *The Breakfast Club* (John Hughes, 1985), five stereotypical high school students who have never met before spend a Saturday together in detention: a "brain" (Anthony Michael Hall), an "athlete" (Emilio Estevez), a "basket case" (Ally Sheedy), a "princess" (Molly Ringwald), and a "criminal" (Judd Nelson). The employment of stereotypes allows the actors to stand out as individuals within the ensemble, and while conflict between them is crucial to the interplay, an overall sense of coherence is achieved with the realization that the vastly different characters have more in common than they initially thought. *The Breakfast Club* achieves this by allowing each actor the opportunity to parade his or her character's stereotype and expose each identity as a constructed front. In an extended twenty-minute sequence toward the end of the film, the camera pans from actor to actor as they reveal their characters' vulnerabilities, gradually letting their guards down and revealing the pressure of maintaining their social roles, for both their parents and their friends. A key sequence shows the five literally and symbolically shaking off the restrictions placed upon them by dancing along to Karla DeVito's "We Are Not Alone." They all emerge liberated and changed. In a subsequent performance montage similar to the Cinderella transformation narratives, Sheedy's Allison morphs from a sullen and disturbed teen with questionable social skills to a sweet, conventional, and decidedly less interesting young woman. With the aid of makeup, a hairbrush, and a flower in her hair, her hostile and closed body language, shifty expression, and monosyllabic mumblings are replaced by a gentle and warm demeanor. While they may not rely on prosthetics or visual effects, these unambiguously moralistic transformations are by no means subtle, but they do depend on the ensemble format to allow them to take shape.

Moments of performative excess are a prominent feature in ensemble films such as *Less Than Zero, St. Elmo's Fire, The Big Chill, Boogie Nights,* and *Magnolia.* In each of these films, excess manifests itself in the actions and mannerisms of at least one central character. Quentin Tarantino employed the ensemble in

Reservoir Dogs (1992), *Pulp Fiction* (1994), and *Jackie Brown* (1997), three films that are clear examples of how transformation and excess are integrated into the ensemble in a narrative format. *Reservoir Dogs* primarily focuses on the interactions among four color-coded criminals, Mr. White (Harvey Keitel), Mr. Orange (Tim Roth), Mr. Blonde (Michael Madsen), and Mr. Pink (Steve Buscemi), and their police hostage (Kirk Baltz) after a heist has gone wrong and they try to ascertain which member of the group gave them away. Roth takes on a dual performance as Mr. Orange and Freddy, an undercover cop trying to convince the group that he can be trusted. In the "Mr. Orange" sequence, Freddy is given "The Commode Story" by an LAPD colleague, Holdaway (Randy Brooks), a scenario to memorize and later perform for the brains behind the operation in order to gain their acceptance. Holdaway's justification to Freddy underscores Tarantino's interest in performance and identity: "Undercover cops gotta be Marlon Brando; to do this job you gotta be a great actor. You gotta be naturalistic. You gotta be naturalistic as hell. Because if you ain't a great actor, you're a bad actor."[64]

Roth performs Freddy performing the four-page script multiple times: first alone while pacing forward and backward in his apartment, then to Holdaway's nodding approval, and finally for Mr. White and others in a nightclub. Roth also performs Freddy in character in a fantasy reconstruction, carrying out the fictionalized commode scenario for the benefit of the film audience. Like the multiple performances discussed earlier in the chapter, the sequence calls attention to performance as a construction, although here it serves an additional function of setting up the framework for the ensemble. The other characters as well as the audience need to be convinced by Roth's rendition in order for the dramatic irony to achieve its maximum effect at the end of the film.

In the ensemble film *Magnolia*, described by Cynthia Fuchs in her review as "a movie about excess that is undeniably excessive," Paul Thomas Anderson also employs excess as both a narrative and performative mode.[65] I have considered elsewhere how Tom Cruise plays out bipolar masculinity as self-help guru Frank T.J. Mackey, and while Cruise's role stands out as particularly excessive, the performance of emotional extremes is evident across the twelve central characters, the majority of whom are defined by their excessive tendencies including love obsession, drug addiction, incest, and misogyny.[66] As with *The Breakfast Club* and *The Big Chill*, *Magnolia* affords the actors at least one scene where their character comes undone and their composed front is called into question. Former child genius and "Quiz Kid" Donnie Smith's (William H. Macy) obsession with a brawny gay barman leads him to a drunken confession of his love. Macy projects Donnie's irrational feelings through nervous stuttering and mumbling that turns into shouted declarations of "I'm sick and in love!" In another declaration of sickness, Linda Partridge (Julianne Moore) shouts expletives at a pharmacist for questioning her prescription; her frantic proclamation "Suck my dick" as she leaves the pharmacy is quite different from the matter-of-fact expletives

FIGURE 36: Layering performative excess in Paul Thomas Anderson's ensemble *Magnolia*.

that punctuate the male dialogue in *Reservoir Dogs*. Molested by her father as a child and now reliant on cocaine to calm her nervous disposition, Melora Walters signals her character's anxiety and paranoia through erratic, breathless panting and spontaneous actions. Cruise performs Mackey's emotional breakdown at his dying father's bedside by hyperventilating, repeatedly shaking his head, and unrestrainedly crying. These are just a few of the numerous scenes of performative excess in *Magnolia* whereby actors hysterically weep or shout as an emotional outlet for their obsessions, marking a turning point for the characters as they allow themselves to express repressed emotion. *Magnolia* manages these numerous examples of excess by framing the narrative as melodrama but also by layering the many performances so that each actor offers a different approach to the presentation of excess (see figure 36).[67]

In a short discussion of ensemble films in 1978, Charles Eidsvik suggested that the characters in the ensemble constitute "an imaginary society" and that "the societies created by film characters are to a great extent extrapolated from real cultures."[68] However, Eidsvik notes that the two key differences between fictional and real cultures are fiction's playfulness and its "rebellion against the real, particularly a rebellion against the everyday."[69] The approach to acting in the 1980s and 1990s taken in this chapter is in line with Eidsvik's argument. The ensembles function as an imaginary society, whereby the culture's excesses are either given space for expression or carefully managed to avoid prolonged disruption. While the 1980s and 1990s ensembles were diverse in style, narrative, and performance, in each film great steps were taken to achieve a coherency of interactions. For *The Big Chill*, one of the defining ensembles of the 1980s, Lawrence Kasdan rehearsed the actors for four weeks to ensure their interactions were as natural as possible. Kevin Kline said the rehearsals helped to show there was "something in the body language of these eight people that gave a sense of physical comfort with one another. It's hard to act that. It kind of happened."[70]

Of course, not all ensembles were looking to achieve a sense of comfort. For "indie" directors such as Paul Thomas Anderson, Wes Anderson, Ethan and Joel Coen, and Todd Solondz, the ensemble is a device used to bring together eccentric, idiosyncratic, and sometimes perverse characters who become even more eccentric and perverse in their interactions. Inverting the idea of having no principal players, Anderson's *Boogie Nights* and *Magnolia* consist of a suite of stars and popular actors.[71] Actors were cast against type and the films reintroduced actors from previous decades to a new generation not familiar with them the first time around, such as Burt Reynolds in *Boogie Nights* and Bill Murray in *Rushmore* (Wes Anderson, 1988). The formation of indie ensembles also took place across a given director's films, with directors frequently collaborating with the same actors in multiple projects. In a number of these ensembles, deadpan, emotionless styles of acting are central to the character-driven narratives and actors are afforded a degree of flexibility in the use of improvisational and semi-improvisational techniques.[72]

With its character- and actor-driven narratives, the 1980s and 1990s ensemble film presents itself as the antithesis of the blockbuster, the action film, and the high-concept film. It offers an example of the synergy of actors, an overriding concept of the film industry during this time, which was evident in mainstream blockbusters and marginal indies alike. With the high-concept film, each aspect of the filmmaking process is dependent upon synergistic relationships and collaboration. Foregrounding the synergistic byplay and interplay of actors and acting, the ensemble films typically comprise different character types that play off each other in order to produce a cohesive overall effect. Each actor has a particular role to play, converging around the central themes. While each role in the ensemble is distinct and actors focus on each character's individual anxieties and identities, they do so by emphasizing their place in the group and wider social community.

The examples of transformation, excess, and the ensemble are all preoccupied by notions of coherence and balance: striking it, upsetting it, attaining it, losing sight of it, and regaining it. Transformative performances seek to maintain coherence during and after any change; excess questions the boundaries of coherence and also challenges expectations about realism; and the ensemble is concerned with maintaining and projecting a coherent collective identity. Collectively, these three modes reveal a period that encompassed much more than the star-led blockbusters or the spectacle-driven high-concept films in which actors recycled characters and performance styles in franchises, sequels, and formulaic narratives. Excess, transformation, and the ensemble, as prevalent modes of acting through the 1980s and 1990s, betray the late capitalist conservatism of the period to reveal an altogether more complex relationship between performance, culture, and an ever-evolving film industry.

6

THE MODERN ENTERTAINMENT MARKETPLACE, 2000–PRESENT

Cynthia Baron

Developments in the American entertainment industry since 2000 have increasingly required professionals to demonstrate their ability to create cogent expressions of compelling human emotions, whether working as actors in Hollywood blockbusters or in niche-market dramas, or as voice talent, motion-capture performers, animators, or videogame designers. Screen performances have always been "hybrids of human agency and technological interventions."[1] Yet today, the multidimensional nature of producing screen performances makes the intersection between actors and technology an especially important area of inquiry.

Since 2000, American films have made expanded use of CGI and performance-capture, which collects data on movement and facial expression. In animated films, "three-dimensional design, virtual camerawork, fabricated cinematic lighting," and vocal performances lead CGA characterizations to be seen as screen performances.[2] One finds "high-concept extravaganzas," often featuring high-definition digital technology, alongside independent "quirky, small-scale dramas" that are sometimes shot on digital video.[3] Also since 2000, screen performances have increasingly been presented in new ways, as theaters offer more immersive 3D adventures, and DVDs and digital television make home viewing a cinematic experience. An array of performances has become available at online sites, starting with Metacafe in 2003, Vimeo in 2004, and YouTube in 2005, and continuing with delivery and programming by Netflix and other video-on-demand providers.

In the current era, "differences between the media of movies, television, and computers are rapidly diminishing";[4] distinctions between film spectator, television viewer, videogame player, and computer user are blurring.[5] Stephen Keane observes that the increasing convergence of film and new media "has simultaneously increased the availability of film and turned it into part of a data stream where images become information that is simply passing through." He explains: while "still concentrated in cinemas and at home, film has also become byte-sized, convenient, and disposable. From watching trailers on the Internet to accessing cinema times on your mobile phone . . . film has also become part of the flow, the previously dominant push [of film and television] and pull [of the Internet] reconfigured into something more approaching scatter and choose."[6] These developments have required professionals charged with creating screen performances to hone their abilities to get and keep audience attention—by increasing their capabilities to cogently convey emotionally engaging human experiences and effectively communicate with people encountering their work in movie theaters and home theater environments, and on laptops, gaming consoles, and smart phones.

The growing convergence between film and new media has involved "a two-way process in which the new benefits from existing modes of information and representation, and the old is updated in such a way as to secure future relevance." Cinematic influences on new forms are quite visible. For example, one finds the use of mobile cameras in first- and third-person videogames. Slow motion, lens flare, motion blur, and shadows add a cinematic feel to the increasingly immersive experience provided by 3D environments presented in continuous takes. Contemporary videogames also often feature "title sequences, closing credits, 'realistic' sound effects, and an overall musical soundtrack that provides narrative- and character-based themes [and serves to] punctuate the in-game action."[7]

Perhaps less noticed but equally significant is that even in the world of videogames, the continuing drive for greater realism, and thus the greater attraction for players, has included development of more sophisticated screen performances. The labor and skill of voice talent have given personality to videogame characters. Building on that practice, since 2000 "videogames have increasingly come to make use of familiar actors, whether Michael Madsen and Michelle Rodriquez in *Driv3r* (2004) or original cast members as in EA Games' *James Bond 007: Everything or Nothing* (2004) and *The Godfather* (2006)."[8] In other words, actors' work has not been replaced by digital technology. Instead, actors' training and skill has made it possible for them to craft screen performances that are an increasingly important part of even videogames.

For contemporary screen actors, drawing on established methods to work effectively in new settings has been central to their success in ensuring that "the old is updated in such a way as to secure future relevance."[9] To offer some insights into developments in acting since 2000, this discussion focuses on ways that film actors are meeting challenges presented by technology-intensive workplaces, spectacle-driven narratives, and the need to craft meaningful performances that engage audiences across a variety of delivery platforms. It describes acting principles that today's actors and digital artists use to communicate with audiences. Examining developments behind the silver screen, my discussion unpacks the paradox that the increasing "computerization of culture"[10] has not only made experienced actors more valuable; it has radically expanded screen professionals' reliance on the acting principles that facilitate embodied expression of thought and feeling, and has increased the influence that screen actors' performances have on the movements, gestures, and expressions people use in contemporary daily life.

There has been heightened professional attention in the twenty-first century to methods for creating physical and vocal expressions that coordinate effectively with filmic elements. That focus is reflected in the growth of training programs and manuals designed for screen acting. It is signaled by the industry's consensus that animators, voice talent, and performance-capture actors create characterizations. It is also highlighted and circulated in the steady stream of interviews with actors who create performances for action-packed blockbusters *and* the era's character- and star-driven Indiewood films produced by specialty divisions such as Sony Pictures Classics, Fox Searchlight, and Paramount Classics.[11]

Actors who work on different types of films are required to continually expand their skills. To collaborate effectively on productions that require performances to integrate into cinematic spectacles, actors craft performances that offer compressed but intense presentation of human emotion, sometimes employing a "bizarrely stressed acting" style that slips "back and forth between low-key naturalism and exaggerated theatricalism."[12] The need to create ensemble performances in niche-market dramas valued for nuanced characterizations requires actors to develop and execute performance choices that interface effectively with the gestures and expressions of the other actors. In blockbuster spectacles or indie dramas, actors depend on acting principles to develop characterizations, and on their expertise in making adjustments for film. Those adjustments make it possible, for example, to create physical and vocal expressions that are coherent when shots are edited together, and that address the specific demands of long, medium, and close shots. Screen actors also develop the expertise to project emotion through physical expression before delivering their lines; this adjustment allows them to effectively communicate the character's thoughts and feelings even when editors cut "away from a speaker just before she has finished speaking in order for [audiences] to see the responder just before she starts to speak."[13]

Landmark events, such as Andy Serkis's MTV Award for Best Virtual Performance for his portrayal of Gollum in *The Lord of the Rings: The Two Towers* (Peter Jackson, 2002), and Marlon Brando's posthumous performance in *Superman Returns* (Bryan Singer, 2006), ostensibly suggest that the current era is marked by "a crisis in the conception of acting."[14] However, as Pamela Robertson Wojcik points out, recent developments in "digital imaging or animation or voice acting [actually] bring to the fore aspects of film acting that need to be more fully taken into account." Observing that screen performance is "a complex and layered process of audiovisual representation," Wojcik notes that scholars "need to consider actor labor as existing within, for, and through mediation," because actors and other professionals charged with creating screen performances are increasingly working with the challenges and opportunities arising, for instance, from the fact that a "fissure between sound and image and the subsequent manipulation of both sound and image, together and apart, is constitutive of film acting."[15]

Looking at contemporary developments from the perspective of a production person, actor and acting teacher Ed Hooks explains that digital technology has not created a crisis in the conception or practice of acting. Instead, he sees the digital age as "an exciting time to be an actor" because it has led a "subculture" of actors, directors, writers, and producers to create performances for global audiences, using digital technology to produce and deliver material.[16] Actor Andy Serkis explains that it's "a very exciting time for actors" because CG characters do not replace them, but instead generate more employment and craft opportunities; he notes that "more actor hours were spent working on Gollum than on any conventional screen character" in *The Lord of the Rings* trilogy.[17]

Films' increasing use of CG characters also leads to additional creative opportunities for actors. Based on changes in technology that have already taken place, Serkis predicts that films will not only make more use of performance-capture, but also that "the technology will become less and less invasive, allowing acting to retain its purity."[18] For actors, that is all good news. As Serkis explains, performance-capture not only demands "pure, truthful acting—no costume, no set, no makeup—but it [also] offers the potential of an infinite range of characters that can be literally mapped onto an actor's interpretation of a role."[19] Thus, the current era rewards actors who embrace the challenge of working in different production settings and on different types of films. Clarifying why the current era provides opportunities for actors to practice and expand their craft, Stanislavsky scholar and acting teacher Sharon Marie Carnicke observes: "Acting is—at base—a discrete art form, which has—over the centuries—variously adapted to the changing technologies that have framed and presented actors' work to audiences, whether those frames be proscenium arches, camera lenses, or computer screens."[20]

Salient Developments since 2000

Screen performances in American cinema since 2000 exemplify the collaborative and complex process of filmmaking. As in other periods, acting choices are keyed to the aesthetic and material demands of individual films. The emphasis of actor training programs and the focus of acting methods reflect the priorities of industry trends and practices. However, by responding to contemporary demands, many of the professionals responsible for the creation of screen performances are exploring new ground. Audience expectations, technological developments, and the desire for economic and critical success by entertainment companies large and small have made the production of screen performances increasingly dependent on a wide range of skilled professionals who are conversant in principles central to the craft of acting.

A glance at the top-grossing films since 2000 reveals the high degree of collaboration between performers and special effects professionals. It also shows that most audiences now encounter screen performances created and presented through high levels of digital-cinematic mediation. The period began with the costume- and makeup-intensive *How the Grinch Stole Christmas* (Ron Howard, 2000) topping the box office. The following year, *Harry Potter and the Sorcerer's Stone* (Chris Columbus, 2001), the first film in the franchise, had the highest gross. In 2002, Sam Raimi and Tobey Maguire got the *Spider-Man* franchise off to a strong start. In 2003, the final piece of Peter Jackson's trilogy, *The Lord of the Rings: The Return of the King*, had the highest gross. *Shrek 2* (Andrew Adamson, Kelly Asbury, Conrad Vernon, 2004) topped the box office the following year. George Lucas's *Star Wars: Episode III: Revenge of the Sith* completed the series and had the highest gross of all films in 2005. *Pirates of the Caribbean: Dead Man's Chest* (Gore Verbinski, 2006), the second film in the franchise, led the field in 2006. Sam Raimi's *Spider-Man 3* had the highest gross in 2007. Christopher Nolan's *The Dark Knight*, starring Christian Bale and Heath Ledger, topped the box office in 2008. James Cameron's 3D computer-animated feature *Avatar* led the box office in 2009. The following year, *Toy Story 3* (Lee Unkrich, 2010) had the highest gross. *Harry Potter and the Deathly Hallows: Part 2* (David Yates, 2011) topped the box office the following year. In 2012, *The Avengers* (Joss Whedon, 2012), featuring a collection of Marvel Entertainment characters, led the field. The following year, *The Hunger Games: Catching Fire* (Francis Lawrence, 2013), the second film in the franchise, secured the top box office position.

The massive scope and scale of these productions have changed industry norms. Whereas actors, directors, and screenwriters have always needed to understand the dramatic principles that make actors' observed behaviors emotionally engaging for audiences, it is now widely accepted that professionals working in 2D and CG animation, mechanical and CG special effects, and motion- and performance-capture must also have a working knowledge of acting principles. That shift is significant. For example, animators create performances that fall along a spectrum that includes what animation historians refer to as figurative performances (portrayal of simple character types) and embodied performances (portrayal of complex, unique characters).[21] However, today's character-driven computer animated films are crafted by professionals who conceive and build screen performances according to basic acting principles, so that the performances reveal the characters' given circumstances, objectives, and series of actions to achieve their objectives.[22] Animators' attention to character development and the physical expression of characters' objectives and actions has been integral to the increasing number of CG-animated films produced since the Motion Picture Academy gave the first Oscar for Best Animated Feature in 2001.

Special interest in screen performances has also informed filmmakers' experiments with digital video. Here, "authentic" performances in low- or no-budget films are designed to offer an alternative to the labor-intensive performances in Hollywood blockbusters and the "quality" ensemble performances associated with independent cinema. For example, building on the Dogme 95 movement that started in the late 1990s, mumblecore films such as *The Puffy Chair* (Jay Duplass, 2005) and *Hannah Takes the Stairs* (Joe Swanberg, 2007) present audiences with ostensibly improvised performances shot on location. This line of work will continue, but the influence of the films' unpolished performances has been curtailed by developments in the independent sector; Thomas Schatz points out that by 2008, "independent films had to be more blatantly 'commercial'—and thus more costly—for any real hope of success in a marketplace ruled by tentpole blockbusters and bloated star vehicles."[23]

However, the digital video aesthetic that combines unpolished performances with static or shaky handheld camerawork has also shaped the viral videos that have become part of the entertainment landscape since 2000. Named the Invention of the Year in 2006 by *Time* magazine, "YouTube has turned the short, homemade video into an art form in and of itself, something to be created and collected."[24] The rise of homemade videos signaled an important shift, in that watching *and* creating screen performances came to be seen as everyday activities. Just as videotapes and DVDs "tamed and domesticated"[25] cinema by transforming the "unapproachable medium that hovered in the distance on the silver screen [into] a household object, intimately and infinitely subject of manipulation in the private sphere,"[26] changes in media technology tamed and domesticated screen performance—to the point that the labor and skill behind screen performances became more visible. As talent agent and entertainment attorney Matt Sugarman points out, the extremely ephemeral fame of YouTube celebrities has shown that while "the freshness of the untrained individual can be refreshing at first, in order to translate to long-term success they need training and time."[27]

Equally important, although "most of the content on YouTube originally fea-tured individual personal videos, media conglomerates [began] to take more and more advantage of this rapidly growing distribution site throughout the 2000s, making both clips of their films and often entire films easily available."[28] The dominance of mainstream product (and performances) on YouTube and other video-on-demand portals was amplified by the "FCC-mandated switchover of commercial television to digital standards" in 2009.[29] The change increased conglomerates' revenue by facilitating the means for ensuring that "the same branded content played out across multiple media."[30] Dana Polan explains: "Dig-ital television gave greater possibilities for home computers to be linked to the television set [thus providing] a new and stronger, more tempting home plat-form for home distribution."[31] With the arrival of digital television, the DVD business lost ground to video-on-demand, which was "shaping up to be the pre-ferred mode for high revenue-generating film distribution on television."[32] Thus, while YouTube and other "amateur" screen performances represent an important development, since 2000 the films that audiences most often encounter continue to depend on the extensive training and experience of professionals charged with creating screen performances.

At the same time, with the arrival of next-generation or super-console games such as Sega Dreamcast in 1999, Sony's PlayStation 2 in 2000, Microsoft's Xbox in 2000, and Nintendo GameCube in 2001, videogame play has become a form of performance that ostensibly competes with performances on the silver screen for audience attention. Today's gamers are "deeply involved in a *physically* active performance" that involves "a pleasure of accessing, witnessing, and perform-ing [in] technologically mediated environments."[33] Contemporary videogames offer "tactile and bodily participation for a growing culture of gamers; *Halo*, released in 2001, promoted its dramatic format of 'first-person shooters'; *Guitar Hero*, released in 2005, allowed players to physically simulate musical perfor-mances; and Wii, released in 2006, introduced 3D interaction between player and screen."[34] By 2011, "the gaming industry for the first time surpassed the film industry in total revenue."[35] As with homemade videos, the growing interest in performing as a videogame player reflects the emerging view of performance as part of everyday life.

It also reflects media conglomerates' success in "extending the commercial range of any particular film or entertainment product."[36] *Newsweek* described 2003 as "The Year of *The Matrix*," after the Wachowskis' *The Matrix Reloaded* and *The Matrix Revolutions* were accompanied by the release of the videogame *Enter the Matrix* and the multi-director piece *The Animatrix*. The "transme-dia extensions" generated revenue by giving fans ways to "fully comprehend the story and appreciate the artistry at work in the *Matrix* saga."[37] However, they also increased the influence that the film actors' performances had on the aesthetic choices made by the animators and videogame designers, and the "performances" of the videogame players. It is widely recognized that block-buster "films regularly translate to commercially successful games," with videogames now based on films such as *"Spider-Man 2, The Incredibles, Harry Potter and the Prisoner of Azkaban, Shrek 2*, and *The Lord of the Rings: The Return of the King.*"[38] Less conspicuously, these videogames and others have created more employment opportunities for actors (voice talent), and more occasions in which actors' performances in films have provided the model for other types of screen performances.

Writing in the 1930s, Prague School theorist Jan Mukařovský observed that while the "influence of acting" on gestures in everyday life had always come from the stage, the influence now occurred "above all through the agency of the film."[39] He explained: "Before our very eyes in the space of a few years this influence has manifested itself [in movements and gestures ranging] from ambulatory gait to the most detailed motions such as opening a powder box or the play of facial muscles."[40] The influence of screen performance is especially powerful today, as media convergence increases, rather than diminishes, the effect that film actors' performances have on the gestures and expressions found in animated films, videogames, and everyday life.

Developments in Actor Training

In the current era, screen professionals see Stanislavsky's system as the foundation for the craft of acting; even books on acting for animation explain that "Stanislavski, of course, is the person who [has had] the greatest influence over acting and performance on stage and screen for the last 100 years or so."[41] Some forms of the American Method also continue to influence contemporary actor training. Sanford Meisner's emphasis on the vital connection between actors in a scene forms the basis for actor training at the Neighborhood Playhouse in New York. It is also integral to actor training programs at universities, conservatories, and professional workshops. Stella Adler's focus on "the actor's commitment to the [character's] circumstances [and the need for] research into the world of the text" informs the training program at the Stella Adler Academy of Acting and Theater in Los Angeles.[42] Adler's attention to script analysis and her understanding that "the physical embodiment of [emotion]—gestures, voice, animation—can be the most effective pathway to feeling" have made her approach a primary vehicle for disseminating Stanislavsky's views.[43] The priorities of her approach have also made the Adler technique foundational knowledge for screen actors. By comparison, the influence of Lee Strasberg and the Actors Studio has waned; training affiliated with the Actors Studio is now offered by Pace University in New York, while the Actors Studio and Actors Studio West serve primarily as places for members, who are well-established actors, to work on scenes.

Preparing individuals to work in "the rapidly evolving landscape of contemporary performance practice" is a primary emphasis of today's actor training programs; for example, the California Institute of the Arts near Los Angeles explains that their "Acting Program has moved beyond the training structures used for preparing actors for repertory theater companies." Cal Arts recognizes that "the actor of the 21st century needs to be highly versatile, able to work in any number of forms, styles and settings. This actor must be technologically literate, have a strong command of body, voice and speech, and be equally adept in theater, film, television, and emerging media."[44]

Today's actors develop foundational knowledge at institutions that include the prestigious programs at Juilliard, Yale, and New York University, and the professional programs at the American Conservatory Theater in San Francisco, the Goodman Theater in Chicago, and the Academy of Dramatic Arts in New York.[45] Actor training is offered by universities across the country. There are also scores of private vendors that have classes for beginning, intermediate, and experienced actors. For example, the New York Film Academy has workshops and degree programs in acting; offerings in Los Angeles include courses at The Actors Workshop, Hollywood Actor's Studio, and David Kagen's School of Film Acting. Acting teachers and coaches, sometimes affiliated with casting companies, offer workshops for actors "who have theatrical experience and are looking to prepare themselves for challenges specific to on-camera work."[46]

The cottage industry that has developed to help actors train for work in film and television generates revenue by playing on people's dreams of being stars. However, it also reflects the acting profession's consensus that screen performance requires actors to master foundational knowledge and various additional techniques. When Tony Barr's *Acting for the Camera* (1986) and Michael Caine's *Acting in Film* (1990) were published, they had little competition. Now the many books about the adjustments required for screen performance include Robert Benedetti's *Action! Professional Acting for Film and Television* (2006), Mel Churcher's *Acting for Film: Truth 24 Times a Second* (2003), Cathy Hasse's *Acting for Film* (2003), and Patrick Tucker's *Secrets of Screen Acting* (2003).

Like contemporary training programs, these manuals emphasize script analysis and rehearsal that enhances embodied performance. They acknowledge that "a move, a way of standing, a gesture, a tone of voice, a dialect, are more than just external refinement; they are often the emotional key to a scene or even to an entire role."[47] That focus is quite different from the priority given to emotion and personal associations in Strasberg's Method, which proposed that "if an actor was really *feeling* inside, all the edges [would] take care of themselves."[48]

Training programs now emphasize that characters' emotions, drives, and psychological complexes become visible only in the qualitative details of actors' observable actions. That perspective has actually been integral to many acting approaches. Bertolt Brecht "recognized that physical positioning on stage, vocal intonations, movements, gestures, and so on, are not mere externals, but that *staging carries meaning.*"[49] In the 1940s, Joan Littlewood and Ewan MacColl's Theater Workshop combined Stanislavskian techniques "to create the inner truth of the characters" and the work of Rudolf Laban "to structure the expressive techniques of performance."[50] Theater Workshop actors developed "the rhythmic patterns" of their performances in theater games and improvisations that allowed actors to test a range of physical and vocal expressions distinguished by their different emphasis in time, weight, direction, and flow.[51] Laban's landmark work, *The Mastery of Movement on the Stage* (1950), which emerged from his collaboration with the Theater Workshop, was the first comprehensive guide to physical characterization for actors.

The physical dimensions of performance have also been emphasized by Jacques Lecoq, whose work combines mime, circus, pantomime, spoken theater, and dance. Lecoq explains that "the great social and psychological upheavals of 1968" created renewed interest in the actor's physical expression.[52] Director Julie Taymor, who studied at Lecoq's mime school, explains that attention to the physical dimension of performance is crucial for contemporary actors. Noting that "the body is a complete resource you can use to express anything, including emotions," Taymor clarifies that for actors "it's not about 'acting' sad" but instead about staying focused on "What is it about 'sad' that makes the body hard or soft? What rhythm does 'sadness' have?"[53]

Movement courses are now a regular part of actor training. They complement courses that highlight Adler's focus on research and script analysis or Meisner's concern with engaged interaction between actors. Movement courses, especially ones grounded in Laban's work, are "a perfect complement" to Stanislavsky's system.[54] For example, actors' use of Laban principles enhances preparation based on Stanislavsky's Method of Physical Actions, which identifies the fact that "emotional life may sometimes be more easily aroused and fixed for performance through work on the physical life of the role, rather than through inner work."[55]

Laban's approach directs actors' attention to "actual movement, rather than its completed result."[56] It reminds actors that the meaning of gestures and expressions is not disclosed by a single frame, but instead by the direction of their movements, the speed of their movements, and the degree of resistance and control in their movements. Laban's approach helps actors think about the spatial design and qualitative energy in their movements. It suggests ways for actors to convey their characters' temperaments, objectives, and responses through the shifting spatial, temporal, weight, and flow qualities carefully crafted into their performances.

To convey characters' thoughts or feelings at any given moment, actors can choose to move in a direct or more flexible fashion, deliver a line in a sudden or sustained way, use gestures that are light or strong/weighted, and physical/vocal expressions that are observably bound or free-flowing. Describing the physical dimension of vocal expression, Laban expert Jean Newlove points out: "Try saying the words 'Yes' and 'No' with thrusting. The voice will be strong, sudden, and direct [and] whatever the bodily movements, the meaning will be quite clear. Here is someone who has made up their mind and is quite emphatic about their decision." Continuing, Newlove explains: "Try a similar exercise with floating. Could you honestly say that this person appears just as emphatic? Does the essence of floating lend itself to such clear and unequivocal decisions?"[57]

The system developed by Rudolf Laban has been useful for screen actors because it provides a comprehensive way to explore and describe the "impelling inner action" that colors the movement an actor performs to convey a character's intention and disposition.[58] Its systematic terminology for describing and classifying movement helps actors plan "exact and minute combinations of space, time, and energy" for their performances.[59] When combined with script analysis that illuminates characters' given circumstances, objectives, and interlocking actions and counteractions, Laban's simple but elegant framework for exploring the spatial, temporal, weight, and flow dimensions of physical and vocal expression helps actors develop what Stanislavsky referred to as the *score of actions* for individual scenes and productions as a whole. Once established by an actor, the score makes it possible to work effectively even when scenes are shot out of sequence. A score of actions also helps screen performers craft coherent and evocative performances composed of identifiable goal-directed actions that (a) distinguish each character, (b) fit coherently and meaningfully with actions performed earlier or later in the narrative, and (c) give individual and meaningful expression to recognizable social gestures.

Acting Principles behind Performances in CG-Animated Films

Acting principles and strategies for creating evocative screen performances have become increasingly important to animators as their industry transitions from traditional to computer-generated animation. CGA became the norm between 1995, when the first CGA feature *Toy Story* (John Lasseter) was released, and 2004, when Disney produced its last traditional animation feature *Home on the Range* (Will Finn and John Sanford). Also that year, in which *Shrek 2* was the top-grossing film, *The Polar Express* (Robert Zemeckis) became the first CGA feature to use performance-capture to create characters, and *The Incredibles* (Brad Bird) would go on to win the Oscar for Best Animated Feature. With CG animation less "geometric in its forms and more fluid and cinematic in terms of action and environments," audiences are presented with what seem to be best described as screen performances.[60]

Today's consensus that "animation is acting" has led animators to import concepts and methods from the craft of acting.[61] For example, *Action! Acting*

Lessons for CG Animators (2009) by John and Kristin Kundert-Gibbs has chapters on "Stanislavski's System," "Commedia dell'Arte," "Bioenergetics," "Using the Work of Michael Chekhov in Animation," "Laban Effort Analysis," and "Alba Emoting." Introducing the need to explore acting strategies, the authors explain that as "an animator, you are basically doing the job of an actor [because you] are creating a living, breathing character that tells a story, shares an experience, and moves an audience."[62] Echoing that point, in *Thinking Animation: Bridging the Gap Between 2D and CG* (2007), Angie Jones and Jamie Oliff explain: "We are character animators [and animated] characters emote, just like live actors."[63]

Jones and Oliff discuss the value of developing animated screen performances using Laban's insights into the spatial, temporal, weight, and flow dimensions of physical and vocal expression and Michael Chekhov's work related to psychological gesture. Reiterating points Ed Hooks makes in his books and acting workshops for animators, Jones and Oliff encourage readers to study Charlie Chaplin's films to see how performances reveal character. They also highlight the ideas of director Peter Brook, who found that in performances, actors should establish and maintain "a tension line between themselves [and their character], a tension line between [themselves and the] other actors, a tension line between themselves and the audience."[64] Acknowledging Hooks's influence, Jones and Oliff highlight the fact that his books and workshops have "made a bridge between the tools actors use" and the methods used by "an animator practicing acting."[65]

Hooks explains that *Acting for Animators* (2011) is designed to assist animators in creating "characters that think and have emotions and play theatrical actions" that reveal characters' objectives as they overcome obstacles arising from situations, other characters, or characters' internal conflicts (see figure 37).[66] To that end, he builds on work by Stanislavsky, Peter Brook, and David Mamet to offer "seven essential acting principles":

1 Thinking tends to lead to conclusions, and emotion tends to lead to action. 2 We humans empathize only with emotion. Your job as a character animator is to create in the audience a sense of empathy with your character. 3 Theatrical reality is not the same thing as regular reality [because theatrical reality necessarily has conflict between characters who play actions in pursuit of objectives while overcoming obstacles]. 4 Acting is doing; acting is also reacting. 5 Your character should play an action until something happens to make him play a different action. 6 Scenes begin in the middle, not at the beginning. 7 A scene is a negotiation [that necessarily involves ways for the characters to win or lose].[67]

Hooks explains that these principles should shape animators' conception of their characters and inform their efforts to give physical expression to their characters' temperaments, circumstances, objectives, and interlocking dramatic

FIGURE 37: Front cover of *Acting for Animators*. The transition to CG animation has increased animators' use of acting principles to create screen performances. Used by permission of Routledge and Ed Hooks.

actions. Highlighting that what characters say is less important than the meaning underlying the dialogue, Hooks observes that especially for animators, acting actually "has very little to do with dialogue." Thus, rather than encourage animators to study the contributions, for example, that Tom Hanks and Tim Allen have made to the *Toy Story* films or that Mike Meyers, Eddie Murphy, and Cameron Diaz have made to the *Shrek* franchise, Hooks emphasizes the need for animators to explore their "character's thoughts, emotions and intentions." He points out that when working with prerecorded dialogue, animators must continually "search for the internal impulse" suggested by the changing qualities in actors' vocal choices.[68]

Hooks's emphasis on the physical dimensions of the performances that animators create reflects the era's increased attention to acting methods that facilitate effective communication of characters' thoughts and feelings. It also reflects values central to animators. As Brad Bird, director of *The Incredibles* and *Ratatouille* (2007), explains, Hooks has been able to establish a bridge between the worlds of acting and animation because he "knows that in the very best animated films movement defines character."[69] That principle becomes especially evident when one considers the degree to which the physical gestures and expressions in animated films are a source of information about characters' inner experiences.

Wall-E (Andrew Stanton, 2008) offers a means for exploring that phenomenon, because in contrast to CGA films that rely on stars' vocal performances, voice artist Elissa Knight and sound guru Ben Burtt did the voice work for the main characters in *Wall-E*. The film's framing, editing, lighting design, and so on contribute to audience interpretations, and yet its cinematic strategies are often designed to feature the gestures and expressions the animators have created for the characters. The film reveals that in each instance, like "actors in the theater or live-action film," the animators have developed the characters "from a script, considering the narrative implications of the role [to determine] the character's design, the range [and type] of movement [and] predominant motivation [that] inevitably [informs the character's] modes of expression and behavior."[70] With acting principles behind screen performances in CG-animated films, the qualities designed into the characters' actions in *Wall-E* are easily illuminated using Laban's terms.

The qualities that the animators have crafted into the movements communicate the central characters' development over the course of the narrative. As in live-action films, character arc in *Wall-E* is conveyed by the observable changes in the qualities of the characters' gestures. For example, low-tech Wall-E starts as a character who is leading a pointless existence, collecting junk and building skyscrapers out of trash. The aimlessness of his daily routine is suggested by the light, sudden, indirect quality of his gestures when, for instance, he flicks a bra into his lunch box. Yet the qualities in his movements are very different once the film reaches its conclusion. Having transformed the characters and situation around him, Wall-E comes into his own. In the final moments of the film, after he has been reassembled by Eve and his memory reactivated by Eve's kiss, the light but focused qualities in his movements show that Wall-E feels a confirmed sense of purpose: he quickly closes his hand around Eve's, he punches out the word "E-Vah" as his eyebrows shoot up, and he then gazes directly and intently at Eve as he continues to hold her hand.

In Eve's case, the strong, direct qualities in her actions early in the film reveal that she is agenda-driven. When she flies, she presses through the air like a bullet. When she encounters Wall-E and other perceived threats, she thrusts out her arm to fire on them. The bound quality of Eve's rigidly vertical stance, combined with the direct quality of the beam she emits as she efficiently searches for life on the trashed planet, suggests that Eve starts off with a fixed and unexamined objective. In the closing scenes, the emotional distance Eve has traveled by the end of the story is communicated by the fact that her gestures now feature entirely different qualities. When she makes her final attempt to restore Wall-E's memory, she gently reaches out and floats lightly next to him as she softly touches her face to his. Then, when it appears he is not going to respond, she slowly turns away in a twisting movement. The wringing quality in Eve's gesture of sorrow shows that her interactions with Wall-E have changed her motivations.

Between the opening and closing scenes, *Wall-E* uses the simple, conventional gesture of holding hands to convey the characters' transformations. Both Wall-E and Eve learn about the gesture of handholding by watching a scene between Cornelius (Michael Crawford) and Irene (Marianne McAndrew) in *Hello, Dolly!* (Gene Kelly, 1969). The first time Eve watches the scene, she has no interest in the gesture. However, the second time she watches it, her movements are infused with the gentle qualities that Wall-E had tried to emulate when he watched the scene between Cornelius and Irene early in the film. The contrast between Eve's

FIGURE 38: Eve clasping hands together in *Wall-E*. Animators use changes in recognizable social gestures to convey the characters' thoughts, values, and feelings.

initial uninterest in the gesture of handholding, and her thorough engagement with it the second time she watches the scene, gives audiences a clear sense of Eve's development. The pivotal scenes in *Wall-E* that center on holding hands are a reminder that animators (and actors) use familiar social gestures to give audiences points of reference. When audiences see which conventional gestures are used and how they are performed, they make inferences about characters' evolving dispositions and motivations (see figure 38).

With acting principles informing animators' choices, the observable qualities in Wall-E's and Eve's gestures in their interactions with emblematic objects, most particularly the plant Wall-E discovers in the abandoned icebox, also convey character. When Wall-E discovers the plant, he taps on the icebox door, then rapidly cuts through it and pulls it aside. However, the qualities in his gestures change completely when he sees the plant. His hands slowly float down to it and then gently scoop it up so that it is surrounded by a handful of soil. The animators have made the way he cradles the plant in his hands as he carries it to the old leather boot that will serve as its pot differ sharply from the quick, irregular rhythm in his movements when audiences first saw him dealing with the trash around him.

The huge contrast between the sudden, jerky qualities in Wall-E's routine gestures early in the film and the soft, sustained qualities in his movements when he encounters the plant signals that Wall-E's discovery changes not only him but the story as well. With the plant's importance established, the qualities in characters' gestures when they interact with the plant communicate key information about their identities: the light, sustained, curving qualities in Wall-E's gestures when he first carries the plant, versus the strong, sudden, linear quality in the beam that shoots out of Eve's body when she sees the plant, give audiences observable evidence about the opposing identities and ideological positions at the heart of the narrative's conflict. Yet rather than present audiences with a simple narrative, the animators convey Eve's complexity by crafting a contrast between the strong, sudden, direct qualities in her initial response to the plant and the soft, sustained, light qualities in the way she later gives the plant to Wall-E. In other words, the animators convey Eve's character development, which brings her motivations in line with Wall-E's, through the physical characterizations.

The demands and opportunities of CG animation have led animators to create screen performances in which the ephemeral qualities of recognizable gestures reveal the circumstances, dispositions, and intentions of the characters. Their collaborations with acting professionals have confirmed that, whether enacted by actors or illustrated by animators, characters' gestures and expressions take on meaning in relation to conventional social gestures, gestures and expressions associated with other characters, and ones shown at different times in the film. Their collaborations with acting professionals have also highlighted that, whether enacted or illustrated, connotations are conveyed by the spatial, temporal, and energy qualities that color gestures, expressions, and movements.

Articulating the contemporary view of screen performances in CGA films, Brad Bird explains "that when you're watching an animated film, the performance you're seeing is the one the *animator* is giving you." He continues: "If an animated character makes you laugh or cry, feel fear, anger, empathy or a million other emotions, it is largely due to the work of these unsung artists, who invest a lot of themselves in the creation of these indelible moments."[71] Animators today recognize that there are many factors that shape audience responses, but in the current CG era, they are honing their understanding of acting principles and calling attention to the fact that the performance details they have created shape audience interpretations.

Acting Opportunities in Performance-Capture Settings

The work of performance-capture actors has also become more visible as a result of publicity surrounding Andy Serkis's portrayal of Gollum in *The Two Towers* (2002) and *The Return of the King* (2003). The character of Gollum emerged from thousands of hours of labor by the entire production team, yet it depended on the vocal and physical performance of Serkis and on his conception of the character "as a complex, tortured soul, whose evil springs from deep suffering."[72] Serkis highlights the collaboration required to create the characterization: "What we achieved collectively was to take a character from literature, filter that through great screenwriters, then take the emotion, physicality and voice of an actor's performance, which had organically grown from acting with other actors on set, and synthesize them with a range of animation and motion capture" (see figure 39).[73]

FIGURE 39: Gollum in *The Two Towers*. Effective collaboration among actors, directors, and CG artists on *The Lord of the Rings* trilogy led the way for performance-capture work to be a new opportunity for actors.

Initially hired to provide the voice for Gollum, Serkis discovered that he could only do the character's voice if he were in character. Moreover, echoing contemporary actors' reliance on the physical dimension of their characters' actions as a means for accessing their characters' emotions, Serkis explains that being in character meant embodying Gollum. Thus, his conception of the character not only emerged from his vocal and physical choices; it also shaped those choices in performances that took place on set, in motion-capture settings, and in ADR sessions where vocal tracks were recorded.[74] In some instances, animators used his performance in the live-action "*animation reference* shots as the basis for their rotoscoping [because] the acting was invariably more convincing in the *animation reference* shots with Serkis than in the *mime passes* without him."[75] In certain cases, work in the motion-capture studio provided the basis for the way live-action scenes would be shot.[76] Identifying a unique acting opportunity he discovered, Serkis explains that motion capture "is very sensitive and can pick up very subtle movement, such as breathing, and also incidental movement, such as a stumble, [which can add] reality by rooting the character in its environment."[77]

In *Acting and Performance for Animation* (2013), Hayes and Webster point out that Serkis's portrayal shows "that the acting of the performance capture actor at this level is about thinking, emotions, and internal dynamics that make up a character's personality and [should be] dealt with in exactly the same way as any other acting job." His work highlights that there is a real "difference between simply capturing motion and capturing a performance." Hayes and Webster describe Serkis as the leading figure in a "new breed of actor" able to work effectively in CG situations. They explain: "In searching for ever more naturalistic animation that includes capturing traits and behaviors of individual personalities, we have seen the rise of the animated performer."[78]

Serkis has continued to expand the role of the actor in performance-capture settings in his work on *King Kong* (Peter Jackson, 2005), *Rise of the Planet of the Apes* (Rupert Wyatt, 2011), and *The Adventures of Tintin* (Steven Spielberg, 2011), which was produced by Peter Jackson and involved the artists who developed performance-capture practices on *The Lord of the Rings* films. Building on his work on *The Polar Express* (2004), Robert Zemeckis has directed other CGA films based on performance-capture: *Beowulf* (2007), with performance-capture work by Ray Winstone, and *A Christmas Carol* (2009), with performance-capture work by Jim Carrey. Digital artists with expertise developed on *The Lord of the Rings* trilogy contributed to the performance-capture-intensive production of *Avatar* (James Cameron, 2009). Willem Dafoe's interviews to support the opening of *John Carter* (Andrew Stanton, 2012) did not help that film's box office, but they highlighted the interesting acting opportunities made available by performance-capture. The positive responses to Mark Ruffalo's performance as the Hulk likely reflect his nuanced conception of the character and the more extensive use of performance-capture to render his portrayal of the character in *The Avengers* (Joss Whedon, 2012).

As performance-capture performances become an increasingly important part of Hollywood cinema, observers like Sharon Carnicke are finding that "Serkis' acting of Gollum was no different that the acting of any other role in a film, where acting provides only one component in the ultimate performance."[79] Echoing the contemporary appreciation for actors' contributions to technology-intensive performances, Pamela Wojcik proposes that "an analysis that considers both the role of technology and its effects might note that Elijah Wood's Frodo is no more natural or authentic than Serkis's Gollum [if only because] Wood's performance as Frodo—whether interacting with Serkis/Gollum, imperiled in volcanic structures, or situated in large-scale battles—depends upon blue-screen, digital effects, and sound design for its ultimate representation."[80]

The era's awareness of actors' contributions to technology-intensive representations is reflected even in contemporary motion-capture research. For example, the Viterbi School of Engineering at the University of Southern California had developed a project designed to assemble data to be used in work on "affective computing, virtual reality, intelligent virtual agents, and robotics." Significantly, "actors, rather than people from other walks of life," were hired to participate in the project, because the researchers recognized that only actors could be relied upon "to create credible emotional behavior through performance." The project revealed that even pared-down physical expression influences interpretations of human interactions, and that individuals generate distinct and identifiable data. It determined that individuals' "emotional states and their interactions with each other are also amazingly legible . . . even when the sound of their words goes unheard" and one can see only the motion capture "dancing skeletons" (the stick figures that emerge when the dots are connected). Most pertinent to a discussion of screen performance, the project revealed that it was by employing acting principles "focusing on the interpersonal dynamics and lines of *impelling actions and*

FIGURE 40: Performance-capture session at the University of Southern California. Use of acting principles led to legible and emotionally expressive movements, gestures, and expressions in the USC Viterbi School of Engineering research project. Used by permission of Sharon Carnicke.

counteractions within each scene or scenario, [that] the actors readily produced emotionally expressive movements that could be successfully captured and digitized" (see figure 40).[81]

Acting Strategies behind Performances in Action Blockbusters

Since 2000, ideas about film acting have been challenged and enriched not only by performances in animated films and CG intensive live-action films, but by performances in action films as well, for despite these performances' failure to adhere to the conventions of realism, audiences and the acting profession recognize that they are not necessarily instances of bad acting. A full discussion about the merits of acting in blockbusters would, for example, consider films from the era's superhero franchises (*Spider-Man, Batman*, Marvel Comic films), fantasy franchises (*Star Wars, Harry Potter, Pirates of the Caribbean*, and *The Lord of the Rings*), and action/thriller franchises (*Die Hard, Bourne*). It would also examine performances in big-budget films with bankable stars, whose leading role in even non-franchise films ensures that those movies have a strong box office opening, and thus generate substantial revenue in subsequent ancillary markets and delivery venues.

Denzel Washington is one of those bankable stars. Prior to the opening of *2 Guns* (Baltasar Kormákur, 2013), Box Office Mojo writer Ray Subers observed: "At 58 years old, Washington is about as much of a sure-thing as one can be at the box office. Excluding *The Great Debaters*—a modest drama—Washington has had ten-straight $20 million debuts."[82] *2 Guns* took the top spot its opening weekend, ahead of *The Wolverine* (James Mangold, 2013), which had secured the top spot when it opened the previous weekend. Washington's star power is reflected in his "Favorite Movie Star" ranking in Harris Interactive Polls. The data posted in 2013 reveals that Washington has been in the top ten every year since 1995 except two; he has been in the top three every year since 2006; he ranked number one in 2006 (tie), 2007, 2008, and 2012; the next best records are held by Tom Hanks (number one in 2002, 2004, and 2005), Clint Eastwood (number one in 1994, 1997, and 2006 [tie]), and Harrison Ford (number one in 1998, 1999, and 2000).[83] Washington's star power is also linked to his two Oscars and six Oscar nominations. Marketing for action films starring Washington consistently highlights the idea that audiences will be presented with the performance of the Academy Award–winning actor.

Washington's performances in the action films directed by Tony Scott, *Man on Fire* (2004), *Déjà Vu* (2006), *The Taking of Pelham 1 2 3* (2009), and *Unstoppable* (2010), provide useful material for considering trends in the era's screen performances, because Scott's films feature minimalist performances punctuated with moments of intense expressivity. By crafting that type of screen performance, Washington has been able to contribute effectively to Scott's action films, which work well on large and small screens because they generate spectacle through "rapid montage-effect editing [that is] combined with 'unstable' camera movements designed to create an impression of subjective immersion in the action, [and] an 'impact aesthetic' often increased by the practice of propelling debris and other objects out toward the viewer."[84] In Scott's editing-intensive films, Washington's use of what Maitland McDonagh once called "bizarrely stressed acting" does not represent a unique style, but rather an approach that is emblematic of (good) performances in contemporary Hollywood action films.

Lead performances in action films with flamboyant camera and editing choices do not reflect the conventions of dramatic realism. Instead, composition and editing choices often amplify the emotion that actors project in comparatively quiet scenes, which are interspersed between spectacular action sequences that involve little if any expression of complex emotion. Scored to suit the films' overall design, performances in explosion-heavy action films have an irregular rhythm and feature hyperbolic shifts in tone. Actors are required to truncate expression of emotion in action sequences, but the films engage audiences emotionally by occasionally lifting the restraint placed on actors' emotional expressivity. Performances in today's male-melodrama action films are not crafted to suit realistic representations in which performance choices build and ebb more slowly. Instead, actors craft performances that convey characters' experiences intermittently, in moments when the emotion they project is often intensified by exaggerated composition, editing, and mise-en-scène selections.

For example, a look at Washington's performance in *Man on Fire* reveals that his evocative facial expressions, poses, movements, and gestures anchor the meaning of scenes that generate spectacle even in ostensibly quiet moments. Former CIA assassin John Creasy (Washington) has been hired to be the bodyguard for a young American girl (Dakota Fanning) living with her mother and stepfather in Mexico City. Although Creasy has been hired to ensure that little Pita does not become another kidnapping-for-ransom victim, she sees him as a new friend. Early in the film, when he is driving her home from school through crowded city streets, Creasy harshly stops her attempts to get to know him. In the next scene, Pita's mother politely asks Creasy about the incident; Washington's bound posture and weighted vocal expressions make the point that Creasy does not want to accommodate Pita's desire for emotional connection.

In the following scene, with Creasy left alone to reflect on his self-imposed isolation, Scott anchors the scene's filmic hijinks with Washington's highly expressive gestures and facial expressions. The sound track is crowded with a cacophony of music fragments and blasts of noise; the camera spins, shots are filled with saturated colors, flares of light appear, shots cut from one to another unexpectedly. Through it all, one sees a crafted sequence of facial expressions: Washington's eyes fill with tears; his mouth turns down in an exaggerated expression of sorrow; he puffs out his cheeks as he fills his mouth with a huge swig of liquor; he rubs his hand across his forehead; he covers his eyes with his outstretched fingers; he squeezes his lips together; he lets spit trickle out of his mouth. Then, cuts and camera movement slow somewhat; Washington stands wavering, laboring several times to load and aim his gun. Cuts and camera movements return to a frenetic pace and feature another series of powerful facial expressions: Washington furrows his eyebrows, covers his face with his hands, bares his lower teeth, breaks into a tight-lipped grin, and then flinches just before putting the gun to his head. The gun fails to fire. In a series of close-ups, Washington takes deep breaths, pauses, and then infuses his movements with quiet purpose as he lowers the gun and checks the bullet. This is a turning point for the character.

Some might argue that the filmic elements in this scene create the screen performance. However, Washington's series of identifiable and communicative facial expressions show that he understands the adjustments necessary for working in films, especially action films filled with rapid editing and flamboyant camera movement. Acting teacher Patrick Tucker explains that while many people imagine that screen performance requires actors to do less with their faces, "if anything, the opposite is true."[85] He points out that effective "screen acting demands *more* reactions from [the actor] (but with less volume)."[86] In fact, "in a

FIGURE 41: In *Déjà Vu*, Denzel Washington's stillness and sustained, direct movements provide emotional connection for audiences, and a counterweight to the film's constant motion.

close-up, you sometimes need to do *more* than you would ever do in real life or on the stage, because the only acting instrument you have for this shot is your face, and *it* has to do what you would normally use your whole body to do."[87]

Washington's performance in *Déjà Vu* reveals the same attention to crafting compelling gestures and expressions that communicate the character's values, objectives, and emotional responses to events despite the film's use of attention-grabbing camera, editing, sound, and set design/photographic color choices. Scott opens this film with a massive explosion that destroys a New Orleans ferry, killing hundreds of people aboard. Then Washington enters the story as ATF agent Doug Carlin; Washington's strong, sustained, and direct gait when he first approaches the crime scene signals that his performance and his character will ground and center the narrative from that point on (see figure 41).

Washington's performance choices in the Tony Scott films of the 2000s are also an effective and representative response to the melodramatic narrative design that informs these films, the era's action films, and its blockbusters as a whole. The Scott films are male melodramas that present audiences with a dynamic hero who is at the center of continuous movement. However, they also employ character-centered structural parallels and dramatic reversals that slow down the narrative's linear trajectory. In these pauses or breaks in the spectacular action, actors' projection of emotion conveys information outside of or even counter to the primary intrigue, and provides an opportunity for audiences' emotional and cognitive involvement. In Scott's films, the melodramatic narrative structure thus involves mood shifts and renewed rather than continuous action. The dovetailing narrative and performance design generates audience involvement by prompting interest in characters' reactions to the underlying significance of high-intensity action situations (which by themselves create an emotional distance from the characters). As in other spectacular male melodramas, in Tony Scott's films it is

FIGURE 42: Denzel Washington in *The Taking of Pelham 1 2 3* holds the film together with his portrayal of the average-guy civil servant and conveys the emotional significance of the final confrontation with the train hijacker.

the lead actors' succinct expression of emotion at selected moments that communicates the characters' experience and thus serves as an emotional lifeline for audiences (see figure 42).

Hollywood's use of rapid "change of image-content . . . to maintain heightened levels of visual stimulus on the [large and] small screen . . . appears to have been learned from formats such as advertising and music videos."[88] Yet there are arguably quite different models for performances in contemporary action films, which need to keep audience attention throughout. For example, Bruce Willis's characterizations in the *Die Hard* films (1988, 1990, 1995, 2007, and 2013) have influenced performances in contemporary action films. Another model for performances that communicate effectively within spectacle-driven narratives has been provided by Hong Kong blood operas such as John Woo's *The Killer* (*Die xue shuang xiong*, 1989), the first Hong Kong film to be a crossover success in the North American market since Wei Lo's *Fists of Fury* (*Tang shan da xiong*, 1971), starring Bruce Lee, made kung fu movies a part of international cinema.

The release of *The Killer* made John Woo "the most exciting cult-icon director from overseas since Sergio Leone put Clint Eastwood in a poncho."[89] Critics described *The Killer* as "*Magnificent Obsession* remade by Sam Peckinpah"[90] and "an unlikely fusion of *The Wild Bunch* and *Dark Victory*."[91] Thus, as Maitland McDonagh noted at the time, the film's "bizarrely stressed acting," where "individual performers slip back and forth between low-key naturalism and exaggerated theatricalism," contrasted with performances in other Hollywood offerings. However, as rapid editing has become integral to American action films, to interface with the dazzling cinematic effects actors have found ways to create performances scored with visibly alternating expressive modes. Washington's work in the Scott films exemplifies the practice of crafting action-film performances that ground films' flamboyant editing and sound-image combinations, and convey intense emotion in intermittent moments when filmic choices support and foreground actors' physical and vocal expression.

Washington's approach to performance also epitomizes the era's consensus that acting principles developed by Stanislavsky and emphasized by Stella Adler are the foundation for creating great screen performances. Interviews on the DVDs of Scott's films with Washington continually highlight the actor's extensive research into his characters and the world of the story. Interviews also reveal that Washington does exhaustive preparation that focuses on the physical embodiment of emotion. Working according to Adler's emphasis, Washington puts "himself in the place of the character,"[92] and crafts a score of actions so he can work effectively out of sequence and in collaboration with editing-intensive scenes. Washington approaches performances believing that "emotion should come from the actor's commitment to the circumstances and that a clear and deep understanding is critical for an actor's expressive truthfulness."[93]

Growing Appreciation for the Craft of Acting

Since 2000, the craft of film acting has become more visible to audiences. Along with fans' continuing interest in movie stars, audiences have become increasingly aware of the techniques that contribute to performances in their favorite films due to behind-the-scenes segments on entertainment programs and DVDs. Action films like *Safe House* (Daniel Espinosa, 2012) have DVD extras with information about the rehearsal period and actors' conception of their characters. Audiences can also discover more about the craft of acting as performance-centered indiewood films increasingly use actors like Viggo Mortensen, who followed his roles in *The Lord of the Rings* trilogy with performances in David Cronenberg's *A History of Violence* (2005), *Eastern Promises* (2007), and *A Dangerous Method* (2011).

Since 2000, actors' labor, craftsmanship, and professionalism have allowed them to interface with Hollywood's increasing use of cinematic effects. Actors' experience, training, and skill have allowed them to create screen performances that get and keep audience attention because the physical and vocal expressions are clear, precise, evocative, and highly legible. Although one might have expected the industry's expanded use of CGI to make film acting and actors obsolete, film professionals' use of actors and acting principles actually expanded during the 2000s, as actors and acting concepts became integrated into CG settings. In addition, whereas critics gave little credence to performances in cinematically flamboyant action films, directors like Scott depended on experienced actors like Washington to create an emotional connection with audiences through minimalist performances punctuated with moments of intense expressivity. As

Sharon Carnicke explains: "The history of acting shows that the basic processes of acting—grounded as they are in the actor's body and voice—remain relatively stable, while the changing technologies of stage and screen continually prompt actors to rethink how they use their bodies and voices in the service of their art."[94] Thus, the remarkable technological changes in contemporary Hollywood cinema have made this an exciting time to be an actor, because the challenges have led to new opportunities to explore and develop the craft of acting.

ACADEMY AWARDS FOR ACTING

All information is from Oscars.org, the website of the Academy of Motion Picture Arts and Sciences (AMPAS).

1927/28 ACTOR: Emil Jannings, *The Last Command*
ACTRESS: Janet Gaynor, *7th Heaven*

1928/29 ACTOR: Warner Baxter, *In Old Arizona*
ACTRESS: Mary Pickford, *Coquette*

1929/30 ACTOR: George Arliss, *Disraeli*
ACTRESS: Norma Shearer, *The Divorcee*

1930/31 ACTOR: Lionel Barrymore, *A Free Soul*
ACTRESS: Marie Dressler, *Min and Bill*

1931/32 ACTOR (tie): Wallace Beery, *The Champ*, and Fredric March, *Dr. Jekyll and Mr. Hyde*
ACTRESS: Helen Hayes, *The Sin of Madelon Claudet*

1932/33   ACTOR: Charles Laughton, *The Private Life of Henry VIII*
    Actress, Katharine Hepburn, *Morning Glory*

1934   ACTOR: Clark Gable, *It Happened One Night*
    ACTRESS: Claudette Colbert, *It Happened One Night*

1935   ACTOR: Victor McLaglen, *The Informer*
    ACTRESS: Bette Davis, *Dangerous*

1936   ACTOR: Paul Muni, *The Story of Louis Pasteur*
    ACTRESS: Luise Rainer, *The Great Ziegfeld*
    ACTOR IN A SUPPORTING ROLE: Walter Brennan, *Come and Get It*
    ACTRESS IN A SUPPORTING ROLE: Gale Sondergaard, *Anthony Adverse*

1937   ACTOR: Spencer Tracy, *Captains Courageous*
    ACTRESS: Luise Rainer, *The Good Earth*
    ACTOR IN A SUPPORTING ROLE: Joseph Schildkraut, *The Life of Emile Zola*
    ACTRESS IN A SUPPORTING ROLE: Alice Brady, *In Old Chicago*

1938   ACTOR: Spencer Tracy, *Boys Town*
    ACTRESS: Bette Davis, *Jezebel*
    ACTOR IN A SUPPORTING ROLE: Walter Brennan, *Kentucky*
    ACTRESS IN A SUPPORTING ROLE: Fay Bainter, *Jezebel*

1939   ACTOR: Robert Donat, *Goodbye Mr. Chips*
    ACTRESS: Vivien Leigh, *Gone with the Wind*
    ACTOR IN A SUPPORTING ROLE: Thomas Mitchell, *Stagecoach*
    ACTRESS IN A SUPPORTING ROLE: Hattie McDaniel, *Gone with the Wind*

1940   ACTOR: Jimmy Stewart, *The Philadelphia Story*
    ACTRESS: Ginger Rogers, *Kitty Foyle*
    ACTOR IN A SUPPORTING ROLE: Walter Brennan, *The Westerner*
    ACTRESS IN A SUPPORTING ROLE: Jane Darwell, *The Grapes of Wrath*

1941   ACTOR: Gary Cooper, *Sergeant York*
    ACTRESS: Joan Fontaine, *Suspicion*
    ACTOR IN A SUPPORTING ROLE: Donald Crisp, *How Green Was My Valley*
    ACTRESS IN A SUPPORTING ROLE: Mary Astor, *The Great Lie*

1942   ACTOR: James Cagney, *Yankee Doodle Dandy*
    ACTRESS: Greer Garson, *Mrs. Miniver*
    ACTOR IN A SUPPORTING ROLE: Van Heflin, *Johnny Eager*
    ACTRESS IN A SUPPORTING ROLE: Teresa Wright, *Mrs. Miniver*

1943   ACTOR: Paul Lukas, *Watch on the Rhine*
       ACTRESS: Jennifer Jones, *The Song of Bernadette*
       ACTOR IN A SUPPORTING ROLE: Charles Coburn, *The More the Merrier*
       ACTRESS IN A SUPPORTING ROLE: Katina Paxinou, *For Whom the Bell Tolls*

1944   ACTOR: Bing Crosby, *Going My Way*
       ACTRESS: Ingrid Bergman, *Gaslight*
       ACTOR IN A SUPPORTING ROLE: Barry Fitzgerald, *Going My Way*
       ACTRESS IN A SUPPORTING ROLE: Ethel Barrymore, *None but the Lonely Heart*

1945   ACTOR: Ray Milland, *The Lost Weekend*
       ACTRESS: Joan Crawford, *Mildred Pierce*
       ACTOR IN A SUPPORTING ROLE: James Dunn, *A Tree Grows in Brooklyn*
       ACTRESS IN A SUPPORTING ROLE: Anne Revere, *National Velvet*

1946   ACTOR: Fredric March, *The Best Years of Our Lives*
       ACTRESS: Olivia de Havilland, *To Each His Own*
       ACTOR IN A SUPPORTING ROLE: Harold Russell, *The Best Years of Our Lives*
       Actress in a Supporting Role, Anne Baxter, *The Razor's Edge*

1947   ACTOR: Ronald Colman, *A Double Life*
       ACTRESS: Loretta Young, *The Farmer's Daughter*
       ACTOR IN A SUPPORTING ROLE: Edmund Gwenn, *Miracle on 34th Street*
       ACTRESS IN A SUPPORTING ROLE: Celeste Holm, *Gentleman's Agreement*

1948   ACTOR: Laurence Olivier, *Hamlet*
       ACTRESS: Jane Wyman, *Johnny Belinda*
       ACTOR IN A SUPPORTING ROLE: Walter Huston, *The Treasure of the Sierra Madre*
       ACTRESS IN A SUPPORTING ROLE: Claire Trevor, *Key Largo*

1949   ACTOR: Broderick Crawford, *All The King's Men*
       ACTRESS: Olivia de Havilland, *The Heiress*
       ACTOR IN A SUPPORTING ROLE: Dean Jagger, *Twelve O'Clock High*
       ACTRESS IN A SUPPORTING ROLE: Mercedes McCambridge, *All the King's Men*

1950   ACTOR: José Ferrer, *Cyrano de Bergerac*
       ACTRESS: Judy Holliday, *Born Yesterday*
       ACTOR IN A SUPPORTING ROLE: George Sanders, *All About Eve*
       ACTRESS IN A SUPPORTING ROLE: Josephine Hull, *Harvey*

1951   ACTOR: Humphrey Bogart, *The African Queen*
       ACTRESS: Vivien Leigh, *A Streetcar Named Desire*
       ACTOR IN A SUPPORTING ROLE: Karl Malden, *A Streetcar Named Desire*
       ACTRESS IN A SUPPORTING ROLE: Kim Hunter, *A Streetcar Named Desire*

1952   ACTOR: Gary Cooper, *High Noon*
       ACTRESS: Shirley Booth, *Come Back, Little Sheba*
       ACTOR IN A SUPPORTING ROLE: Anthony Quinn, *Viva Zapata!*
       ACTRESS IN A SUPPORTING ROLE: Gloria Grahame, *The Bad and the Beautiful*

1953   ACTOR: William Holden, *Stalag 17*
       ACTRESS: Audrey Hepburn, *Roman Holiday*
       ACTOR IN A SUPPORTING ROLE: Frank Sinatra, *From Here to Eternity*
       ACTRESS IN A SUPPORTING ROLE: Donna Reed, *From Here to Eternity*

1954   ACTOR: Marlon Brando, *On the Waterfront*
       ACTRESS: Grace Kelly, *The Country Girl*
       ACTOR IN A SUPPORTING ROLE: Edmond O'Brien, *The Barefoot Contessa*
       ACTRESS IN A SUPPORTING ROLE: Eva Marie Saint, *On the Waterfront*

1955   ACTOR: Earnest Borgnine, *Marty*
       ACTRESS: Anna Magnani, *The Rose Tattoo*
       ACTOR IN A SUPPORTING ROLE: Jack Lemmon, *Mister Roberts*
       ACTRESS IN A SUPPORTING ROLE: Jo Van Fleet, *East of Eden*

1956   ACTOR: Yul Brynner, *The King and I*
       ACTRESS: Ingrid Bergman, *Anastasia*
       ACTOR IN A SUPPORTING ROLE: Anthony Quinn, *Lust for Life*
       ACTRESS IN A SUPPORTING ROLE: Dorothy Malone, *Written on the Wind*

1957   ACTOR: Alec Guinness, *The Bridge on the River Kwai*
       ACTRESS: Joanne Woodward, *The Three Faces of Eve*
       ACTOR IN A SUPPORTING ROLE: Red Buttons, *Sayonara*
       ACTRESS IN A SUPPORTING ROLE: Miyoshi Umeki, *Sayonara*

1958   ACTOR: David Niven, *Separate Tables*
       ACTRESS: Susan Hayward, *I Want to Live!*
       ACTOR IN A SUPPORTING ROLE: Burl Ives, *The Big Country*
       ACTRESS IN A SUPPORTING ROLE: Wendy Hiller, *Separate Tables*

1959   ACTOR: Charlton Heston, *Ben-Hur*
       ACTRESS: Simone Signoret, *Room at the Top*
       ACTOR IN A SUPPORTING ROLE: Hugh Griffith, *Ben-Hur*
       ACTRESS IN A SUPPORTING ROLE: Shelley Winters, *The Diary of Anne Frank*

1960   ACTOR: Burt Lancaster, *Elmer Gantry*
       ACTRESS: Elizabeth Taylor, *BUtterfield 8*
       ACTOR IN A SUPPORTING ROLE: Peter Ustinov, *Spartacus*
       ACTRESS IN A SUPPORTING ROLE: Shirley Jones, *Elmer Gantry*

1961   ACTOR: Maximilian Schell, *Judgment at Nuremberg*
       ACTRESS: Sophia Loren, *Two Women*
       ACTOR IN A SUPPORTING ROLE: George Chakiris, *West Side Story*
       ACTRESS IN A SUPPORTING ROLE: Rita Moreno, *West Side Story*

1962   ACTOR: Gregory Peck, *To Kill a Mockingbird*
       ACTRESS: Anne Bancroft, *The Miracle Worker*
       ACTOR IN A SUPPORTING ROLE: Ed Begley, *Sweet Bird of Youth*
       ACTRESS IN A SUPPORTING ROLE: Patty Duke, *The Miracle Worker*

1963   ACTOR: Sidney Poitier, *Lilies of the Field*
       ACTRESS: Patricia Neal, *Hud*
       ACTOR IN A SUPPORTING ROLE: Melvyn Douglas, *Hud*
       ACTRESS IN A SUPPORTING ROLE: Margaret Rutherford, *The V.I.P.s*

1964   ACTOR: Rex Harrison, *My Fair Lady*
       ACTRESS: Julie Andrews, *Mary Poppins*
       ACTOR IN A SUPPORTING ROLE: Peter Ustinov, *Topkapi*
       ACTRESS IN A SUPPORTING ROLE: Lila Kedrova, *Zorba the Greek*

1965   ACTOR: Lee Marvin, *Cat Ballou*
       ACTRESS: Julie Christie, *Darling*
       ACTOR IN A SUPPORTING ROLE: Martin Balsam, *A Thousand Clowns*
       ACTRESS IN A SUPPORTING ROLE: Shelley Winters, *A Patch of Blue*

1966   ACTOR: Paul Scofield, *A Man for All Seasons*
       ACTRESS: Elizabeth Taylor, *Who's Afraid of Virginia Woolf?*
       ACTOR IN A SUPPORTING ROLE: Walter Matthau, *The Fortune Cookie*
       ACTRESS IN A SUPPORTING ROLE: Sandy Dennis, *Who's Afraid of Virginia Woolf?*

1967   ACTOR: Rod Steiger, *In the Heat of the Night*
       ACTRESS: Katharine Hepburn, *Guess Who's Coming to Dinner*
       ACTOR IN A SUPPORTING ROLE: George Kennedy, *Cool Hand Luke*
       ACTRESS IN A SUPPORTING ROLE: Estelle Parsons, *Bonnie and Clyde*

1968   ACTOR: Cliff Robertson, *Charly*
       ACTRESS (tie): Barbra Streisand, *Funny Girl*, and Katharine Hepburn, *The Lion in Winter*
       ACTOR IN A SUPPORTING ROLE: Jack Albertson, *The Subject Was Roses*
       ACTRESS IN A SUPPORTING ROLE: Ruth Gordon, *Rosemary's Baby*

1969   ACTOR: John Wayne, *True Grit*
       ACTRESS: Maggie Smith, *The Prime of Miss Jean Brodie*
       ACTOR IN A SUPPORTING ROLE: Gig Young, *They Shoot Horses, Don't They?*
       ACTRESS IN A SUPPORTING ROLE: Goldie Hawn, *Cactus Flower*

1970   ACTOR: George C. Scott, *Patton*
ACTRESS: Glenda Jackson, *Women in Love*
ACTOR IN A SUPPORTING ROLE: John Mills, *Ryan's Daughter*
ACTRESS IN A SUPPORTING ROLE: Helen Hayes, Airport

1971   ACTOR: Gene Hackman, *The French Connection*
ACTRESS: Jane Fonda, *Klute*
ACTOR IN A SUPPORTING ROLE: Ben Johnson, *The Last Picture Show*
ACTRESS IN A SUPPORTING ROLE: Cloris Leachman, *The Last Picture Show*

1972   ACTOR: Marlon Brando, *The Godfather*
ACTRESS: Liza Minnelli, *Cabaret*
ACTOR IN A SUPPORTING ROLE: Joel Grey, *Cabaret*
ACTRESS IN A SUPPORTING ROLE: Eileen Heckart, *Butterflies Are Free*

1973   ACTOR: Jack Lemmon, *Save the Tiger*
ACTRESS: Glenda Jackson, *A Touch of Class*
ACTOR IN A SUPPORTING ROLE: John Houseman, *The Paper Chase*
ACTRESS IN A SUPPORTING ROLE: Tatum O'Neal, *Paper Moon*

1974   ACTOR: Art Carney, *Harry and Tonto*
ACTRESS: Ellen Burstyn, *Alice Doesn't Live Here Anymore*
ACTOR IN A SUPPORTING ROLE: Robert De Niro, *The Godfather Part II*
ACTRESS IN A SUPPORTING ROLE: Ingrid Bergman, *Murder on the Orient Express*

1975   ACTOR: Jack Nicholson, *One Flew Over the Cuckoo's Nest*
ACTRESS: Louise Fletcher, *One Flew Over the Cuckoo's Nest*
ACTOR IN A SUPPORTING ROLE: George Burns, *The Sunshine Boys*
ACTRESS IN A SUPPORTING ROLE: Lee Grant, *Shampoo*

1976   ACTOR IN A LEADING ROLE: Peter Finch, *Network*
ACTRESS IN A LEADING ROLE: Faye Dunaway, *Network*
ACTOR IN A SUPPORTING ROLE: Jason Robards, *All the President's Men*
ACTRESS IN A SUPPORTING ROLE: Beatrice Straight, *Network*

1977   ACTOR IN A LEADING ROLE: Richard Dreyfuss, *The Goodbye Girl*
ACTRESS IN A LEADING ROLE: Diane Keaton, *Annie Hall*
ACTOR IN A SUPPORTING ROLE: Jason Robards, *Julia*
ACTRESS IN A SUPPORTING ROLE: Vanessa Redgrave, *Julia*

1978   ACTOR IN A LEADING ROLE: Jon Voight, *Coming Home*
ACTRESS IN A LEADING ROLE: Jane Fonda, *Coming Home*
ACTOR IN A SUPPORTING ROLE: Christopher Walken, *The Deer Hunter*
ACTRESS IN A SUPPORTING ROLE: Maggie Smith, *California Suite*

1979   ACTOR IN A LEADING ROLE: Dustin Hoffman, *Kramer vs. Kramer*
       ACTRESS IN A LEADING ROLE: Sally Field, *Norma Rae*
       ACTOR IN A SUPPORTING ROLE: Melvyn Douglas, *Being There*
       ACTRESS IN A SUPPORTING ROLE: Meryl Streep, *Kramer vs. Kramer*

1980   ACTOR IN A LEADING ROLE: Robert De Niro, *Raging Bull*
       ACTRESS IN A LEADING ROLE: Sissy Spacek, *Coal Miner's Daughter*
       ACTOR IN A SUPPORTING ROLE: Timothy Hutton, *Ordinary People*
       ACTRESS IN A SUPPORTING ROLE: Mary Steenburgen, *Melvin and Howard*

1981   ACTOR IN A LEADING ROLE: Henry Fonda, *On Golden Pond*
       ACTRESS IN A LEADING ROLE: Katharine Hepburn, *On Golden Pond*
       ACTOR IN A SUPPORTING ROLE: John Gielgud, *Arthur*
       ACTRESS IN A SUPPORTING ROLE: Maureen Stapleton, *Reds*

1982   ACTOR IN A LEADING ROLE: Ben Kingsley, *Gandhi*
       ACTRESS IN A LEADING ROLE: Meryl Streep, *Sophie's Choice*
       ACTOR IN A SUPPORTING ROLE: Lou Gossett Jr., *An Officer and a Gentleman*
       ACTRESS IN A SUPPORTING ROLE: Jessica Lange, *Tootsie*

1983   ACTOR IN A LEADING ROLE: Robert Duvall, *Tender Mercies*
       ACTRESS IN A LEADING ROLE: Shirley MacLaine, *Terms of Endearment*
       ACTOR IN A SUPPORTING ROLE: Jack Nicholson, *Terms of Endearment*
       ACTRESS IN A SUPPORTING ROLE: Linda Hunt, *The Year of Living Dangerously*

1984   ACTOR IN A LEADING ROLE: F. Murray Abraham, *Amadeus*
       ACTRESS IN A LEADING ROLE: Sally Field, *Places in the Heart*
       ACTOR IN A SUPPORTING ROLE: Haing S. Ngor, *The Killing Fields*
       ACTRESS IN A SUPPORTING ROLE: Peggy Ashcroft, *A Passage to India*

1985   ACTOR IN A LEADING ROLE: William Hurt, *Kiss of the Spider Woman*
       ACTRESS IN A LEADING ROLE: Geraldine Page, *The Trip to Bountiful*
       ACTOR IN A SUPPORTING ROLE: Don Ameche, *Cocoon*
       ACTRESS IN A SUPPORTING ROLE: Anjelica Huston, *Prizzi's Honor*

1986   ACTOR IN A LEADING ROLE: Paul Newman, *The Color of Money*
       ACTRESS IN A LEADING ROLE: Marlee Matlin, *Children of a Lesser God*
       ACTOR IN A SUPPORTING ROLE: Michael Caine, *Hannah and Her Sisters*
       ACTRESS IN A SUPPORTING ROLE: Dianne Wiest, *Hannah and Her Sisters*

1987   ACTOR IN A LEADING ROLE: Michael Douglas, *Wall Street*
       ACTRESS IN A LEADING ROLE: Cher, *Moonstruck*
       ACTOR IN A SUPPORTING ROLE: Sean Connery, *The Untouchables*
       ACTRESS IN A SUPPORTING ROLE: Olympia Dukakis, *Moonstruck*

1988 ACTOR IN A LEADING ROLE: Dustin Hoffman, *Rainman*
ACTRESS IN A LEADING ROLE: Jodie Foster, *The Accused*
ACTOR IN A SUPPORTING ROLE: Kevin Kline, *A Fish Called Wanda*
ACTRESS IN A SUPPORTING ROLE: Geena Davis, *The Accidental Tourist*

1989 ACTOR IN A LEADING ROLE: Daniel Day-Lewis, *My Left Foot*
ACTRESS IN A LEADING ROLE: Jessica Tandy, *Driving Miss Daisy*
ACTOR IN A SUPPORTING ROLE: Denzel Washington, *Glory*
ACTRESS IN A SUPPORTING ROLE: Brenda Fricker, *My Left Foot*

1990 ACTOR IN A LEADING ROLE: Jeremy Irons, *Reversal of Fortune*
ACTRESS IN A LEADING ROLE: Kathy Bates, *Misery*
ACTOR IN A SUPPORTING ROLE: Joe Pesci, *Good Fellas*
ACTRESS IN A SUPPORTING ROLE: Whoopi Goldberg, *Ghost*

1991 ACTOR IN A LEADING ROLE: Anthony Hopkins, *The Silence of the Lambs*
ACTRESS IN A LEADING ROLE: Jodie Foster, *The Silence of the Lambs*
ACTOR IN A SUPPORTING ROLE: Jack Palance, *City Slickers*
ACTRESS IN A SUPPORTING ROLE: Mercedes Ruehl, *The Fisher King*

1992 ACTOR IN A LEADING ROLE: Al Pacino, *Scent of a Woman*
ACTRESS IN A LEADING ROLE: Emma Thompson, *Howards End*
ACTOR IN A SUPPORTING ROLE: Gene Hackman, *Unforgiven*
ACTRESS IN A SUPPORTING ROLE: Marisa Tomei, *My Cousin Vinny*

1993 ACTOR IN A LEADING ROLE: Tom Hanks, *Philadelphia*
ACTRESS IN A LEADING ROLE: Holly Hunter, *The Piano*
ACTOR IN A SUPPORTING ROLE: Tommy Lee Jones, *The Fugitive*
ACTRESS IN A SUPPORTING ROLE: Anna Paquin, *The Piano*

1994 ACTOR IN A LEADING ROLE: Tom Hanks, *Forrest Gump*
ACTRESS IN A LEADING ROLE: Jessica Lange, *Blue Sky*
ACTOR IN A SUPPORTING ROLE: Martin Landau, *Ed Wood*
ACTRESS IN A SUPPORTING ROLE: Dianne Wiest, *Bullets Over Broadway*

1995 ACTOR IN A LEADING ROLE: Nicolas Cage, *Leaving Las Vegas*
ACTRESS IN A LEADING ROLE: Susan Sarandon, *Dead Man Walking*
ACTOR IN A SUPPORTING ROLE: Kevin Spacey, *The Usual Suspects*
ACTRESS IN A SUPPORTING ROLE: Mira Sorvino, *Mighty Aphrodite*

1996 ACTOR IN A LEADING ROLE: Geoffrey Rush, *Shine*
ACTRESS IN A LEADING ROLE: Frances McDormand, *Fargo*
ACTOR IN A SUPPORTING ROLE: Cuba Gooding Jr., *Jerry Maguire*
ACTRESS IN A SUPPORTING ROLE: Juliette Binoche, *The English Patient*

1997   ACTOR IN A LEADING ROLE: Jack Nicholson, *As Good as It Gets*
ACTRESS IN A LEADING ROLE: Helen Hunt, *As Good as It Gets*
ACTOR IN A SUPPORTING ROLE: Robin Williams, *Good Will Hunting*
ACTRESS IN A SUPPORTING ROLE: Kim Basinger, *L.A. Confidential*

1998   ACTOR IN A LEADING ROLE: Roberto Benigni, *Life Is Beautiful*
ACTRESS IN A LEADING ROLE: Gwyneth Paltrow, *Shakespeare in Love*
ACTOR IN A SUPPORTING ROLE: James Coburn, *Affliction*
ACTRESS IN A SUPPORTING ROLE: Judi Dench, *Shakespeare in Love*

1999   ACTOR IN A LEADING ROLE: Kevin Spacey, *American Beauty*
ACTRESS IN A LEADING ROLE: Hilary Swank, *Boys Don't Cry*
ACTOR IN A SUPPORTING ROLE: Michael Caine, *The Cider House Rules*
ACTRESS IN A SUPPORTING ROLE: Angelina Jolie, *Girl, Interrupted*

2000   ACTOR IN A LEADING ROLE: Russell Crowe, *Gladiator*
ACTRESS IN A LEADING ROLE: Julia Roberts, *Erin Brockovich*
ACTOR IN A SUPPORTING ROLE: Benicio Del Toro, *Traffic*
ACTRESS IN A SUPPORTING ROLE: Marcia Gay Harden, *Pollock*

2001   ACTOR IN A LEADING ROLE: Denzel Washington, *Training Day*
ACTRESS IN A LEADING ROLE: Halle Berry, *Monster's Ball*
ACTOR IN A SUPPORTING ROLE: Jim Broadbent, *Iris*
ACTRESS IN A SUPPORTING ROLE: Jennifer Connelly, *A Beautiful Mind*

2002   ACTOR IN A LEADING ROLE: Adrien Brody, *The Pianist*
ACTRESS IN A LEADING ROLE: Nicole Kidman, *The Hours*
ACTOR IN A SUPPORTING ROLE: Chris Cooper, *Adaptation*
ACTRESS IN A SUPPORTING ROLE: Catherina Zeta-Jones, *Chicago*

2003   ACTOR IN A LEADING ROLE: Sean Penn, *Mystic River*
ACTRESS IN A LEADING ROLE: Charlize Theron, *Monster*
ACTOR IN A SUPPORTING ROLE: Tim Robbins, *Mystic River*
ACTRESS IN A SUPPORTING ROLE: Renee Zellweger, *Cold Mountain*

2004   ACTOR IN A LEADING ROLE: Jamie Foxx, *Ray*
ACTRESS IN A LEADING ROLE: Hilary Swank, *Million Dollar Baby*
ACTOR IN A SUPPORTING ROLE: Morgan Freeman, *Million Dollar Baby*
ACTRESS IN A SUPPORTING ROLE: Cate Blanchett, *The Aviator*

2005   ACTOR IN A LEADING ROLE: Philip Seymour Hoffman, *Capote*
ACTRESS IN A LEADING ROLE: Reese Witherspoon, *Walk the Line*
ACTOR IN A SUPPORTING ROLE: George Clooney, *Syriana*
ACTRESS IN A SUPPORTING ROLE: Rachel Weisz, *The Constant Gardener*

2006   ACTOR IN A LEADING ROLE: Forest Whitaker, *The Last King of Scotland*
       ACTRESS IN A LEADING ROLE: Helen Mirren, *The Queen*
       ACTOR IN A SUPPORTING ROLE: Alan Arkin, *Little Miss Sunshine*
       ACTRESS IN A SUPPORTING ROLE: Jennifer Hudson, *Dreamgirls*

2007   ACTOR IN A LEADING ROLE: Daniel Day-Lewis, *There Will Be Blood*
       ACTRESS IN A LEADING ROLE: Marion Cotillard, *La Vie en Rose*
       ACTOR IN A SUPPORTING ROLE: Javier Bardem, *No Country for Old Men*
       ACTRESS IN A SUPPORTING ROLE: Tilda Swinton, *Michael Clayton*

2008   ACTOR IN A LEADING ROLE: Sean Penn, *Milk*
       ACTRESS IN A LEADING ROLE: Kate Winslet, *The Reader*
       ACTOR IN A SUPPORTING ROLE: Heath Ledger, *The Dark Knight*
       ACTRESS IN A SUPPORTING ROLE: Penelope Cruz, *Vicky Cristina Barcelona*

2009   ACTOR IN A LEADING ROLE: Jeff Bridges, *Crazy Heart*
       ACTRESS IN A LEADING ROLE: Sandra Bullock, *The Blind Side*
       ACTOR IN A SUPPORTING ROLE: Christoph Waltz, *Inglourious Basterds*
       ACTRESS IN A SUPPORTING ROLE: Mo'Nique, *Precious, Based on the Novel 'Push' by Sapphire*

2010   ACTOR IN A LEADING ROLE: Colin Firth, *The King's Speech*
       ACTRESS IN A LEADING ROLE: Natalie Portman, *Black Swan*
       ACTOR IN A SUPPORTING ROLE: Christian Bale, *The Fighter*
       ACTRESS IN A SUPPORTING ROLE: Melissa Leo, *The Fighter*

2011   ACTOR IN A LEADING ROLE: Jean Dujardin, *The Artist*
       ACTRESS IN A LEADING ROLE: Meryl Streep, *The Iron Lady*
       ACTOR IN A SUPPORTING ROLE: Christopher Plummer, *Beginners*
       ACTRESS IN A SUPPORTING ROLE: Octavia Spencer, *The Help*

2012   ACTOR IN A LEADING ROLE: Daniel Day-Lewis, *Lincoln*
       ACTRESS IN A LEADING ROLE: Jennifer Lawrence, *Silver Linings Playbook*
       ACTOR IN A SUPPORTING ROLE: Christoph Waltz, *Django Unchained*
       ACTRESS IN A SUPPORTING ROLE: Anne Hathaway, *Les Misérables*

2013   ACTOR IN A LEADING ROLE: Matthew McConaughey, *Dallas Buyers Club*
       ACTRESS IN A LEADING ROLE: Cate Blanchett, *Blue Jasmine*
       ACTOR IN A SUPPORTING ROLE: Jared Leto, *Dallas Buyers Club*
       ACTRESS IN A SUPPORTING ROLE: Lupita Nyong'o, *12 Years a Slave*

2014   ACTOR IN A LEADING ROLE: Eddie Redmayne, *The Theory of Everything*
       ACTRESS IN A LEADING ROLE: Julianne Moore, *Still Alice*
       ACTOR IN A SUPPORTING ROLE: J. K. Simmons, *Whiplash*
       ACTRESS IN A SUPPORTING ROLE: Patricia Arquette, *Boyhood*

NOTES

Introduction

1 Leon Wieseltier, review of *The Second Plane: September 11: Terror and Boredom*, by Martin Amis, *New York Times Sunday Book Review*, April 27, 2008, www.nytimes.com/2008/04/27/books/review/Wieseltier-t.html?_r=2&oref=slogin&.

2 Cynthia Baron, Diane Carson, and Frank P. Tomasulo, "Introduction," in *More Than a Method: Trends and Traditions in Contemporary Film Performance*, ed. Cynthia Baron, Diane Carson, and Frank P. Tomasulo (Detroit: Wayne State University Press, 2004), 12.

3 James Naremore, *Acting in the Cinema* (Berkeley: University of California Press, 1988), 43.

4 Ibid., 65–67.

5 Scholarship engaged in reevaluating the distinctions between Stanislavsky's and Brecht's approaches includes Baron, Carson, and Tomasulo, *More Than a Method*; Dennis C. Beck, "The Paradox of the Method Actor: Rethinking the Stanislavsky Legacy," in *Method Acting Reconsidered*, ed. David Krasner (New York: St. Martin's, 2000), 261–282; Rhonda Blair, "The Method and the Computational Theory of the Mind," in *Method Acting Reconsidered*, 201–218; Sharon M. Carnicke, *Stanislavsky in Focus*, 2nd ed. (London: Routledge, 2009).

6 Ed Ulbrich, "How Benjamin Button Got His Face," TED: Ideas Worth Spreading, www.ted.com/talks/ed_ulbrich_shows_how_benjamin_button_got_his_face.html.

7 Laura Sydell, "Building the Curious Faces of 'Benjamin Button,'" National Public Radio, February 17, 2009, www.npr.org/templates/story/story.php?storyld=100668766.

8   Charlie Kei., "Acting Like a Star: Florence Turner, Picture Personality," in *Theorizing Film Acting*, ed. Aaron Taylor (New York: Routledge, 2012), 203.

9   Charles Musser, "The Changing Status of the Actor," in *Movie Acting, The Film Reader*, ed. Pamela Robertson Wojcik (New York: Routledge, 2004), 53.

10 Aaron Taylor, "Introduction: Acting, Casually and Theoretically Speaking," in Taylor, *Theorizing Film Acting*, 5.

11 Cynthia Baron and Sharon Marie Carnicke, *Reframing Screen Performance* (Ann Arbor: University of Michigan Press, 2008), 17.

12 Alexander Walker, *Stardom: The Hollywood Phenomenon* (New York: Stein and Day, 1970).

13 Ibid., 233.

14 Richard Dyer, *Stars* (London: British Film Institute, 1979), 151.

15 Ibid., 73.

16 Richard Dyer, *Heavenly Bodies: Film Stars and Society* (New York: St. Martin's Press, 1986).

17 Dyer, *Stars*, 175.

18 Naremore, *Acting in the Cinema*, 76.

19 Ronald L. Davis, *The Glamour Factory: Inside Hollywood's Big Studio System* (Dallas: Southern Methodist University Press, 1993), 132.

20 Thomas Schatz, "'A Triumph of Bitchery': Warner Bros., Bette Davis, and *Jezebel*," in *The Studio System*, ed. Janet Staiger (New Brunswick, NJ: Rutgers University Press, 1995), 80–82.

21 Thomas Schatz, *The Genius of the System: Hollywood Filmmaking in the Studio Era* (New York: Pantheon Books, 1988), 318.

22 Davis, *The Glamour Factory*, 134.

23 Richard B. Jewell, *The Golden Age of Cinema: Hollywood, 1929–1945* (Malden, MA: Blackwell Publishing, 2007), 72–73.

24 Ibid., 257.

25 Davis, *The Glamour Factory*, 80–81.

26 Ibid., 81–82.

27 Ibid., 84.

28 Larry Ceplair, "SAG and the Motion Picture Blacklist," *Special Edition of the National Screen Actor: 50 Years: SAG Remembers the Blacklist*, January 1998, www.cobbles.com/simpp_archive/linkbackups/huac_blacklist.htm.

29 Davis, *The Glamour Factory*, 378.

30 Alva Johnston, "Hollywood's Ten Per Centers," *Saturday Evening Post* 215, no. 8 (August 22, 1942): 23–45.

31 Connie Bruck, *When Hollywood Had a King: The Reign of Lew Wasserman, Who Leveraged Talent into Power and Influence* (New York: Random House, 2004).

32 Jewell, *The Golden Age of Cinema*, 118.

33 Donald Bogle, *Toms, Coons, Mulattoes, Mammies, & Bucks: An Interpretive History of Blacks in American Films* (New York: Viking Press, 1973), 31.

34 Ibid., 44.

35 V. I. Pudovkin, *Film Technique and Film Acting*, trans. Ivor Montagu (London: Newnes, 1933), quoted in David A. Cook, *A History of Narrative Film*, 4th ed. (New York: W. W. Norton, 2004), 119.

36 Dick Powell, qtd. in Karen Burroughs Hannsberry, *Bad Boys: The Actors of Film Noir* (Jefferson, NC: McFarland, 2003), 524.

37 Qtd. in Tony Thomas, *The Dick Powell Story* (Burbank, CA: Riverwood Press, 1993), 15.

38 Ibid., 15.

39 Hannsberry, *Bad Boys*, 526.

40 Kevin Esch, "The Bond That Unbinds by Binding: Acting Mythology and the Film Community," in Taylor, *Theorizing Film Acting*, 127–128.

41 Hannsberry, *Bad Boys*, 523.

42 John O. Thompson, "Screen Acting and the Commutation Test," in Wojcik, *Movie Acting*, 37–48.

1 The Silent Screen, 1894-1927

1 Vachel Lindsay, *The Art of the Moving Picture* (New York: Modern Library, 2000), 18–20, 55–57.

2 Ibid., 108.

3 Ibid.

4 See John Burrows, *Legitimate Cinema: Theatre Stars in Silent British Films, 1908–1918* (Devon: University of Exeter Press, 2003); Eric de Kuyper, "Le théâtre comme 'mauvais objet,'" *Cinémathèque*, no. 11 (1997): 60–72; Annette Förster, "A Pendulum of Performances: Asta Nielsen on Stage and Screen," in *Researching Women in Silent Cinema: New Findings and Perspectives*, ed. Monica Dall'Asta, Victoria Duckett, and Lucia Tralli (Bologna: University of Bologna Press, 2013), 303–317; Christine Gledhill, *Reframing British Cinema 1918–1928: Between Restraint and Passion* (London: British Film Institute, 2003), especially chapter 1, "Theatricalising British Cinema"; and David Mayer, "Learning to See in the Dark," *Nineteenth Century Theatre* 25, no. 2 (Winter 1997).

5 David Mayer, "Acting in Silent Cinema: Which Legacy of the Theatre?," in *Screen Acting*, ed. Alan Lovell and Peter Krämer (London: Routledge, 1999), 10.

6 Ibid., 96–97.

7 Joseph R. Roach, *The Player's Passion: Studies in the Science of Acting* (Newark: University of Delaware Press, 1985), 60. See in general chapter 2, "Nature Still, But Nature Mechanized."

8 Ibid., 60.

9 Ibid., 70.

10 See Gustave Garcia, *The Actor's Art: A Practical Treatise on Stage Declamation, Public Speaking and Deportment* (London: Simpkin, Marshall & Co., 1888; reprint, Milton Keynes, UK: BiblioBazaar, 2010), 86–97.

11 See Cooper C. Graham's discussion (and citation of Edward Barrett Warman's *Gestures and Attitudes: An Exposition of the Delsarte Philosophy of Expression*, 1892) in "Unmasking Feelings: The Portrayal of Emotions in the Biograph Films of 1908–1911," *Performing Arts Annual 1988* (Washington, DC: Library of Congress, 1989), 100.

12 Nancy Lee Chalfa Ruyter, in *The Cultivation of Body and Mind in Nineteenth-Century American Delsartism* (Westport, CT: Greenwood Press, 1999), 8, cites the Abbé Delaumosne's *Delsarte System of Oratory* (1885), where Delsarte's lectures were included from the 3rd edition on, and Genevieve Stebbins's *Delsarte System of Expression* (1887), where his lectures were included from the 2nd edition on. These references provide evidence of Delsarte's work being published and reaching audiences in America in the 1880s.

13 *The Home and School Speaker: A Practical Manual of Delsarte Exercises and Elocution* (Chicago: W. B. Conkey Company, 1897). I would like to thank David Mayer for bringing this reader to my attention and giving me access to it.

14 Ibid., 3–16.

15 Nancy Lee Chalfa Ruyter, "Antique Longings: Genevieve Stebbins and American Delsartean Performance," in *Corporealities: Dancing, Knowledge, Culture, and Power*, ed. Susan Leigh Foster (London: Routledge, 1996), 74.

16 Ibid., 74.

17 Stebbins, cited in Wendell Stone, "Expressing Delsarte," *Pioneering North America: Mediators of European Culture and Literature*, ed. Klaus Martens (Würzburg: Königshausen and Neumann, 2000), 219.

18 See the brief biographical account of her life given in "Genevieve Stebbins," in *Rhetorical Theory by Women Before 1900: An Anthology*, ed. Jane Donawerth (Lanham, MD: Rowman and Littlefield, 2002), 195–196.

19 Ruyter, "Antique Longings," 80.

20 Percy MacKaye, cited in Wendell Stone, "Expressing Delsarte," 216.

21 "Chronique Théâtrale" [theatrical review], *Le Temps*, November 25, 1887, 1.

22 *L'Art du Théâtre* (1923; reprint, Paris: L'Harmattan, 1993), 116. (Bernhardt is developing her teacher Georges Antoine Élie's principle of gesture preceding speech; Élie was her teacher in deportment at the Conservatoire.)

23 Ibid., 116–117. See also Gerda Taranow's discussion of this in *Sarah Bernhardt: The Art within the Legend* (Princeton, NJ: Princeton University Press, 1972), 85–87.

24 This sequence might also suggest why Bernhardt considered *Tosca* a suitable vehicle for film and indeed a suitable subject for her first narrative film. Although made in 1908, *Tosca* was not released until after *Camille* and is today considered lost. See G. F. Blaisdell's review of the film, "Bernhardt in La Tosca (Universal Feature's Release)," *Moving Picture World*, October 19, 1912, 230–231; also see mention of it in later discussion, for example in "Sarah Bernhardt's 'La Tosca,'" November 2, 1912, 441.

25 Cited in Ruyter, "Antique Longings," 80.

26 Note also how photographs of movement also tied in to gesture in the theater.

27 "Letters to the Editor," *Motion Picture Story Magazine* 3, no. 5 (June 1912): 168.

28 Erwin Panofsky, "Style and Medium in the Motion Pictures," in *Film Theory and Criticism: Introductory Readings*, ed. Gerald Mast and Marshall Cohen (London: Oxford, 1974), 153.

29 *Moving Picture World*, February 10, 1912, 498–499.

30 Two-page advertisement, *Moving Picture World*, March 16, 1912, 982–983.

31 Two-page advertisement, *Moving Picture World*, March 23, 1912, 1088–1089.

32 Two-page advertisement, *Moving Picture World*, February 24, 1912, 700–701.

33 Advertisement, *Moving Picture World*, March 2, 1912, 799.

34 Advertisement, *Moving Picture World*, March 9, 1912, 833.

35 Two-page advertisement, *Moving Picture World*, February 17, 1912, 596–597.

36 "Bernhardt Brings Tears as Camille," *New York Times*, December 8, 1910, 13.

37 "The French Plays," *Times*, June 13, 1881, 13.

38 Francisque Sarcey, "Les représentations françaises a Londres," *Le Temps*, June 20, 1881, 2.

39 See the poster reproduced in Charles Musser, "Conversions and Convergences: Sarah Bernhardt in the Era of Technological Reproducibility, 1910–1913," *Film History* 25, no. 1–2 (2013): 162.

40 See David Mayer, "*Why Girls Leave Home*: Victorian and Edwardian 'Bad Girl' Melodrama Parodied in Early Film," *Theatre Journal* 58 (2006): 590–591.

41 "Reviews of Feature Subjects: Bernhardt in Camille," *New York Dramatic Mirror*, April 10, 1912, 26.

42 W. Stephen Bush, "Bernhardt and Réjane in Pictures," *Moving Picture World*, March 2, 1912, 760. I am aware that this might not be the precise moment he was indicating.

43 "Bernhardt as Marguerite Gautier," *New York Times*, November 16, 1880.

44 *Moving Picture World*, September 21, 1912, 1174.

45 "Bernhardt Conquers New World," *Moving Picture World*, March 9, 1912, 874–875.

46 G. Dureau, "Madame Sarah Bernhardt sur l'écran," *Ciné-Journal*, February 24, 1912, 3–4.

47 W. B. Yeats, "Notes," *Samhain* (Dublin: Searly Bryers, October 1902), 4.

48 See "The Reform of the Theatre," *Samhain*, October 1901, 10: "We must simplify acting, especially poetical drama. . . . We must get rid of everything that is restless, everything that draws the attention away from the sound of the voice, or from the few moments of intense expression, whether that expression is through the voice or through the hands; we must from time to time substitute for the movements that the eye sees the nobler movements that the heart sees, the rhythmical movements that seem to flow up into the imagination from some deeper life than that of the individual soul."

49 See the comment of A.E. (George William Russell) in "The Dramatic Treatment of Heroic Literature," in *Samhain*, October 1901, 13: "Man, when he has returned to himself, and to the knowledge of himself, may find a greater power in his voice than in those powers which he has painfully harnessed to perform his will, in steamship or railway. It is through drama alone that the writer can summon, even if vicariously, so great a power to his aid; and it is possible that we may yet hear on the stage, not merely the mimicry of human speech, but the old forgotten music which was heard in the drums of kings, which made the reveller grow silent and great warriors to bow low their face on their hands."

50 *Moving Picture World*, February 24, 1912, 700–701.

51 Advertisement, *Moving Picture World*, March 2, 1912, 799.

52 Georges Michel, "Sarah-Bernhard [*sic*] au Cinématographe," *Ciné-Journal*, March 16, 1912, 13. Translation mine.

53 "Bernhardt Conquers New World," *Moving Picture World*, March 9, 1912, 875.

54 David Mayer, "Acting in Silent Cinema: Which Legacy of the Theatre?," in *Screen Acting*, ed. Alan Lovell and Peter Krämer (London: Routledge, 1999), 18, 20.

55 "Sarah Bernhardt's Rehearsals," *Sporting Times*, in *New York Herald*, December 18, 1880, 6.

56 Martin Marks, *Music and the Silent Film* (New York: Oxford University Press, 1997), 100.

57 Clarence E. Sinn, "Music for the Picture," *Moving Picture World*, August 31, 1912, 871.

58 See Gish's own account of the nomadic lifestyle she and her sister Dorothy Gish endured as children in Lillian Gish, *The Movies, Mr. Griffith, and Me* (London: Columbus Books, 1969). See especially 14, where she states, "I learned early to be flexible."

59 Charles Affron, *Lillian Gish: Her Legend, Her Life* (New York: Scribner, 2001), 27.

60 James Naremore, *Acting in the Cinema* (Berkeley: University of California Press, 1988), 107.

61 Ibid., 104–105.

62 Affron, *Lillian Gish*, 45.

63 "Answers to Inquiries," *Motion Picture Story Magazine*, June 1913, 160.

64 *Motion Picture Story Magazine*, July 1913, 6.

65 Lindsay, *The Art of the Moving Picture*, 4, 8–9.

66 Kristen Hatch, "Lillian Gish: Clean, and White, and Pure as the Lily," in *Flickers of Desire: Movie Stars of the 1910s*, ed. Jennifer M. Bean (New Brunswick, NJ: Rutgers University Press, 2011), 70–71. (Note that Hatch cites Affron, *Lillian Gish*, 117, as the source for this, but it is on 125 that Affron speaks of Gish as "a great screen tragedienne.")

67 Affron, *Lillian Gish*, 125.

68 Scott Simmon, *The Films of D. W. Griffith* (New York: Cambridge University Press, 1993), 8.

69 Eileen Bowser, *The Transformation of the Cinema, A History of the American Cinema* 2 (Berkeley: University of California Press, 1994), 220.

70 Richard Koszarski, *An Evening's Entertainment: The Age of the Silent Feature Picture, 1915–1928* (Berkeley: University of California Press, 1994), 291.

71 Advertisement for Pathé's *La Dame aux camélias* starring Vittoria Lepanto, *Moving Picture World*, December 31, 1909, 961. I would like to thank Helen Day Mayer for her discussion with me about Gish's acting, particularly in *Broken Blossoms*.

72 See Ross Forman, *China and the Victorian Imagination: Empires Entwined* (New York: Cambridge University Press, 2013), 261n17, for original journal source; the first American publication is *Limehouse Nights* (New York: Robert M. McBride & Co., 1917).

73 Thomas Burke, "The Chink and the Child," *Limehouse Nights* (London: Cassell, 1916), 18, 27, 29.

74 Ibid., 18.

75 Naremore, *Acting in the Cinema*, 101.

76 Ibid., 106.

77 Burke, "The Chink and the Child," 20, 29.

78 Gish, *The Movies, Mr. Griffith, and Me*, 219–220.

79 Sandy Flitterman-Lewis, "The Blossom and the Bole: Narrative and Visual Spectacle in Early Film Melodrama," *Cinema Journal* 33, no. 3 (Spring 1994): 5.

80 Note that in the actual shot of the pan hitting her father's hand, Lucy is not covering the handle of the pan with this cloth. This is odd, as this is precisely when we see the pan's danger (in terms of burning). It is also odd as all of the previous and subsequent shots feature the cloth.

81 Tom Gunning, "The Mothering Heart," *The Griffith Project* 7 (London: British Film Institute, 2003), 76. See also Bryony Dixon's discussion of Victor Sjöström's *The Wind* (1928) in *100 Silent Films* (London: Palgrave Macmillan, 2011), 238, where she also notes that Gish is "almost driven demented" by the wind that shakes the shack and, realizing that the battering is a person, fatefully lets Roddy in.

82 Mayer, "*Why Girls Leave Home*," 593.

83 Ibid., 590.

2   Classical Hollywood, 1928–1946

1 Richard B. Jewell, *The Golden Age of Cinema: Hollywood, 1929–1945* (Malden, MA: Blackwell Publishing, 2007), 29.

2 Ibid., 33.

3 Ibid.

4 Ibid., 32.

5 Donald Crafton, *The Talkies: American Cinema's Transition to Sound, 1926–1931*, History of the American Cinema, vol. 4 (Berkeley: University of California Press, 1977), 178.

6 James F. Scott, *Film: The Medium and the Maker* (New York: Holt, Rinehart and Winston, 1975), 240.

7 Cynthia Baron, "Crafting Film Performances: Acting in the Hollywood Studio Era," in *Movie Acting: The Film Reader*, ed. Pamela Robertson Wojcik (New York: Routledge, 2004), 90–91. Also see James Naremore's classic study *Acting in the Cinema* (Berkeley: University of California Press, 1988).

8 Lillian Albertson, quoted in Baron, "Crafting Film Performances," 91.

9 André Loiselle and Jeremy Maron, "Introduction," in *Stages of Reality: Theatricality in Cinema*, ed. Loiselle and Maron (Toronto: University of Toronto Press, 2012), 5.

10 Richard Dyer, *Stars* (London: British Film Institute, 1979), 151.

11 For a listing and discussion of the "Top Ten" money making stars from 1932 through 1945, see Jewell, *The Golden Age of Cinema*, 268–298.

12 Lotte H. Eisner, *The Haunted Screen: Expressionism in the German Cinema and the Influence of Max Reinhardt* (Berkeley: University of California Press, 1969), 141.

13 See John Belton, *American Cinema/American Culture*, 2nd ed. (Boston: McGraw-Hill, 2005), 73.

14 Ibid.

15 Bette Davis, "The Actress Plays Her Part," in *Playing to the Camera: Film Actors Discuss Their Craft*, ed. Bert Cardullo, Harry Geduld, Ronald Gottesman, and Leigh Woods (New Haven, CT: Yale University Press, 1988), 183.

16 David Shipman, *The Great Movie Stars: The Golden Years* (New York: Crown Publishers, 1970), 253, 363.

17 Cynthia Baron, "Crafting Film Performances," 84–85.

18 Paul McDonald, *The Star System: Hollywood's Production of Popular Identities* (London: Wallflower Press, 2000), quoted in Erica Carter, "Stars after Sound," in *The Cinema Book*, ed. Pam Cook, 3rd ed. (London: British Film Institute, 2007), 125.

19 James Stewart, "The Many-Splendored Actor," in Cardullo et al., *Playing to the Camera*, 201.

20 Neil Doyle, "Olivia de Havilland Was Not Content to Be Merely a Beautiful Costumed Prop," *Films in Review* 13, no. 2 (February 1962): 77–79.

21 Thomas Schatz, *Boom and Bust: American Cinema in the 1940s*, vol. 6 (Berkeley: University of California Press, 1999), 3.

22 Peter Lucia, "Beulah Bondi: 'Perhaps the Most Consummate of Character Players,'" Nowever Then, noweverthen.com/many/bondi.html (accessed May 2, 2014).

23 Patrick McGilligan, *Alfred Hitchcock: A Life in Darkness and Light* (New York: Regan Books, 2004), 319–320.

24 Henry Fonda, "Reflections on Forty Years of Make-Believe," in Cardullo et al., *Playing to the Camera*, 213.

25 David Thomson, *America in the Dark: The Impact of Hollywood Films on American Culture* (New York: William Morrow, 1977), 115–116.

26 Cynthia Baron and Sharon Marie Carnicke, *Reframing Screen Performance* (Ann Arbor: University of Michigan Press, 2008), 236.

27 Linda J. Obalil, "Muni, Paul," in *The International Dictionary of Films and Filmmakers*, vol. 3, *Actors and Actresses*, ed. James Vinson (Chicago: St. James Press, 1986), 459.

28 Joan Crawford, "The Player: A Profile of an Art," in Cardullo et al., *Playing to the Camera*, 190–191.

29 Shipman, "Spencer Tracy," in *The Great Movie Stars*, 525–526.

30 Scott, *Film: The Medium and the Maker*, 242.

31 Ibid., 242, and Belton, *American Cinema/American Culture*, 115.

32 Carter, "Stars after Sound," 124.

33 Mike Mashon, "Pre-Code Hollywood," *Sight and Sound* 24, no. 5 (May 2014): 20.

34 Thomas Doherty, *Pre-Code Hollywood: Sex, Immorality, and Insurrection in American Cinema, 1930–1934* (New York: Columbia University Press, 1999), 3.

35 James Bell, "Pre-Code Hollywood," *Sight and Sound* 24, no. 5 (May 2014): 25.

36 Ibid., 23.

37 William Paul, *Ernst Lubitsch's American Comedy* (New York: Columbia University Press, 1983), 24.

38 Dan Callahan, "The Jezebel Swagger of Miriam Hopkins," *Sight and Sound* 22, no. 12 (December 2012): 38.

39 Paul, *Ernst Lubitsch's American Comedy*, 56.

40 Ibid., 65.

41 Steve Vineberg, *High Comedy in American Movies: Class and Humor from the 1920s to the Present* (Lanham, MD: Rowman and Littlefield, 2005), 11.

42 Ginger Rogers, *Ginger, My Story* (New York: HarperCollins, 1991), 129.

43 Ibid., 136.

44 Ibid., 161.

45 Stanley Solomon, *Beyond Formula: American Film Genres* (New York: Harcourt Brace Jovanovich, 1976), 63.

46 Elizabeth Kendall, *The Runaway Bride: Hollywood Romantic Comedy of the 1930s* (New York: Cooper Square Press, 2002), 96.

47 Ibid., 104.

48 Edward Gallafent, *Astaire and Rogers* (New York: Columbia University Press, 2002), 59.

49 Hannah Hyam, *Fred & Ginger: The Astaire-Rogers Partnership, 1934–1938* (Brighton: Pen Press Publishers, 2007), 78.

50 Arlene Croce, *The Fred Astaire and Ginger Rogers Book* (1972; reprint, E. P. Dutton, 1987), 108.

51 Hyam, *Fred & Ginger*, 209–210.

52 Leo Braudy, *The World in a Frame: What We See in Films* (Garden City, NY: Anchor Press/Doubleday, 1976), 200.

53 See Lucia, "Beulah Bondi," noweverthen.com/many/many.html.

54 John Spring, Letter: Beulah Bondi, *Films in Review* 14, no. 6 (June–July 1963): 374.

55 Richard de Cordova, "Genre and Performance: An Overview," in *Film Genre Reader II*, ed. Barry Keith Grant (Austin: University of Texas Press, 1995), 135, 137.

56 Nick Bradshaw, "Killing with Kindness [on *Make Way for Tomorrow*]," *Sight and Sound* 20, no. 11 (November 2010): 40.

57 Robin Wood, *Sexual Politics and Narrative Film: Hollywood and Beyond* (New York: Columbia University Press, 1998), 157. Also see my essay "Ozu's *Tokyo Story* and the 'Recasting' of McCarey's *Make Way for Tomorrow*," in *Ozu's Tokyo Story*, ed. David Desser (New York: Cambridge University Press, 1997), 25–52.

58 Murray Pomerance, "Performed Performance and *The Man Who Knew Too Much*," in *Theorizing Film Acting*, ed. Aaron Taylor (New York: Routledge, 2012), 64.

59 Ibid., 64. Another notable example of performed performance occurs in *The Letter* (William Wyler, 1940), in which Bette Davis murders her lover, then acts out a wholly false account of the events leading up to it to her husband, her lawyer, and a local official. Only the movie audience is suspicious of her performance. See Charles Affron, *Star Acting: Gish, Garbo, Davis* (New York: E. P. Dutton, 1977), 240–241.

60 Bradshaw, "Killing with Kindness," 40.

61 Dennis Brown, *Actors Talk: Profiles and Stories from the Acting Trade* (New York: Limelight Editions, 1999), 151.

62 For a discussion of how the film challenged Code standards "to suggest the fragility of middle-class norms and, consequently, of Hollywood's wartime vision of an ideal America,"

see Gaylyn Studlar, "*Double Indemnity* (1944): Hard-Boiled *Film Noir*," in *Film Analysis: A Norton Reader*, ed. Jeffrey Geiger and R. L. Rutsky (New York: W. W. Norton, 2005), 394.

63 Mary Ann Doane, cited in Richard de Cordova, "Genre and Performance: An Overview," 133.

64 De Cordova, "Genre and Performance," 133.

65 Richard Schickel, *Double Indemnity*, BFI Classics (London: British Film Institute, 1992), 44.

66 J. P. Telotte, "The Double Indemnity of *Noir* Discourse," in *Voices in the Dark: The Narrative Patterns of Film Noir* (Urbana: University of Illinois Press, 1989), 49–50.

67 Schickel, *Double Indemnity*, 59.

68 Ibid., 52.

69 Gene D. Phillips, *Some Like It Wilder: The Life and Controversial Films of Billy Wilder* (Lexington: University Press of Kentucky, 2010), 62.

3 Postwar Hollywood, 1947–1967

1 The most widely read of these was Constantin Stanislavski, *An Actor Prepares*, trans. Elizabeth Reynolds Hapgood (New York: Theatre Arts Books, 1936).

2 Mel Gordon, *Stanislavsky in America: An Actor's Workbook* (New York: Routledge, 2010), 10.

3 Rick Kemp, *Embodied Acting: What Neuroscience Tells Us about Performance* (New York: Routledge, 2012), 147.

4 Film critic David Thomson somewhat reductively labels this "the old English style of acting in which young players were taught elocution, fencing, manners, and pretending." David Thomson, "The Death of Method Acting," *Wall Street Journal,* December 5, 2009, online. wsj.com/article/SB10001424052748704107104574571821619515590.html.

5 David Sterritt, "From Stage Actor to Film Star," *Christian Science Monitor*, March 10, 1977, 22.

6 David Sheward, *Rage and Glory: The Volatile Life and Career of George C. Scott* (New York: Applause, 2008), 132.

7 Bruce McConachie, "Method Acting and the Cold War, *Theatre Survey* 41 (2000): 47–68, cited at 47.

8 Michael L. Quinn, "Self-Reliance and Ritual Renewal: Anti-Theatrical Ideology in American Method Acting," *Journal of Dramatic Theory and Criticism* 10, no. 1 (Fall 1995): 5–20, cited at 16.

9 *Shadows* has a complex history. It was completed in two considerably different versions, only one of which went into release. More important, it is not "an improvisation," even though an onscreen text declares it to be; it was developed from acting workshops in which improvisation was an oft-used technique. See Ray Carney, *Shadows* (London: British Film Institute, 2008).

10 Gaile McGregor, "Domestic Blitz: A Revisionist History of the Fifties," *American Studies* 34, no. 1 (Spring 1993): 5–33, cited at 20.

11 Norman Mailer, *Marilyn: A Biography* (New York: Gosset & Dunlap, 1973), 115.

12 Information on budgets and earnings in this essay is drawn from *The Numbers* (www.the-numbers.com/person/320401-Marilyn-Monroe) and other standard sources.

13 David Sterritt, "Shelley Became a Star and Then She Studied Acting," *Christian Science Monitor,* August 6, 1980, www.csmonitor.com/1980/0806/080601.html.

14 Carl E. Rollyson Jr., *Marilyn Monroe: A Life of the Actress* (Ann Arbor, MI: UMI Research Press, 1986), 77.

15 Shelley Winters, *Shelley: Also Known as Shirley* (New York: William Morrow and Company, 1980), 196, 208.

16 Ibid., 459–460.

17 Burton was nominated for seven Oscars, none of which he won. Winters was nominated four times, winning twice for supporting performances. Monroe was never nominated for an Academy Award.

18 Williams adapted *Boom!* from his 1963 play *The Milk Train Doesn't Stop Here Anymore.*

19 Harry M. Benshoff, "Movies and Camp," in *American Cinema of the 1960s: Themes and Variations*, ed. Barry Keith Grant (New Brunswick, NJ: Rutgers University Press, 2008), 150–171, cited at 162.

20 Kristen Hatch, "Movies and the New Faces of Masculinity," in *American Cinema of the 1950s: Themes and Variations*, ed. Murray Pomerance (New Brunswick, NJ: Rutgers University Press, 2005), 43–64, cited at 45.

21 Vito Russo. *The Celluloid Closet: Homosexuality in the Movies*, rev. ed. (New York: Harper Perennial, 1987), 78.

22 Hatch, "Movies and the New Faces of Masculinity," 50.

23 David Gritten, "From Here to Eternity: Why 'Eternity' Will Endure For Ever," *The Telegraph*, September 9, 2010, www.telegraph.co.uk/culture/film/classic-movies/7992727/From-Here-to-Eternity-Why-Eternity-will-endure-for-ever.html.

24 Hatch, "Movies and the New Faces of Masculinity," 50.

25 Elia Kazan. *Elia Kazan: A Life* (New York: Knopf, 1988), 342–343, 346.

26 Budd Schulberg, "The King Who Would Be Man," *Vanity Fair* (March 2005), www.vanityfair.com/culture/features/2005/03/brand0200503. *On the Waterfront* was something of a Method family reunion: Brando, Malden, Steiger, Cobb, and Kazan were all certified members of the clan.

27 Arthur Miller, "Introduction," in Tennessee Williams, *A Streetcar Named Desire* (New York: New Directions, 2004), ix–xiv, cited at xii.

28 Quinn, "Self-Reliance and Ritual Renewal," 11.

29 Schulberg writes that as early as the Broadway run of *A Streetcar Named Desire*, Brando would tell his friend Malden that "checking in every night and pretending to be someone you weren't really wasn't respectable work for a grown man. . . . That was the beginning of Brando's lifelong put-down of the profession." Schulberg, "The King Who Would Be Man."

30 For extended discussion of performance tropes in *One-Eyed Jacks* see David Sterritt, "Defining the Situation: Brando, Role-Playing, and the Western as Performance Art," in *Guiltless Pleasures: A David Sterritt Film Reader* (Jackson: University Press of Mississippi, 2005), 50–65.

31 Pauline Kael, *5001 Nights at the Movies: A Guide from A to Z* (New York: Holt, Rinehart and Winston, 1982), 432. Raymond Durgnat, *Films and Feelings* (Cambridge, MA: MIT Press, 1967), 269–270.

32 Oscar Brockett and Robert Findlay, *Century of Innovation* (Englewood Cliffs, NJ: Prentice Hall, 1971). 573. Cited in Richard A. Blum, *American Film Acting: The Stanislavski Heritage* (Ann Arbor, MI: UMI Research Press, 1977), 59.

33 James Naremore, *Acting in the Cinema* (Berkeley: University of California Press, 1988), 202.

34 Peter Manso, *Brando: The Biography* (New York: Hyperion, 1994), 484.

35 Elia Kazan. *Kazan on Directing* (New York: Vintage, 2010), 185–186.

36 Patrick McGilligan, *Nicholas Ray: The Glorious Failure of an American Director* (New York: HarperCollins, 2011), 274.

37 Lawrence Frascella and Al Weisel, *Live Fast, Die Young: The Wild Ride of Making "Rebel Without a Cause"* (New York: Touchstone, 2005), 27; cited in McGilligan, *Nicholas Ray*, 276.

38 Dean received no screen credits for his bit parts in the early 1950s. He worked on the stage and in television before reaching stardom in *East of Eden* and then *Rebel Without a Cause*. He died (in a car crash at age twenty-four) in September 1955.

39 Kazan, *Kazan on Directing*, 186–187.

40 Claudia Springer, *James Dean Transfigured: The Many Faces of Rebel Iconography* (Austin: University of Texas Press, 2007), 14–15.

41 Joseph Humphreys, ed., *Jimmy Dean on Jimmy Dean* (London: Plexus Publishing, 1990), 122–123, 124; cited in Springer, *James Dean Transfigured*, 87.

42 Springer, *James Dean Transfigured*, 28.

43 "I cannot concur in an impression that has some currency," Kazan said, "that [Dean] fell into [Brando's] mannerisms; he had his own and they were ample." Kazan, *Kazan on Directing*, 187.

44 Matthew Sewell, "James Dean's Clumsy Punch." *Bright Lights Film Journal* 70 (November 2010), brightlightsfilm.com/70/70jamesdean_sewell.php#.UhaRmrzHQwy.

45 Kazan, *Elia Kazan*, 538. Sewell acknowledges Kazan's remark in "James Dean's Clumsy Punch."

46 Brando's films of this period include *Guys and Dolls* (Joseph L. Mankiewicz, 1955), *Mutiny on the Bounty* (Lewis Milestone, 1962), *The Chase* (Arthur Penn, 1966), *A Countess from Hong Kong* (Charles Chaplin, 1967), and *Candy* (Christian Marquand, 1968).

47 Steve Vineberg, *Method Actors: Three Generations of an American Acting Style* (New York: Schirmer Books, 1991), 91.

4 The Auteur Renaissance, 1968–1980

1 See Jon Lewis, "The Perfect Money Machine(s): George Lucas, Steven Spielberg, and Auteurism in the New Hollywood," in *Looking Past the Screen: Case Studies in American Film History and Method*, ed. Jon Lewis and Eric Smoodin (Durham, NC: Duke University Press, 2007), 61–86.

2 David A. Cook, *Lost Illusions: American Cinema in the Shadow of Watergate and Vietnam, 1970–1979* (Berkeley: University of California Press, 2000), xvii. For another discussion of the two "New Hollywoods," see Thomas Elsaesser, Alexander Horwath, and Noel King, eds., *The Last Great American Picture Show: New Hollywood Cinema in the 1970s* (Amsterdam: Amsterdam University Press, 2004), 19–35.

3 Hoffman claims that he himself was the first to tell the story and he then debunks it in his interview with James Lipton on *Inside the Actor's Studio*, season 12, episode 16, June 18, 2006.

4 For example, while shooting *East of Eden* (Elia Kazan, 1955), James Dean's extensive Method preparations and lack of technical skill greatly irritated Raymond Massey. See Raymond Massey, *A Hundred Different Lives* (Boston: Little, Brown, 1979), 376–378.

5 Laurence Olivier interview with Kenneth Tynan in *Great Acting*, ed. Hal Burton (New York: Hill and Wang, 1967), 123.

6 Cynthia Baron, Diane Carson, and Frank P. Tomasulo, eds., *More Than a Method: Trends and Traditions in Contemporary Film Performance* (Detroit: Wayne State University Press, 2004), 1–2.

7   David A. Cook writes that between 1969 and 1971, the major Hollywood studios lost $600 million. Cook, *Lost Illusions*, 3.

8   For statistical details of the decline in box office revenues see Jim Hillier, *The New Hollywood* (New York: Continuum, 1994), 13.

9   Paul McDonald, *The Star System: Hollywood's Production of Popular Identities* (London: Wallflower 2000), 75–76.

10 Barry King, "Embodying an Elastic Self: The Parametrics of Contemporary Stardom," in *Contemporary Hollywood Stardom*, ed. Thomas Austin and Martin Baker (London: Arnold, 2003), 49.

11 Maureen Orth, "How to Succeed: Fail, Lose, Die," *Newsweek*, March 4, 1974, 51.

12 Axel Madsen, *The New Hollywood* (New York: Thomas Y. Crowell, 1975), 47.

13 Jeff Lenburg, *Dustin Hoffman: Hollywood's Anti-Hero* (New York: St. Martin's Press, 1983), 119.

14 Andrew J. Rausch, *Martin Scorsese and Robert De Niro* (Lanham, MD: Scarecrow Press, 2010), 32.

15 Ibid., 79.

16 Richard Schickel, "Brutal Attraction: The Making of *Raging Bull*," *Vanity Fair* 52, no. 3 (March 2010): 292.

17 Jack Kroll, "De Niro: A Star for the 70s," *Newsweek*, May 16, 1977, 82.

18 Rausch, *Martin Scorsese and Robert De Niro*, 50.

19 George Hickenlooper, *Real Conversations: Candid Interviews with Film's Foremost Directors and Critics* (New York: Citadel Press, 1991), 27.

20 Rausch, *Martin Scorsese and Robert De Niro*, 51–52.

21 Steve Vineberg, *Method Actors: Three Generations of an American Acting Style* (New York: Schirmer Books, 1991), 275.

22 Rehearsal notes and transcripts of talks among Hal Ashby, Bruce Dern, Jane Fonda, and Jon Voight. March 24, 1977, to April 3, 1977, Margaret Herrick Library, Academy of Motion Picture Arts and Sciences, Beverly Hills, CA. See also David Thomson, *Overexposures: The Crisis in American Filmmaking* (New York: William Morrow, 1981), 228–230.

23 Warren Beatty, interview by Mike Wilmington and Gerald Peary for *The Daily Cardinal* and *The Velvet Light Trap* (Winter 1972/73).

24 Pamela Robertson Wojcik gives a brief overview of the scholarly discussion of actors as auteurs in her editor's introduction to *Movie Acting: The Film Reader* (New York: Routledge, 2004), 1–13.

25 Several scholars have made the point that the promotion of an auteurist pantheon in the 1970s was as much a marketing ploy on the part of the studios as it was an artistic designation on the part of film critics and historians. See, for example, Jon Lewis, "The Perfect Money Machine(s)," 68–69.

26 For a good introduction to the critical debate about film authorship, see Virginia Wright Wexman, ed., *Film and Authorship* (New Brunswick, NJ: Rutgers University Press, 2002).

27 Andrew Sarris, "The Actor as Auteur," *American Film* 2, no. 7 (May 1977): 16–19.

28 Richard Dyer's book *Stars* (London: British Film Institute, 1979) was one of the first studies of stardom and performance to explore the idea of actors as auteurs. Dyer insisted that theories of authorship needed to consider the ways in which the star persona, force of personality, and performing style play a substantial role in the overall design and vision of a movie.

29 Sharon Marie Carnicke, "Screen Performance and Directors' Visions," in Baron, Carson, and Tomasulo, *More Than a Method*, 57.

30 For a discussion of how the use of the Steadicam in films of this period affected actors and directors, see Serena Ferrara, *Steadicam: Techniques and Aesthetics* (Oxford: Focal Press), 2001.

31 Peter Biskind, *Easy Riders, Raging Bulls: How the Sex-Drugs-and-Rock 'n' Roll Generation Saved Hollywood* (New York: Simon & Schuster, 1998), 103–104.

32 Interview with Doug Tomlinson, February 19, 1982. Quoted in *Actors on Acting for the Screen: Roles and Collaborations*, ed. Doug Tomlinson (New York: Garland, 1994), 50.

33 See *Casting By*, directed by Tom Donahue (HBO Documentary Films, 2013).

34 See Shyon Baumann, *Hollywood Highbrow: From Entertainment to Art* (Princeton, NJ: Princeton University Press, 2007), and Tino Balio, *Foreign Film Renaissance on American Screens: 1946–73* (Madison: University of Wisconsin Press, 2010).

35 See Jonathan Rosenbaum, "New Hollywood and the Sixties Melting Pot," in Elsaesser, Horwath, and King, *The Last Great American Picture Show*, 131–152.

36 For testimonies from directors of 1970s films about their debt to New Wave cinema, see the documentary *A Decade under the Influence*, directed by Ted Demme and Richard LaGravanese (IFC Films, 2003).

37 For a discussion of the process of audience engagement and identification with characters, see Murray Smith, *Engaging Characters: Fiction, Emotion, and the Cinema* (Oxford: Oxford University Press, 1995).

38 In *Hollywood Incoherent: Narration in Seventies Cinema* (Austin: University of Texas Press, 2010), 217, Todd Berliner refers to the "characterological inconsistency" of many performances of that decade. He writes about the films that contain those performances as "something of a Golden Age of narrative perversity in Hollywood cinema."

39 Sarah Kozloff, *Overhearing Film Dialogue* (Berkeley: University of California Press, 2000).

40 For discussions of the primacy of the notion of authenticity in 1970s American culture and politics, see Bruce J. Shulman, *The Seventies: The Great Shift in American Culture, Society and Politics* (Cambridge: Da Capo Press, 2002), and the introduction to Erica J. Seifert, *The Politics of Authenticity in Presidential Campaigns, 1976 to 2008* (Jefferson, NC: McFarland, 2012).

41 See *For the Love of Movies: The Story of American Film Criticism*, directed by Gerald Peary (AG Films, 2009).

42 Brian Kellow, *Pauline Kael: A Life in the Dark* (New York: Viking, 2011), 269–273.

43 Richard Dyer, *Stars* (London: British Film Institute, 1979); Richard Dyer, *Heavenly Bodies: Film Stars and Society* (New York: St. Martin's Press, 1986).

44 King, "Embodying an Elastic Self: The Parametrics of Contemporary Stardom," 46–47.

45 Pauline Kael, "Goodbar, or How Nice Girls Go Wrong," *The New Yorker*, October 24, 1977, 147–150.

46 In "Reexamining Stardom: Questions of Texts, Bodies, and Performances," Christine Geraghty distinguishes among performers, professionals, and celebrities; the essential distinction has to do with the extent to which an actor's fame derives from one's work as opposed to one's public persona. See *Reinventing Film Studies*, ed. Christine Gledhill and Linda Williams (London: Arnold Publishers, 2000), 183–201.

47 Biskind, *Easy Riders, Raging Bulls*; Cook, *Lost Illusions*; Elsaesser, Horwath, and King, *The Last Great American Picture Show*; Lester Friedman, ed., *American Cinema in the 1970s: Themes and Variations* (New Brunswick, NJ: Rutgers University Press, 2007); Geoff King, ed., *New Hollywood Cinema: An Introduction* (New York: Columbia University Press, 2002); Jonathan Kirschner, *Hollywood's Last Golden Age: Politics, Society, and the Seventies Film in America* (Ithaca, NY: Cornell University Press, 2012); Peter Lev, *American Films of the 70s: Conflicting Visions* (Austin: University of Texas Press, 2000); William J. Palmer, *The Films of the Seventies: A Social History* (Metuchen, NJ: Scarecrow Press, 1987); Thomas Schatz, *Old Hollywood/New Hollywood: Ritual, Art, and Industry* (Ann Arbor, MI: UMI Research Press, 1983).

48   Cited in Cook, *Lost Illusions*, 67.

49   Ibid., 67–69.

50   Ibid., 70–71.

51   Elliott Gould interview by Danny Peary, *Bijou* 1, no. 3 (August 1977): 31.

52   Elliott Gould interview by Richard Warren Lewis, *Playboy* 17, no. 11 (November 1970): 262–264.

53   For an analysis of *The Godfather*'s correlation of ethnicity and authenticity, see Michael DeAngelis, "Movies and Confession," in Friedman, *American Cinema in the 1970s*, 71–94.

54   *A Decade under the Influence*, dir. Demme and LaGravanese.

55   Ibid.

56   Micki McGee, *Self-Help, Inc.: Makeover Culture in American Life* (Oxford: Oxford University Press, 2005), 171.

57   Vineberg, *Method Actors*, 7.

58   James Naremore, *Acting in the Cinema* (Berkeley: University of California Press, 1988), 2.

59   Vineberg, *Method Actors*, 110.

60   See ibid. and also Foster Hirsch, *A Method to Their Madness: The History of the Actors Studio* (New York: W. W. Norton, 1984).

61   Eric Morris and Joan Hotchkis, *No Acting Please: Beyond the Method: A Revolutionary Approach to Acting and Living* (Burbank, CA: Whitehouse/Spelling Publications, 1977).

62   In addition to the transcripts for *Coming Home* cited above, see Eleanor Coppola, *Notes: The Making of Apocalypse Now* (New York: Simon and Schuster, 1979), and Peter Cowie, *The Apocalypse Now Book* (New York: Da Capo Press, 2000).

63   Cynthia Baron, in "Crafting Film Performances: Acting in the Hollywood Studio Era," details how studio-hired acting coaches worked with contract players to develop their characters' backstories. In *Screen Acting*, ed. Alan Lovell and Peter Krämer (London: Routledge, 1999), 40.

64   Unpublished letter from Jill Clayburgh to Alan J. Pakula, October 20, 1978, file 673, Margaret Herrick Library, Academy of Motion Picture Arts and Sciences, Beverly Hills, CA.

65   Richard Maltby, *Hollywood Cinema*, 2nd ed. (Malden, MA: Wiley-Blackwell, 2003), 394.

66   Bert Cardullo et al., eds., *Playing to the Camera: Film Actors Discuss Their Craft* (New Haven, CT: Yale University Press, 1998), 281.

67   Ibid., 301.

68   Diane Carson, "Plain and Simple: Masculinity through John Sayles's Lens," in Baron, Carson, and Tomasulo, *More Than a Method*, 173–174.

69   Barry King, "Articulating Stardom," in *Stardom: Industry of Desire*, ed. Christine Gledhill (London: Routledge, 1991), 167–182.

70   Andrew Higson, "Film Acting and Independent Cinema," in Wojcik, *Movie Acting: The Film Reader*, 161.

71   Naremore, *Acting*, 19.

72   Jerzy Grotowski, *Towards a Poor Theatre* (New York: Simon and Schuster, 1970).

73   For an analysis of how such an acting style revealed itself in films of the period, see Virginia Wright Wexman's discussion of *Nashville* (Robert Altman, 1975) in *Creating the Couple: Love, Marriage, and Hollywood Performance* (Princeton, NJ: Princeton University Press, 1993), 183–201.

74   Naremore, *Acting*, 27–30.

75   Nick Davis, "Julie Christie and Vanessa Redgrave: Performance and the Politics of

Singularity," in *Hollywood Reborn: Movie Stars of the 1970s*, ed. James Morrison (New Brunswick, NJ: Rutgers University Press, 2010), 187.

76 Ibid., 189.

5 The New Hollywood, 1981–1999

1 Jon Lewis, *American Film: A History* (New York: W. W. Norton, 2008), 351–352.

2 Ibid., 399.

3 Stephen Prince, "Introduction: Movies and the 1980s," in *American Cinema of the 1980s: Themes and Variations,* ed. Stephen Prince (New Brunswick, NJ: Rutgers University Press, 2007), 2.

4 Barry Langford, *Post-Classical Hollywood: Film Industry, Style and Ideology since 1945* (Edinburgh: Edinburgh University Press, 2010), 246.

5 David Thomson, "The Decade When Movies Mattered," in *The Last Great American Picture Show: New Hollywood Cinema in the 1970s*, ed. Thomas Elsaesser, Alexander Horwath, and Noel King (Amsterdam: Amsterdam University Press, 2004), 73–82.

6 James Kendrick, *Hollywood Bloodshed: Violence in 1980s American Cinema* (Carbondale: Southern Illinois University Press, 2009), ix.

7 Linda Ruth Williams and Michael Hammond, "Introduction: The 1990s," in *Contemporary American Cinema*, ed. Linda Ruth Williams and Michael Hammond (Maidenhead: Open University Press, 2006), 325.

8 See Yvonne Tasker, "Action Heroines in the 1980s: The Limits of 'Musculinity,'" in *Spectacular Bodies: Gender, Genre and Action Cinema* (London: Routledge, 1993), 132-152.

9 Linda Ruth Williams, "Arnold Schwarzenegger: Corporeal Charisma," in *Pretty People: Movie Stars of the 1990s*, ed. Anna Everett (New Brunswick, NJ: Rutgers University Press, 2012), 21.

10 Prince, "Introduction," 1, 20.

11 Jon Lewis, ed., *The End of Cinema as We Know It: American Film in the Nineties* (London: Pluto Press, 2002).

12 Kevin Esch, "'I Don't See Any Method at All': The Problem of Actorly Transformation," *Journal of Film and Video* 58, no. 1–2 (Spring/Summer 2006): 96.

13 Ibid., 96–97.

14 Ibid.

15 Ibid.

16 Janet Maslin, "Review/Film; A Mirror Image of Disintegration," *New York Times*, September 23, 1988, 18.

17 James Naremore, *Acting in the Cinema* (Berkeley: University of California Press, 1988), 69.

18 Cynthia Baron and Sharon Marie Carnicke, *Reframing Screen Performance* (Ann Arbor: University of Michigan Press, 2008), 186.

19 Ibid., 185.

20 Graham Fuller, "Getting Out of My Head: An Interview with Edward Norton," *Cineaste* 25, no. 1 (Winter 1999): 6.

21 Lynn Norment, "Why Will Smith Is Hollywood's Biggest Summer Attraction," *Ebony* 54, no. 9 (July 1999): 46.

22 Ibid.

23 Barry King, "Embodying an Elastic Self: The Parametrics of Contemporary Stardom," in *Contemporary Hollywood Stardom*, ed. Thomas Austin and Martin Barker (London: Arnold, 2003), 60.

24 For a detailed discussion of Smith's "crossover" stardom see Geoff King, "Stardom in the Willennium," in Austin and Barker, *Contemporary Hollywood Stardom*, 62–73.

25 While it would seem to be quite a leap from serious acting, Smith has noted that his career as a rap artist prepared him for acting: "My training has a lot to do with the nature of rap music . . . there's a certain level of confidence that you have to have to survive as a rapper. You can't be shy and you can't be insecure as a rapper. Those are the same parameters and the same tenets necessary to be successful as an actor." Lori Talley, "Will to Power: How a Fresh-Faced Philly Rapper Became One of America's Best and Biggest Actors," *Back Stage West* 9, no. 3 (January 17, 2002): 1.

26 Michael Hofferber, "Renaissance in American Schools: Training for Actors in the 1980s Changing," *Back Stage*, January 25, 1985, 40.

27 Esther Walker, "The Tall Guy: Jeff Goldblum Gets Personal," *The Independent*, April 8, 2008.

28 Vic Ziegel, "*The Big Chill* Makes Jeff Goldblum a Contender," *New York Magazine*, September 26, 1983, 78.

29 A separate award did not exist until the following year when the category was introduced as a result of criticisms about *The Elephant Man*'s Christopher Tucker being overlooked.

30 Vincent Canby, "*The Elephant Man* (1980)," *New York Times*, October 3, 1980.

31 Roderick Mann, "A Tale of Misery," *Los Angeles Times*, October 7, 1980, 1–5.

32 Geoff Andrew, "John Hurt: The Guardian Interview," *Guardian*, April 27, 2000.

33 Variety Staff, "Review: The Elephant Man," *Variety*, December 31, 1979.

34 Roger Ebert, "The Elephant Man," *Chicago Sun-Times*, January 1, 1980.

35 "Inside the Actors Studio: Billy Bob Thornton," season 8, episode 18, August 18, 2002, Bravo TV.

36 Susan Linfield, "Zen and the Art of Film Acting," *American Film* (July/August 1986): 28–33. With thanks to Abraham Tetenbaum from the AFI for tracking down this interview.

37 Ibid., 30.

38 Roger Ebert, "*Kiss of the Spider Woman*," *Chicago Sun-Times*, August 9, 1985; Linfield, "Zen," 32.

39 Dan Yakir, "Had Time Hurt," *Film Comment* 21, no. 4 (July/August, 1985): 57.

40 Lisa Cholodenko, "Girl Interrupted (Interview with Kimberly Peirce)," *Filmmaker Magazine* (Fall 1999).

41 Elizabeth Bronfen, *The Knotted Subject: Hysteria and Its Discontents* (Princeton, NJ: Princeton University Press, 1998), 382, 385.

42 Linda Badley, *Film, Horror and the Body Fantastic* (Westport, CT: Greenwood Press, 1995), 25.

43 Kristin Thompson, "The Concept of Cinematic Excess," *Cine-Tracts* 1, no. 2 (Summer 1977): 62–63.

44 Ibid., 56, 63.

45 Carole Zucker, "The Concept of 'Excess' in Film Acting," *Post Script* 12, no. 2 (1993): 61.

46 Variety Staff, "Review: The Shining," *Variety*, December 31, 1979.

47 Pauline Kael, "Devolution: *The Shining*," in *Taking It All In: Film Writings 1980–1983* (London: Arrow Books, 1987), 3.

48 Zucker, "The Concept of 'Excess,'" 61.

49 Variety Staff, "*Vampire's Kiss*," *Variety*, December 31, 1987.

50 Caryn James, "*Vampire's Kiss*," *New York Times*, June 2, 1989.

51 Hal Hinson, "*Vampire's Kiss*," *Washington Post*, June 2, 1989.

52 Emma Brockes, "People Think I'm Not in on the Joke," *Guardian*, July 29, 2013, 24.

53 For more on expressionist acting see Lotte H. Eisner, *The Haunted Screen: Expressionism in the German Cinema and the Influence of Max Reinhardt* (Berkeley: University of California Press, 1952), 137–150.

54 Brian D. Johnson, "*Leaving Las Vegas*," *Macleans* 108, no. 44 (October 30, 1995): 57.

55 Janet Maslin, "*Leaving Las Vegas* Is Voted Best Film by Critics Circle," *New York Times*, December 15, 1995.

56 David Thomson, "The Hole You're In," *Film Comment* 3, no. 6 (November 1995): 38.

57 Philip Kemp, "*Leaving Las Vegas*," *Sight & Sound* (January 1996): 44–45. Not all reviews were positive about Cage's performance. In his review of the film for the *National Review*, John Simon noted that he had seen "better acting in a chimpanzee." John Simon, "*Leaving Las Vegas*," *National Review* 47, no. 22 (November 27, 1995): 67.

58 James Bone, "De Vil Incarnate: Interview," *Times*, December 7, 1996, 8.

59 David Sacks, "I Never Was an Ingénue," *New York Times*, January 27, 1991, 24.

60 Ibid.

61 Emanuel Levy, "Oscar History: Disregarding Ensemble Acting," *Cinema 24/7* (2013): www.emanuellevy.com.

62 David Blum, "Hollywood's Brat Pack," *New York Magazine*, June 10, 1985, 46.

63 V. I. Pudovkin, *Film Technique and Film Acting* (London: Vision Press, 1968), 111–112.

64 The notion of actors playing characters who are themselves performing also occurs in *Pulp Fiction* and *Jackie Brown*, as well as Tarantino's later films *Inglourious Basterds* (2009) and *Django Unchained* (2012), both resulting in Oscars for Best Supporting Actor for Christoph Waltz.

65 Cynthia Fuchs, "Interview with Paul Thomas Anderson: *Magnolia*," PopMatters, 1999, www.popmatters.com/feature/anderson-paulthomas.

66 Donna Peberdy, *Masculinity and Film Performance: Male Angst in Contemporary American Cinema* (Basingstoke: Palgrave Macmillan, 2011), 95–120.

67 For more on *Magnolia* as melodrama see Joanne Clarke Dillman, "*Magnolia* Masquerading as Soap Opera," *Journal of Popular Film and Television* 33, no. 3 (Fall 2005): 143, 146.

68 Charles Eidsvik, *Cineliteracy: Film amongst the Arts* (New York: Random House, 1978), 93, 100.

69 Ibid.

70 Jeff Gordinier, "A Time to Chill," *Entertainment Weekly*, November 6, 1998, 36.

71 Wes Anderson increasingly followed suit in the 2000s with his all-star ensembles *The Royal Tenenbaums* (2001), *The Life Aquatic with Steve Zissou* (2004), and *The Grand Budapest Hotel* (2014).

72 I consider acting in the films of Wes Anderson in more detail in "'I'm Just a Character in Your Film': Acting and Performance from Autism to Zissou," *New Review of Film and Television Studies* 10, no. 1, (2012): 46–67, special issue on Wes Anderson and Co.

6 The Modern Entertainment Marketplace, 2000–Present

1 Sharon Marie Carnicke, "Emotional Expressivity in Motion Capture Technology," in *Acting and Performance in Moving Image Culture: Bodies, Screens, Renderings*, ed. Jörg Sternagel, Deborah Levitt, and Dieter Mersch (Piscataway, NJ: Transaction Publishers, 2012), 331.

2 Christine Cornea, "2-D Performance and the Re-animated Actor in Science Fiction Cinema," in *Genre and Performance: Film and Television*, ed. Christine Cornea (New York: Manchester University Press), 150.

3 Murray Pomerance, "Introduction: Stardom in the 2000s," in *Shining in the Shadows: Movie Stars of the 2000s*, ed. Murray Pomerance (New Brunswick, NJ: Rutgers University Press, 2012), 3.

4 Anne Friedberg, "The End of Cinema: Multi-media and Technological Change," in *Reinventing Film Studies*, ed. Christine Gledhill and Linda Williams (London: Arnold, 2000), 439.

5 Stephen Keane, *CineTech: Film, Convergence, and New Media* (New York: Palgrave Macmillan, 2007), 29.

6 Ibid., 150.

7 Ibid., 10, 107.

8 Ibid., 107–108.

9 Ibid., 10.

10 Lev Manovich, *The Language of New Media* (Cambridge, MA: MIT Press, 2001), 9.

11 Geoff King, *Indiewood, USA: Where Hollywood Meets Independent Cinema* (New York: I. B. Tauris, 2009), 4.

12 Maitland McDonagh, "Action Painter John Woo," *Film Comment* 29, no. 5 (September 1993): 48.

13 Patrick Tucker, *Secrets of Screen Acting*, 2nd ed. (New York: Routledge, 2003), 57.

14 Pamela Robertson Wojcik, "The Sound of Film Acting," *Journal of Film and Video* 58, nos. 1–2 (Spring/Summer 2006): 71. See Lisa Bode, "No Longer Themselves? Framing Digitally Enabled Posthumous 'Performances,'" *Cinema Journal* 49, no. 4 (Summer 2010): 46–70.

15 Ibid., 72, 78, 75.

16 Ed Hooks, *Acting Strategies for the Cyber Age* (Portsmouth, NH: Heinemann, 2001), 1.

17 Andy Serkis, *Gollum: How We Made Movie Magic* (New York: Houghton Mifflin, 2003), 110.

18 Ibid., 117.

19 Ibid.

20 Carnicke, "Emotional Expressivity in Motion Capture Technology," 322.

21 Donald Crafton, *Shadow of a Mouse: Performance, Belief, and World-Making in Animation* (Berkeley: University of California Press, 2013), 15–57.

22 See Derek Hayes and Chris Webster, *Acting and Performance for Animation* (New York: Focal Press, 2013); Ed Hooks, *Acting for Animators*, 3rd ed. (Portsmouth, NH: Heinemann, 2011); Angie Jones and Jamie Oliff, *Thinking Animation: Bridging the Gap between 2D and CG* (Boston: Thomson, 2007); and John Kundert-Gibbs and Kristin Kundert-Gibbs, *Action! Acting Lessons for CG Animators* (Indianapolis: Wiley, 2009).

23 Thomas Schatz, "2008: Movies and a Hollywood Too Big to Fail," in *American Cinema in the 2000s: Themes and Variations*, ed. Timothy Corrigan (New Brunswick, NJ: Rutgers University Press, 2012), 208.

24 Frederick Levy, *15 Minutes of Fame: Becoming a Star in the YouTube Revolution* (New York: Alpha Books, 2008), 31.

25 Keane, *CineTech*, 22.

26 Barbara Klinger, "The Contemporary Cinephile: Film Collecting in the Post-Video Era," in *Hollywood Spectatorship: Changing Perceptions of Cinema Audiences*, ed. Melvin Stokes and Richard Maltby (London: British Film Institute, 2001), 133–134.

27 Quoted in Levy, *15 Minutes of Fame*, 147.

28 Timothy Corrigan, "Introduction: Movies and the 2000s," in Corrigan, *American Cinema in the 2000s*, 4.

29 Dana Polan, "2009: Movies, a Nation, and New Identities," in Corrigan, *American Cinema in the 2000s*, 236.

30 Keane, *CineTech*, 2.

31 Polan, "2009: Movies, a Nation, and New Identities," 236.

32 Ibid.

33 Andrew Mactavish, "Technological Pleasure: The Performance and Narrative of Technology in *Half-Life* and Other High-Tech Computer Games," in *ScreenPlay: Cinema/Videogames/Interfaces*, ed. Geoff King and Tanya Krzywinska (London: Wallflower, 2002), 45, 46.

34 Corrigan, "Introduction: Movies and the 2000s," 4.

35 Nora Alter, "2000: Movies, Anti-Climaxes, and Disenchantments," in Corrigan, *American Cinema in the 2000s*, 39.

36 Keane, *CineTech*, 2.

37 Bob Rehak, "2003: Movies, 'Shock and Awe,' and the Troubled Blockbuster," in Corrigan, *American Cinema of the 2000s*, 89.

38 Keane, *CineTech*, 98.

39 Jan Mukařovský, *Aesthetic Function, Norm and Value as Social Facts*, trans. Mark E. Suino (Ann Arbor: University of Michigan Press, 1970), 40.

40 Ibid.

41 Hayes and Webster, *Acting and Performance for Animation*, 29.

42 Robert Barton, *Acting Onstage and Off*, 4th ed. (Belmont, CA: Thomson Wadsworth, 2006), 159.

43 Ibid., 160.

44 "Acting Program," *School of Theater, California Institute of the Arts*, theater.calarts.edu/programs/acting (accessed October 11, 2013).

45 Hooks, *Acting Strategies for the Cyber Age*, 24–27.

46 "FAQs," *Peter Kelly Acting*, actingonfilm.com/faq.html (accessed October 10, 2013).

47 Richard Hornby, *The End of Acting: A Radical View* (New York: Applause, 1992), 245.

48 Jean Sabatine, *Movement Training for the Stage and Screen* (New York: Back Stage Books, 1995), 14.

49 Hornby, *The End of Acting*, 204.

50 Clive Barker, "Joan Littlewood," in *Twentieth Century Actor Training*, ed. Alison Hodge (New York: Routledge, 2000), 115.

51 Ibid., 119.

52 Jacques Lecoq, "Theatre of Gesture and Image," in *The Intercultural Performance Reader*, ed. Patrice Pavis (New York: Routledge, 1996), 142.

53 Quoted in Richard Schechner, "Julie Taymor: From Jacques Lecoq to *The Lion King*: An Interview," in *Popular Theatre: A Sourcebook*, ed. Joel Schechter (New York: Routledge, 2003), 64.

54 Valerie Preston-Dunlap, *Rudolf Laban: An Extraordinary Life* (London: Dance Books, 1998), 273.

55 Sharon Marie Carnicke, "Stanislavsky's System: Pathways for the Actor," in *Twentieth Century Actor Training*, ed. Alison Hodge (New York: Routledge, 2000), 26. By 1913, Laban had developed a vision of dance based on body rhythm (not musical meter). Capturing attention for choreographing open-air movement choirs, Laban made modern

dance a distinct art form. His appointment in 1921 at the National Theater in Mannheim, Germany, confirmed his reputation as a founder of modern dance. Working in Germany during the Bauhaus and Expressionist periods, he established dance programs and schools; he wrote books, journals, and other publications. Forced to leave Nazi Germany at the height of his career, Laban fled to the United Kingdom and continued to expand his exploration of human movement through collaborations with theater directors, educators, and industrialists.

56 Warren Lamb and Elizabeth Watson, *Body Code: The Meaning in Movement* (London: Routledge, 1979), 7.

57 Jean Newlove, *Laban for Actors and Dancers* (New York: Routledge, 1993), 99.

58 Valentia Litvinoff, "The Natural and the Stylized: In Conflict or Harmony?," in *Movement for the Actor*, ed. Lucille S. Rubin (New York: Drama Book Specialists, 1980), 107.

59 Sabatine, *Movement Training for the Stage and Screen*, 112. Today's movement specialists see a clear distinction between specialized skill training and movement training that facilitates creating and presenting characters. Sabatine explains: training in mime, "ballet, modern dance, jazz dance, T'ai Chi, karate, physical education, rolfing, fencing, stage combat, approaches like Alexander technique and effort-shape, and so on" helps actors gain specialized skills (14). By comparison, movement training gives actors systematic tools for locating movements appropriate to the dramatic situation and character's given circumstances (Litvinoff, "The Natural and the Stylized," 106).

60 Keane, *CineTech*, 64.

61 Jones and Cliff, *Thinking Animation*, 295.

62 Kundert-Gibbs and Kundert-Gibbs, *Action! Acting Lessons for CG Animators*, 15.

63 Jones and Cliff, *Thinking Animation*, 67.

64 Ibid., 188.

65 Ibid., 182.

66 Hooks, *Acting for Animators*, 8.

67 Ibid., 11–12

68 Ibid., 29.

69 Brad Bird, "Foreword," *Acting for Animators*, 3rd ed. (New York: Routledge, 2011), xi.

70 Paul Wells, *Understanding Animation* (New York: Routledge, 1998), 104.

71 Bird, "Foreword," x.

72 Carnicke, "Emotional Expressivity in Motion Capture Technology," 329.

73 Serkis, *Gollum*, 108.

74 Ibid., 22, 34.

75 Carnicke, "Emotional Expressivity in Motion Capture Technology," 328; see Serkis, *Gollum*, 51–52.

76 Serkis, *Gollum*, 88.

77 Ibid., 84.

78 Hayes and Webster, *Acting and Performance for Animation*, 185–186.

79 Carnicke, "Emotional Expressivity in Motion Capture Technology," 331.

80 Wojcik, "The Sound of Film Acting," 81.

81 Carnicke, "Emotional Expressivity in Motion Capture Technology," 322, 330, 325.

82 Ray Subers, "Forecast: '2 Guns' Takes Aim at First Ahead of 'Smurfs 2,'" *Box Office Mojo*, August 1, 2013, www.boxofficemojo.com/news/?id=3709&p=.htm (accessed August 6, 2013).

83 "Denzel Flies to Number One and Is America's Favorite Movie Star," *Harris Interactive: Harris Polls*, January 3, 2013, www.harrisinteractive.com/NewsRoom/HarrisPolls/tabid/447/mid/1508/articleId/114 (accessed August 6, 2013).

84 Geoff King, "Spectacle, Narrative, and Spectacular Blockbuster," in *Movie Blockbusters*, ed. Julian Stringer (New York: Routledge, 2003), 117.

85 Tucker, *Secrets of Screen Acting*, xiii.

86 Ibid., 188.

87 Ibid., 38.

88 King, "Spectacle, Narrative, and the Spectacular Blockbuster," 117.

89 James Wolcott, "Blood Test," *New Yorker*, August 23, 1993, 63.

90 J. Hoberman, "Hong Kong Blood and Guts," *Premiere* 3, no. 12 (August 1990): 33.

91 McDonagh, "Action Painter John Woo," 47.

92 Barton, *Acting Onstage and Off*, 160.

93 Ibid., 159.

94 Carnicke, "Emotional Expressivity in Motion Capture Technology," 322.

SELECTED BIBLIOGRAPHY

Affron, Charles. *Star Acting: Gish, Garbo, Davis*. New York: Dutton, 1977.

Austin, Thomas, and Martin Baker, ed. *Contemporary Hollywood Stardom*. London: Arnold 2003.

Baron, Cynthia, and Sharon Marie Carnicke. *Reframing Screen Performance*. Ann Arbor: University of Michigan Press, 2008.

Baron, Cynthia, and Diane Carson, eds. *Journal of Film and Video* (Special Issue on Screen Performance) 58: 1–2 (Spring/Summer 2006).

Baron, Cynthia, Diane Carson, and Frank P. Tomasulo, eds. *More Than a Method: Trends and Traditions in Contemporary Film Performance*. Detroit: Wayne State University Press, 2004.

Barton, Robert. *Acting Onstage and Off*. 4th ed. Belmont, CA: Thomson Wadsworth, 2006.

Bean, Jennifer M., ed. *Flickers of Desire: Movie Stars of the 1920s*. New Brunswick, NJ: Rutgers University Press, 2011.

Bernhardt, Sarah. *L'Art du théâtre*. 1923. Reprint, Paris: L'Harmattan, 1993.

Bogle, Donald. *Toms, Coons, Mulattoes, Mammies, & Bucks: An Interpretive History of Blacks in American Films*. New York: Viking Press, 1973.

Braudy, Leo. *The World in a Frame: What We See in Films*. Garden City, NY: Anchor Press/Doubleday, 1976.

Butler, Jeremy, ed. *Star Texts: Image and Performance in Film and Television*. Detroit: Wayne State University Press, 1991.

Cardullo, Bert, et al., eds. *Playing to the Camera: Film Actors Discuss Their Craft*. New Haven, CT: Yale University Press, 1998.

Cornea, Christine, ed. *Genre and Performance: Film and Television*. Manchester: Manchester University Press, 2010.

Crafton, Donald. *Shadow of a Mouse: Performance, Belief, and World-Making in Animation*. Berkeley: University of California Press, 2013.

Davis, Ronald L. *The Glamour Factory: Inside Hollywood's Big Studio System*. Dallas: Southern Methodist University Press, 1993.

de Cordova, Richard. "Genre and Performance: An Overview." In *Film Genre Reader III*, edited by Barry Keith Grant. Austin: University of Texas Press, 1995.

Duckett, Victoria, and Monica Dall'Asta. *Researching Women in Silent Cinema: New Findings and Perspectives*. Bologna: University of Bologna online monograph, 2013.

Dyer, Richard. *Heavenly Bodies: Film Stars and Society*. New York: St. Martin's Press, 1986.

———. *Stars*. London: British Film Institute, 1979.

Esch, Kevin. "'I Don't See Any Method at All': The Problem of Actorly Transformation." *Journal of Film and Video* 58, no. 1–2 (Spring/Summer 2006): 95–107.

Gish, Lillian. *The Movies, Mr. Griffith, and Me*. London: Columbus Books, 1969.

Gledhill, Christine, ed. *Stardom: Industry of Desire*. London: Routledge, 1991.

Hatch, Kristen. "Lillian Gish: Clean, and White, and Pure as the Lily." In *Flickers of Desire: Movie Stars of the 1910s*, edited by Jennifer M. Bean, 69–90. New Brunswick, NJ: Rutgers University Press, 2011.

———. "Movies and the New Faces of Masculinity." In *American Cinema of the 1950s: Themes and Variations*, edited by Murray Pomerance, 43–64. New Brunswick, NJ: Rutgers University Press, 2005.

Hayes, Derek, and Chris Webster. *Acting and Performance for Animation*. New York: Focal Press, 2013.

Hodge, Alison, ed. *Twentieth Century Actor Training*. New York: Routledge, 2000.

Hollinger, Karen. *The Actress: Hollywood Acting and the Female Star*. New York: Routledge, 2013.

The Home and School Speaker: A Practical Manual of Delsarte Exercises and Elocution. Chicago: W. B. Conkey Company, 1897.

Hooks, Ed. *Acting for Animators*, 3rd ed. Portsmouth, NH: Heinemann, 2011.

Hornby, Richard. *The End of Acting: A Radical View*. New York: Applause, 1992.

Jewell, Richard B. *The Golden Age of Cinema: Hollywood, 1929–1945*. Malden, MA: Wiley-Blackwell, 2007.

Kazan, Elia. *Kazan on Directing*. New York: Vintage, 2010.

Keane, Stephen. *CineTech: Film, Convergence and New Media*. New York: Palgrave Macmillan, 2007.

Kemp, Rick. *Embodied Acting: What Neuroscience Tells Us about Performance*. New York: Routledge, 2012.

King, Barry. "Embodying an Elastic Self: The Parametrics of Contemporary Stardom." In *Contemporary Hollywood Stardom*, edited by Thomas Austin and Martin Baker, 46–47. London: Arnold, 2003.

Klevan, Andrew. *Film Acting: From Achievement to Appreciation*. London: Wallflower Press, 2005.

Kozloff, Sarah. *Overhearing Film Dialogue*. Berkeley: University of California Press, 2000.

Lindsay, Vachel. *The Art of the Moving Picture*. 1915. Reprint, New York: Modern Library, 2000.

Loiselle, André, and Jeremy Maron. *Stages of Reality: Theatricality in Cinema*. Toronto: University of Toronto Press, 2012.

Lovell, Alan, and Peter Krämer, ed. *Screen Acting*. New York: Routledge, 1999.

Mayer, David. "Learning to See in the Dark." *Nineteenth Century Theatre* 25, no. 2 (Winter 1997): 92–114.

McDonald, Paul. *Hollywood Stardom*. Hoboken, NJ: Wiley-Blackwell, 2013.

———. *The Star System: Hollywood's Production of Popular Identities*. London: Wallflower Press, 2000.

Morin, Edgar. *The Stars*. London: Transatlantic Book Service, 1960.

Naremore, James. *Acting in the Cinema*. Berkeley: University of California Press, 1988.

Newlove, Jean. *Laban for Actors and Dancers*. London: Nick Hern Books, 2007.

Pearson, Roberta. *Eloquent Gestures: The Transformation of Performance Style in the Griffith Biograph Films*. Berkeley: University of California Press, 1992.

Peberdy, Donna. *Masculinity and Film Performance: Male Angst in Contemporary American Cinema*. Basingstoke, UK: Palgrave Macmillan, 2011.

Pudovkin, V. I. *Film Technique and Film Acting*. London: Vision Press, 1954.

Quinn, Michael L. "Self-Reliance and Ritual Renewal: Anti-theatrical Ideology in American Method Acting." *Journal of Dramatic Theory and Criticism* 10, no. 1 (Fall 1995): 5–20.

Roach, Joseph R. *The Player's Passion: Studies in the Science of Acting*. Newark: University of Delaware Press, 1985.

Ruyter, Nancy Lee Chalfa. "Antique Longings: Genevieve Stebbins and American Delsartean Performance." In *Corporealities: Dancing, Knowledge, Culture, and Power*, edited by Susan Leigh Foster, 72–91. London: Routledge, 1996.

Sabatine, Jean. *Movement Training for the Stage and Screen*. New York: Back Stage Books, 1995.

Schatz, Thomas. *The Genius of the System: Hollywood Filmmaking in the Studio Era.* Minneapolis: University of Minnesota Press, 2010.

Stanislavski, Constantin. *An Actor Prepares.* Translated by Elizabeth Reynolds Hapgood. New York: Theatre Arts Books, 1936.

Sternagel, Jörg, Deborah Levitt, and Dieter Mersch, eds. *Acting and Performance in Moving Image Culture: Bodies, Screens, Renderings.* Piscataway, NJ: Transaction Publishers, 2012.

Taylor, Aaron, ed. *Theorizing Film Acting.* New York: Routledge, 2012.

Thompson, Kristin. "The Concept of Cinematic Excess." *Cine-Tracts* 1, no. 2 (Summer 1977): 54–64.

Tomlinson, Doug. *Actors on Acting for the Screen: Roles and Collaborations.* New York: Garland Press, 1994.

Tucker, Patrick. *Secrets of Screen Acting.* 2nd ed. New York: Routledge, 2003.

Vineberg, Steve. *Method Actors: Three Generations of an American Acting Style.* New York: Schirmer Books, 1991.

Walker, Alexander. *Stardom: The Hollywood Phenomenon.* New York: Stein and Day, 1970.

Wexman, Virginia Wright, ed. *Cinema Journal,* Special Issue on Film Acting 20, no. 1 (Fall 1980).

Wojcik, Pamela Robertson, ed. *Movie Acting, the Film Reader.* New York: Routledge, 2004.

Zucker, Carole. "The Concept of 'Excess' in Film Acting." *Post Script* 12, no. 2 (1993): 54–62.

———. *Making Visible the Invisible.* Lanham, MD: Scarecrow Press, 1991.

NOTES ON CONTRIBUTORS

Cynthia Baron is a professor in the Department of Theatre and Film and an Affiliated Faculty in the American Culture Studies Graduate Program at Bowling
Green State University. She is the author of *Denzel Washington* and co-author
of *Reframing Screen Performance* and *Appetites and Anxieties: Food, Film, and
the Politics of Representation*. She is co-editor of *More Than a Method* and a
special issue of the *Journal of Film and Video* on screen performance. Her
essays on actors and acting include articles in *Cineaste, Theatre Annual: A
Journal of Performance Studies*, and *Journal of Film and Video*, and chapters in
*Movie Acting: The Film Reader; Genre and Performance: Film and Television;
New Constellations: Movie Stars of the 1960s; The Wiley-Blackwell History of
American Film*, vol. 3: *1946–1975*; and *Cult Film Stardom*. She is the editor
of the Palgrave Studies in Screen Industries and Performance Series and the
founding editor of *The Projector: A Journal on Film, Media, and Culture*.

Victoria Duckett is a lecturer in media studies at Deakin University, Melbourne. She
has published extensively in the areas of performance, film, and media studies.
She is on the steering committee of Women and Film History International,

on the editorial board of *Nineteenth Century Theatre and Film*, and a member of the founding editorial board of *Feminist Media Histories: An International Journal*. In 2013 she was co-convener of the seventh international "Women and Silent Screen" conference in Melbourne. She is co-editor of *Researching Women in Silent Film: New Findings and Perspectives*. Her book *Performing Passion: Sarah Bernhardt and Silent Film* is forthcoming from the University of Illinois Press.

Julie Levinson is a professor of film at Babson College. She is the author of *The American Success Myth on Film* and editor of *Alexander Payne: Interviews*. Her published work in journals and edited collections has covered a range of topics including genre and gender, documentary film, and metafiction. She was the curator of film at the Institute of Contemporary Art in Boston as well as at the Boston Film/Video Foundation and the New England Foundation for the Arts. She has also been a guest curator for several film presenters, including the Flaherty Film Seminar, the Celebration of Black Cinema, and the Davis Museum at Wellesley College. Her curatorial work was awarded a special citation from the Boston Society of Film Critics. She has served on panels and juries for the National Endowment for the Arts, the Radcliffe Institute at Harvard University, and many other arts organizations and film festivals.

Arthur Nolletti Jr. is a professor emeritus of film studies and English at Framingham State University, where he initiated the concentration in film studies. He is the author of *The Cinema of Gosho Heinosuke: Laughter through Tears*, the editor of *The Films of Fred Zinnemann*, and the co-editor of *Reframing Japanese Cinema*. Nolletti has published and lectured widely and is the recipient of numerous awards; in addition, he participated in the first NEH summer seminar devoted to film study and is on the Advisory Committee of *Film Criticism*. He recently edited the special double issue of *Film Criticism* devoted to Japanese director Kore-eda Hirokazu.

Donna Peberdy is a senior lecturer in film and television studies at Southampton Solent University, UK. Her research and publications focus on acting and performance, masculinity, and sexuality in American cinema, and she is the author of *Masculinity and Film Performance: Male Angst in Contemporary American Cinema* and co-editor of *Tainted Love: Screening Sexual Perversities*. Peberdy has published articles in journals such as *Celebrity Studies, Men & Masculinities, New Review of Film and Television Studies,* and *Screening the Past*, and she has guest-edited a special issue on acting and performance for *Transnational Cinemas*. She has also contributed chapters to *The Blackwell Companion to Film Noir; Pretty People: Movie Stars of the 1990s; Millennial Masculinity: Men in Contemporary American Cinema;* and *Film Dialogue*.

Claudia Springer is in the English department at Framingham State University, where she teaches film studies and literature. She is the author of *Electronic Eros: Bodies and Desire in the Postindustrial Age* and *James Dean Transfigured: The Many Faces of Rebel Iconography*. She contributed chapters to the anthologies *The Matrix Trilogy: Cyberpunk Reloaded; Rebel Without a Cause: Approaches to a Maverick Masterwork; Alien Zone II: The Spaces of Science Fiction Cinema; Unspeakable Images: Ethnicity and the American Cinema; The Virtual Dimension: Architecture, Representation, and Crash Culture; Flame Wars: The Discourse of Cyberculture*; and *American Representations of Vietnam*. She has published articles in the journals *Screen, Genders, Explorations in Media Ecology, Cultural Critique, Jump Cut, Woman's Art Journal*, and *Wide Angle*, among others.

David Sterritt is a film professor at Columbia University, where he also co-chairs the University Seminar on Cinema and Interdisciplinary Interpretation. He is a humanistic studies and art history professor at the Maryland Institute College of Art and professor emeritus of theater and film at Long Island University as well editor-in-chief of the *Quarterly Review of Film and Video*, chair of the National Society of Film Critics, past chair of the New York Film Critics Circle, and a former member of the New York Film Festival selection committee. He serves on the editorial boards of *Cinema Journal*, the *Journal of Beat Studies*, and other publications, and has authored many film-related books, including *The Films of Alfred Hitchcock, Spike Lee's America*, and *The Cinema of Clint Eastwood: Chronicles of America*.

INDEX